A Head Full of Music

The soundtrack to my life

CLIFF RICHARD

with Ian Gittins

EBURY
SPOTLIGHT

I

Ebury Spotlight, an imprint of Ebury Publishing
20 Vauxhall Bridge Road
London SW1V 2SA

Ebury Spotlight is part of the Penguin Random House group of companies
whose addresses can be found at global.penguinrandomhouse.com

First published by Ebury Spotlight in 2023

www.penguin.co.uk

A CIP catalogue record for this book is available from the British Library

Hardback ISBN 9781529907346
Trade Paperback ISBN 9781529907353

Typeset in 11.5/19 pt SabonNext LT Regular by Jouve UK, Milton Keynes
Printed and bound in Great Britain by Clays Ltd, Elcograf S.p.A.

The authorised representative in the EEA is Penguin Random House Ireland,
Morrison Chambers, 32 Nassau Street, Dublin D02 YH68

Penguin Random House is committed to a sustainable future for our
business, our readers and our planet. This book is made from
Forest Stewardship Council® certified paper.

*I was not the only one affected by the tsunami of
rock and roll that came from the USA to Britain. It not only changed
our lives but also shaped our futures.
So, I dedicate this book to Norman Mitham, Terry Smart,
Ian Samwell . . . my first band.*

*To Hank B Marvin, who influenced countless, now world-famous
guitarists. To Bruce Welch and Brian Bennett. To my competitors
Marty Wilde and Billy Fury and, of course, The Beatles, a formidable
force . . . with admiration and love . . . Cliff.*

CONTENTS

FOREWORD BY BOB STANLEY

What do you think was the best year for music? I'd plump for 1981. I was sixteen, after all, and the world was a peach. There was the summer breeze of Britfunk from Freeez, Level 42 and Linx; the proto-indie 12-string reveries of Orange Juice; the chart takeover of synthpop, with unlikely oddballs Soft Cell and the Human League going all the way to Number 1 and the exciting new technology of the Walkman, which meant you could listen to all of these records on the bus without bothering the other passengers. In 1981, the Walkman even inspired a Number 4 hit called 'Wired For Sound'. Records you hear as a teenager are so affecting, and aged sixteen you're open to everything – any guitar, or any bass drum as Paul Weller put it. Your ears are tuned in to anything new.

In January 1957, Cliff Richard was sixteen. The year before, his head had been turned by a song he had caught wafting out of a car window in Waltham Cross. It was a mesmeric sound, all echo and mood, which seemed to have come from another planet – 'Heartbreak Hotel' by Elvis Presley. Cliff has said many times how that moment literally changed his life. He sought out pictures of Elvis, bought every Elvis record he could find from his local record shop, grew his hair and slicked it into a pompadour, practised his Presley moves in the mirror. Elvis's look, his attitude, his sound transmitted a message so powerful it caused a youthquake in Britain – he didn't even need to set foot in this country to transform it. There was no bigger fan than teenager Harry Webb from Hertfordshire. He wanted to be Elvis – not to be *like* him, but to get inside his skin and actually *be* him.

Elvis, it turned out, was just the beginning. January 1957 saw 'Hound Dog' in the Top 10 nuzzled up alongside Tommy Steele's wobbly 'Singing The Blues' (Cliff was apparently not impressed) and Malcolm Vaughan's keening 'St Therese of the Roses' (Cliff's thoughts on this record have never been recorded). February was the month when Little Richard's 'Long Tall Sally' entered the UK chart. Imagine hearing Richard's ear-splitting Venusian wail for the first time on the radio, straight after some pre-rock ballad like David Whitfield's 'The Adoration Waltz'! Well, you probably wouldn't have, not on the BBC's Light Programme anyway. Happily, 16-year-old Cliff had discovered the American Forces Network – or AFN – which would also have introduced him to another record that was in the charts in February 1957 – Fats Domino's rolling, relaxed New Orleans beauty 'Blueberry Hill'. Every month, it seemed like there was a fresh, new, ever more outlandish rock and roll 45. In June it was the turn of The Diamonds' falsetto doo-wop 'Little Darlin''; then along came Chuck

Berry, seeming to duet with his own guitar on 'School Day'; and in July The Everly Brothers appeared on the British hit parade for the very first time with 'Bye Bye Love' their harmonies going on to inspire The Beatles, Cliff's favourites The Bee Gees, and his future bandmates Brian Rankin and Bruce Welch, back then just a pair of spotty skifflers in Newcastle upon Tyne.

What an unimaginable thrill it must have been to be sixteen in 1957. Elvis's 'All Shook Up' was Number 1 right through the summer holidays. By the end of the year, Jerry Lee Lewis had stormed the chart with 'Whole Lotta Shakin' Goin' On'. And when Cliff turned seventeen, Buddy Holly's band, The Crickets, were Number 1 with their breakthrough hit, 'That'll Be the Day'. *Imagine being there!* The wonderful thing about this book is that you can. Cliff's enthusiasm for this music is completely undimmed. Sometimes he can hardly get the words out, the love for the music is so great. You're there with him in Cheshunt, kicking your heels through school, waiting for the latest piece of teenage news ('Have you heard? Bill Haley is playing in Edmonton! *Let's go!*'). You're there with him outside the record shop in Waltham Cross, hearing 'Heartbreak Hotel' for the first time. You're there at the Kilburn State, with a handful of die-hard Jerry Lee Lewis fans, as the sweat-drenched Killer gives the performance of his life.

I can guarantee you won't be able to get through this book without pausing to dig out your Eddie Cochran 45s – or your *Best Of* album, or at least without tapping his name into Spotify. Cliff is and was, first and foremost, a music fan. Just a year after all these seismic singles were released, he had one of his own – 'Move It!' – and there he was, translating his fandom, his love of rock and roll, into something tangible, a record on the green Columbia label – just like Frankie Lymon & The Teenagers! – that you could buy from Marsden's in Waltham Cross alongside those Jerry Lee and Elvis 45s, or those Sammy Davis Jr and Frank Sinatra albums. Talk about making your dreams come true.

INTRODUCTION

The title of this book may ring a bell for you. In fact, you know what? I hope it does! It's taken from the chorus of one of my biggest hits, 1981's 'Wired for Sound'. That's the song where I sing about 'Walking around with a head full of music . . .' – and, in so many ways, that is what I've been doing for my entire life.

It's a simple fact. When you're a musician, an artist, music *consumes* you. The love of music is what makes you want to be a performer; then, when you get started, it's what fills your head every waking day. You hear music everywhere you go, and it constantly sets questions pinballing around your mind:

Wow! That's a great song – I wonder what it is?
I love that singer's voice – who is he?
That's a brilliant melody – what could I do with it?
Oh, I know that song! It's fantastic – what is it, again?

The part of your brain that responds to music never switches off, and nor would you want it to. Songs are the soundtrack to our lives: the music that moves us and lifts us; the music that we fall in love to, and break up to. Music was my first love, and it will be my last . . . oh, hang on, isn't that a song, too?!

Artists live in, and *for*, music. I'm no exception. I have been a singer for sixty-five years now, and done Lord knows how many thousands of interviews, yet for some reason, journalists always prefer to ask me about my private life, or nonsense like that. Why? Who knows! Because, frankly, I'd *much* rather talk about music.

Well, this book is my chance. I've had a head full of music for most of my life and here, laid out, are the contents. This book is, roughly speaking, thirty songs that I have played regularly since the first day that I heard them. They sound as fresh and exciting to me as they did on first listen, even if that was many decades ago.

You will soon notice that there are two main themes that unite the majority of the songs in this book. And I make no excuses for either of them! The first is that much of the music dates from the first wave of rock and roll, right back in the late fifties. And the second is that most of the songs came out of America.

America will always be the fatherland of rock and roll. I have always said that the day my life changed was the Saturday morning in May 1956 when I was mooching down Waltham Cross High Street, aged fifteen, with two mates. We heard some music blaring out of a parked car . . . and it simply stopped us in our tracks.

The song was 'Heartbreak Hotel' by Elvis Presley and it sounded like nothing I had ever heard before. In that instant, I fell in love with rock and roll, and it gave me the thrill, the purpose and the mission that has shaped my life ever since. As I've always said, if there had been no Elvis Presley, there'd have been no Cliff Richard.

Before rock and roll, it felt like there was nothing much happening in music. We were all listening to Frank Sinatra and Alma Cogan and Max Bygraves, and then suddenly ... *boom*! Along came Elvis and Jerry Lee Lewis and Little Richard and Buddy Holly! I'm not exaggerating: it felt like the world had changed overnight.

It was a truly extraordinary time and, luckily, I was just the right age to appreciate it and lap it all up. Being alive, being *young* at that time, meant you knew that you were in at the start of something truly special. The advent of rock and roll changed so many British lives. It certainly altered mine beyond all recognition.

How do I mean? Well, I came to England from India in 1948, a wide-eyed, seven-year-old boy named Harry Webb. Just ten years later, I was a teenage rock star called Cliff Richard who was fronting a band called The Drifters, riding high in the hit parade, and on tour playing live to thousands of screaming fans every night.

How did *that* happen? Well, it happened because I heard the amazing music being made by the people in this book, and I wanted to make my own. And it happened because I was lucky enough to catch a few breaks, make the first ever British rock and roll record, and work like crazy to make my dream come true.

I hope this book serves another purpose. So many people believe that British pop music began in the early sixties with The Beatles. *Well, no, it didn't, thank you very much!* We had homegrown rockers making terrific tunes much earlier than that: not just me, but Billy Fury, Marty Wilde, Adam Faith . . .

In any case, The Beatles only really took off five years after I did, but they were listening to exactly the same artists that I was taking inspiration from: that first generation of American rock and rollers. The first time that I ever bumped into the Liverpool lads, we compared notes:

'What do you think of Chuck Berry?'

'Hey, man, we *love* Chuck Berry!'

'What about John Lee Hooker?'

'Wow, yeah – he's fantastic!'

We had the same musical education, the same schooling, as each other. And I think that The Beatles would be as happy as I am that this book is celebrating that great music.

This book is meaningful to me on a number of levels. It's not just that I love the songs, although obviously I *do*. I was also fortunate enough to meet, and even get to know, some of the legendary artists who created them, and I'll share those stories and memories with you in these pages as well.

The songs in *A Head Full of Music* are arranged in rough chronological order – but not strictly. It's the sequence in which the songs impacted on me. I didn't hear a few of them until a while after they came out. I also get diverted here and there, but that's OK: rock and roll rarely proceeds in a straight line from A to Z!

I'm eighty-three this year. I've been alive for a very long time, which means that not all of the music filling my head dates from that first era of rock and roll. I also want to take this chance to pay homage to other artists whose songs have deeply moved me over the years.

It's a broad category, and it includes great soul stars such as Aretha Franklin, long-time colleagues like Elton John, dear friends who have passed away, such as Cilla Black and Olivia Newton-John, and, of course, my all-time favourite band, The Bee Gees . . . and some of the great gospel music that is so close to my heart.

It's a lot to fit in – well, of course it is! I have lived my entire life in music! So, let's get started, and delve in to my *Head Full of Music*. I hope you enjoy it and I hope, by the end, that the music is playing inside your head, too.

ONE

'IN A PERSIAN MARKET' – SAMMY DAVIS JR

A tune from before I'd even heard of rock and roll

Before Elvis shoved rock and roll to the very centre of my life, music was really just background noise for me: pleasant, diverting and inconsequential. An occasional tune might catch my fancy, but nothing about the ditties that I was hearing on the radio sounded remotely important or life-changing.

As I explained in my life story, *The Dreamer*, my first musical memory as a boy, growing up in India, was being put in my church school's choir. I can't remember which hymns we sang, just how mortified I felt at having to wear a cassock, which to me felt like putting on a girl's dress!

We had some music at home. My dad worked for a catering company but he was also a hobby musician, playing banjo in his firm's jazz band. In our apartment we had a gramophone, which had what looked like a huge old hearing aid sticking out of it: an ancient wooden contraption that played my parents' records.

My mum and dad would listen to singers such as Frank

Sinatra and Ella Fitzgerald on there, as well as big bands like Stan Kenton & His Orchestra. And, when I was only four years old, I had my own little party piece.

Whenever my parents had friends over for dinner, Dad would tell me, 'Harry, go and get "Chewing a Piece of Straw"!' This was a 10" single by Jack Payne & His Orchestra. I would scurry over to Mum and Dad's record collection, stacked neatly by the gramophone, fish it out, and proudly run back and hand it to them.

I couldn't read yet, of course, but I could recognise the shape of the writing on the label on the middle of the record. Nearly eighty years on, I can still picture it – and still remember the guests all saying 'Look at that!' as they praised me for being so clever. I liked that!

That gramophone got sold and left behind when my family moved to England in 1948, after partition had divided British India into India and Pakistan. We lived in relatives' spare rooms for two years and were very poor. We didn't even have enough money for a radio, let alone a record player!

My dad was nothing if not ingenious, and brilliant with his hands, and when my parents, my three sisters and I were all living in one room at my Aunty Dorothy's house in Waltham Cross in 1950, he built us a crystal radio set. This was a basic radio receiver, with valves, and a big pair of headphones attached to it.

We took it with us when we got given our own council house, down the road in Cheshunt, at the end of that year. I would sometimes sit in the front room and listen to it after school or at the weekends but, if I am honest, I wasn't all that excited about the music I was hearing on the BBC Light Programme.*

When you're a kid, I guess you're attracted to novelty tunes. I liked a fun 1951 single by Dean Martin and Helen O'Connell called 'How D'ya Like Your Eggs in the Morning' ('I like mine with a kiss!' sang Dino). I can remember Patti Page's '(How Much Is) That Doggie in the Window?', which basically sounded like a nursery rhyme set to music.

The first British weekly singles chart came out in 1952, with Al Martino at Number 1 with 'Here in My Heart'. Every week, it was full of what, nowadays, we would call 'easy-listening' music. I remember Frankie Laine's trembly voiced 'I Believe', and Guy Mitchell's clip-clopping cowboy song, 'A Dime and a Dollar'.

There was Doris Day's 'Secret Love', which I liked because I'd been to the flicks to see her sing it in *Calamity Jane*. I didn't mind big 1955 Number 1 'Dreamboat' by Alma Cogan† ('The girl with the giggle in her voice') or Jimmy Young singing 'The Man from Laramie' or 'Unchained Melody'. But they didn't mean much to me.

There were a lot of crooners. Frank Sinatra was being chased around America by the bobby-soxers, and Perry Como and Matt Monro were always on the radio. I was pretty indifferent to them. Only years later, as a singer myself, did I listen to them more closely and think, *Wow, they really know what they're doing!*

---

* Before I got into music, my favourite show on the BBC Light Programme was *The Goons*. My friends and I would all listen to it at home, then go to school and impersonate Neddie Seagoon, Eccles and Bluebottle.

† I was to meet Alma many years later. She was a lovely lady who, sadly, died of cancer when she was only thirty-four.

Like a lot of kids, as I got into my mid-teens I started to grow more interested in music. I began tuning that crystal radio into Radio Luxembourg, when I could hear it through the crackle and static. It launched a lot of DJs who were later to become famous on the BBC, such as Pete Murray, David Jacob and, sadly, Jimmy Savile.

Far better than Luxembourg, because I could actually hear it clearly, was the American Forces Network, or AFN, which broadcast out of Germany. And when I was about fourteen, I began to hear music on that station which drew me in a little more.

I liked the stuff that the DJs called 'doo-wop' that was coming out of New York. Even as a gawky teenager who knew nothing about music, I loved the easy grace and smooth harmonies of groups like The Moonglows and The Cadillacs. As you'll soon learn from *A Head Full of Music*, I'm a sucker for a great harmony!

I liked The Moonglows' 'Sincerely', The Cadillacs' 'Gloria', 'A Thousand Miles Away' by The Heartbeats and The Flamingos' 'I Only Have Eyes for You'. Some of it was almost like barbershop-quartet music, but it had an extra edge and a little bit of attitude about it, which appealed to me.

The other music scene that was going on at the time, and which I used to hear on the BBC Light Programme, was home-grown skiffle music. Skiffle was a bit of a weird one. It was originally a kind of American folk-blues music, which had been popular in the US early in the century then got revived in Britain in the fifties.

I didn't *mind* skiffle but I didn't love it either. Its big selling point was that it used very cheap, homemade instruments. People would bang on washboards or make a tea-chest bass: a tea chest with a broom handle tied to one corner with a piece of string, which the player would vigorously twang away on.

The first big UK skiffle hit was 'Rock Island Line' by Lonnie Donegan, which went into the chart in 1956 and stayed there for months and months. It was OK but it sounded lightweight to me. It was a cover of an old US folk song previously sung by bluesman Lead Belly. I only heard his version recently, and I much prefer it.

Lonnie Donegan had a pretty good voice, I suppose, but I had no interest in buying skiffle records. I only got a thruppenny bit* pocket money each week and, in any case, there would have been no point. We were still too poor as a family to own a record player – or even a television, come to that!

In the very unlikely event that I wanted to hear a record, I'd cycle to my auntie's house, in Waltham Abbey, to play it on their radiogram. If I wanted to watch TV, I'd get on my bike and pedal in the opposite direction to my Aunty Dorothy's, in Waltham Cross. At least it all kept me fit!

Sometimes, my cousins from Waltham Abbey – Gerald, Derek, Keith and Gordon – joined me at Aunty Dorothy's to watch telly. She only had a small set, but she put a magnifying-glass-like contraption on the front of it to make the picture bigger. It meant that we didn't have to squint as we gawped at *The Quatermass Experiment*.

On the rare occasions when I *did* buy singles at fifteen, I got them from a shop called Marsden's in Waltham Cross, next to the Embassy cinema. Marsden's was a local institution: a family-run

---

* A thruppenny bit was a pre-decimal twelve-sided coin worth the mighty sum of three old pence (just over 1p).

business that sold TVs and electrical goods, and also stocked all of the latest hits and records by almost any artist you could think of.

The cool thing about Marsden's, in common with most record shops in those days, was that you could listen to songs and decide whether you wanted to buy them or not. It had three little booths at the back of the store, and you'd go to the counter and tell the assistant what you wanted to hear:

'Excuse me, can I listen to "Sixteen Tons" by Tennessee Ernie Ford, please?'

They would nod, put the record on the turntable on the counter, and you would go to a booth and sit and listen to it through headphones, or via a speaker. If the shop was quiet, they might play you two songs. But, after that, they'd be knocking on the door of the booth to kick you out!

I wasn't buying many singles when I was fifteen, but one that I *did* get, after I heard it on our crystal radio, was 'In a Persian Market' by Sammy Davis Jr.* It was a jaunty little number, and I suppose a bit of a novelty tune, with its bursts of trumpet and saxophone across what sounded like exotic, snake-charming music.

What really got me, though, was the *rhythm* that ran beneath it all. The song had a swing to it, yet also quite a hard-edged beat that was almost rock and roll, in its own way. It chugged along a lot like Fats Domino's 'The Fat Man' had done a few years earlier, which I thought was tremendous.

Sammy Davis Jr was one of the Hollywood Rat Pack, of

---

* I heard it on AFN in 1955, when it was a US double A-side single for Sammy with 'The Man with the Golden Arm'.

course, with Frank Sinatra and Dean Martin. He was a true global superstar. Six years later, in 1961, after my career had taken off, he came over to play more than fifty nights at the Prince of Wales Theatre in London. My then manager, Tito Burns, took me to see him.

Sammy was *unbelievable*. He had the crowd in the palm of his hand as soon as he walked on and said, in his gravelly voice: 'Look at me – I'm the only broken-nosed, black Jew in the world!' He was an amazing showman who could do everything. He could act, sing, tap-dance, tell jokes, and he was terrific at all of them.

That was the big thing with the generation of entertainers before mine: they had all been to stage school, so they were complete all-round showbiz entertainers. Sammy was terrific to watch, but I remember turning to Tito and saying, 'I think I might as well give up and retire now!' Because I felt that I just couldn't compete.

So, back in 1955, I bought 'In a Persian Market' and went off, on my bike, to my aunt's house to listen to it. It was sweet, but it certainly wasn't a song to blow my head off my shoulders and turn my entire world upside-down. *That* came along on that fateful afternoon on Waltham Cross High Street . . .

TWO

'HEARTBREAK HOTEL'
– ELVIS PRESLEY

I heard it through a car window ... and my life changed

It used to take us about twenty-five minutes to walk from Cheshunt to Waltham Cross. We did it a lot of Saturdays. There wasn't a lot for a teenager to do in Cheshunt, so a few school-friends and I would meet up and mosey on down to Waltham Cross, where there was ... well, not a lot, but *slightly* more to do.

That Saturday in May 1956, Norman Mitham, Terry Smart and I did the walk. We were planning to do the usual: hang out in the park, look in a couple of shops, have a cup of tea in a café, maybe call in at Marsden's to listen to a new single or two. And then, outside the newsagents, Aspland's, we saw the parked car.

I must have told this story a thousand times, but I never tire of telling it. It was a French car, a green Citroën, with a funky curved back. You didn't see many of *those* in rural Hertfordshire, so we headed over to it for a gawp. And then, wafting through the open front window, we heard the song playing on the car radio.

'We-e-e-e-ll, *since my baby left me ...*'

Huh? What. Is. That? Norman, Terry and I stared at each other, open-mouthed. And as we did, a guy ran out of Aspland's, jumped into the car, threw his fags and newspaper onto the front passenger seat, started the motor, and drove off. The alien-sounding music vanished down the road with the Citroën.

Wow! I had never heard anything like it in my life! Norman, Terry and I spent the whole afternoon gabbling about how great it had sounded, and how we had to find out what it was. As soon as I got home and had had my tea that evening, I glued myself to the crystal radio to try to track it down.

I had no luck, but Norman was more successful. When I saw him at school that Monday morning, he was grinning in triumph. 'I heard that song again, on AFN!' he proclaimed. 'It's called "Heartbreak Hotel", and it's by some guy called Elvis Presley!'

Well, we all had a good hoot about what a daft name that was – *Elvis? Who gets called Elvis?* – but, more to the point, I knew I had to get the song. I would never have dared ask my parents for money for a record, so I saved up my thruppenny bits for a couple of weeks to get the shilling that I needed to buy it.

I marched back to Waltham Cross, and didn't even bother asking the assistant in Marsden's if I could hear 'Heartbreak Hotel' first – there was no way that I wasn't going to get it! And one very cool thing was that, by now, I didn't have to climb on my bike and head off to my auntie's house to listen to it.

We were still quite impoverished as a family, and my dad was always very careful with the purse strings, but we had recently invested in a record player. It was the basic, classic Dansette, a turntable in a sturdy square box with a hinged lid, and it now took pride of place on the sideboard in our front room.

The turntable had a spindle and you could stack five records on it that would drop down and play, one at a time. Next to the turntable, in the bottom-left corner of the open box, was a knob that you had to set to control the speed the records played at: 16rpm (revolutions per minute), 33, 45 or 78.

Why was this? Because records were changing. Singles had always been pressed on what was called shellac, and rotated at 78rpm. But technology had moved on – and there'd apparently been a shellac shortage, since the war – so now they were being increasingly pressed on vinyl, which played at 45rpm.*

The 33 – or, strictly speaking, 33⅓ – setting was for albums, which in those days were called long-players, or LPs. I gather that 16rpm was intended for playing spoken-word records, such as talking books, but never really took off. I certainly don't recall us ever using it!

My copy of 'Heartbreak Hotel' was a 10" single in the old-fashioned shellac format and played at 78rpm. It didn't come in a picture sleeve: they hardly existed yet! It had a plain cardboard cover and a blue label with Elvis's name, the song title, and the famous His Master's Voice logo of the dog sitting by a gramophone.

I couldn't wait to get the record out of its cover and onto the player. And, when I did, the music that came out of the Dansette

---

* Shellac was largely dying out by the late fifties but someone recently wrote to me to tell me they'd found a 10" shellac version of my 1962 single 'The Young Ones' in an American antique shop. *An antique shop!* Oh, dear . . .

transfixed me just as much as it had blaring through the window of the green Citroën.

I'd heard American rock and roll before. Like everybody, I'd enjoyed Bill Haley & His Comets' 'Rock Around the Clock' – '*One, two, three o'clock, four o'clock, rock!*' – when it had been a big hit a year earlier, and I'll talk about that song, and about Bill, later in this book. But *this . . . Elvis . . .* was something else again.

It's always hard to explain exactly why you love a piece of music. It's like trying to describe why you fall in love with somebody – you just do! But what I can say, for sure, was that Elvis Presley sounded like nobody we had ever heard before.

This was new. It was fresh. It was unique. It was nothing like Frank Sinatra or Bing Crosby or Dean Martin, or any of the male singers that I was familiar with. Those guys, with their smooth voices and their gentle melodies, sounded like they were singing for my mum and dad. Elvis sounded like he was singing for me. *To me*.

Nobody my age, no teenager, would ever have been inspired by Sinatra or Bing, or wanted to be like them. Elvis was different. He sounded so young, so cool and so *now*, and his voice cut through everything else. He sounded passionate, and powerful. He sounded like he had . . . secrets that you needed to learn.

Oddly, I wasn't that bothered about the lyrics of 'Heartbreak Hotel'. It was exactly what it said on the tin: a heartbreak song, as so many great rock and roll tunes are. But what excited me about it was the rhythms of the music, the beats, the feel, the *attitude*. The sense of something being born.

Here, right before my ears, Elvis was giving rock and roll a new shape. Yes, he sounded like nothing I had heard before, but suddenly I wanted to hear nothing *but* him. And, a whole lifetime on, I still remember exactly how thrilling, how life-changing, hearing Elvis Presley for the first time was.

Immediately, he obsessed me. I started trying to find out everything about Elvis that I could. When I first saw a photograph of him, I couldn't believe how cool he looked – that quiff! That curled lip! And when I realised that he had an album out already, I absolutely *had* to have it.

LPs cost four-and-six (22.5p) in those days, an absolute fortune for a schoolboy who got a thruppenny bit pocket money a week. But I started frantically saving up. I got a holiday job picking potatoes on a local farm. There I was, all day long, bent double and yanking spuds out of the dirt for a shilling an hour.

The boredom and backache were all worth it when I had saved up the cash and was back down Marsden's to buy *Elvis Presley*. 'Heartbreak Hotel' wasn't on the record, but I didn't mind: there were so, so many new songs to love.

I loved the opener, 'Blue Suede Shoes', with its urgent vocal and frantic rhythms. I adored 'I'm Left, You're Right, She's Gone', where Elvis's trembling voice told tales of desertion. I worshipped 'Lawdy Miss Clawdy', with its honky-tonk piano, crazy twang and aching vocal. Heck, I loved every single note on the record!*

Listening back to that debut album now, I still think there is a distinct Black-music influence on it, especially on one track,

---

* I even loved the distinctive font that Elvis's name was in on the album sleeve, in pink and green letters. I used that lettering on my own records in years to come.

'Mystery Train'. I used to imagine Elvis sitting on his stoop, at home in Memphis, with a Black guy hanging out with him. If you close your eyes, I think you can easily imagine Elvis was a Black guy singing.

Not everybody agrees with me. I used to have friendly arguments about this with Pearly Gates, the great Black American singer who sometimes guested on my TV show in the seventies. 'Elvis Presley could be a Black singer,' I'd tell her.

'No, he couldn't,' Pearly would say. 'He sounds white.'

'Well, his influences were Black music, and he sounds Black to me!' I'd reply. We had to agree to disagree. But I thought of trying to track dear old Pearly down to call her when I saw the Baz Luhrmann movie, *Elvis*, in 2022.

The film has a scene where the young Elvis, played by Austin Butler, goes into a Black church. He is blown away and transported by the passion and spirituality of the gospel music he hears, and goes wild, singing and clapping along. *A-ha!* I thought, when I saw it. *Yes! That's the Elvis that I know and love!*

Back in the summer of 1956, I played that *Elvis Presley* album to death. Because the Dansette was in our front room, my parents and sisters got very used to me running home from school and dropping the needle on the start of the record. Mum would laughingly say, 'Oh, please, Harry! Don't play it *again*!'

My parents didn't really mind, though. Back in the day, they had loved Sinatra and Ella Fitzgerald, so they indulged my passion. Their only negative comment was, now and then, to shake their heads and say, 'Hmph! I can't tell a word that he is singing!' Well, that was fine, because every line was crystal clear to me.

I wasn't the only family member hooked on Elvis. My eldest sister, Donna, who was thirteen then, adored him. At the end of 1956, I took her to the pictures to see him star in *Love Me Tender*. She *sobbed*. 'Harry, can I borrow your handkerchief?' When she gave it back, it wasn't just wet through. It was *torn*!

Whenever I could afford them, I bought magazines like *Melody Maker* and the *New Musical Express* and scoured them for articles about Elvis and, best of all, photographs of him. He was such big news seemingly overnight that they, and even the daily newspapers, were suddenly full of stories about him.

They talked about how Elvis looked like a Greek god, and ran photos of him next to pictures of statues. They started calling him 'Elvis the Pelvis', and said that his gyrations on stage were so sexual that American television would only show him from the waist up. *Wow!* Obviously, this only made me marvel at him even more!

Elvis Presley quickly became the poster boy of rock and roll. From not knowing what he looked like only a few weeks earlier, suddenly I was seeing his picture everywhere. And I set off on a determined one-man mission to make myself look as identical to him as was humanly possible.

The quiff came first, of course. I began spending hours in front of the bathroom mirror, sweeping my hair to the back of my head and trying to fix it in place with Brylcreem. I wasn't the only lad in Cheshunt doing that. A couple of other boys also turned up at school sporting would-be Elvis quiffs.

You need thick hair to make a quiff (I could do it in those days; I'd certainly have no chance now!). I was quite pleased with my Brylcreem skills, but it never looked as good as when Elvis had just a few strands that broke loose from his quiff and hung over his forehead. I never managed to reproduce that.

I wanted to dress like Elvis as well. I appeared in a school production of Dickens's *A Christmas Carol* as Bob Cratchit, Tiny Tim's father, and my costume included a pair of tight, tapered Edwardian-style trousers. They looked like the drainpipe trousers that the Teddy Boys, who were into Elvis, wore, so I got a pair of those.

I'd have loved a leather jacket, but there was no chance that would happen, both because of the cost, and because my parents might have looked askance at me dressing like that. Instead, my mum got me a duffle coat. All the other kids at school had black or blue ones, so I chose brown.*

My love for Elvis even influenced my diet! When I read in *Girlfriend* magazine that he liked putting peanut butter *and* jam (or 'jelly', as the Americans call it) on his toast, I started eating mine like that too. It was an . . . acquired taste, but I managed to acquire it. *This is how Elvis eats it!* I told myself. *It MUST taste great!*

I was so infatuated with Elvis Presley that, really, it was hero worship. There is no other term for it. Seriously, some nights I used to dream that I *was* Elvis: singing on stage in front of thousands of screaming fans, or signing autographs. I would be *so* disappointed when I woke up in the morning!

It was all great, but combing my hair like Elvis, dressing like him, and even eating like him weren't enough. As I said in my

---

* I've been like that for my entire life. Whether I'm on stage or off, I don't like just wearing what everybody else is wearing.

memoir *The Dreamer*, I didn't just want to be like Elvis: I wanted to *be* him. From the second I heard 'Heartbreak Hotel' blasting out of that Citroën, I knew in my heart that I wanted to be a singer.

No: I wanted to be a rock and roll star.

How did a teenage boy from Hertfordshire begin to go about this? I didn't have a clue, but I did find a way to start making music. I had begun to go, with a few friends, to a youth club in Waltham Cross on Saturday nights. It was fun: we'd dance to chart hits and sing along.

It was a small step from that to five of us – me, a boy called John, and three girls – Freda, Beryl and my sort-of first girlfriend, Betty – forming an a cappella group that we called The Quintones. My English teacher, Jay Norris, let us practise our harmonies in a classroom after school.

We'd sing doo-wop songs like 'Eddie My Love' by The Teen Queens and 'Only You' by The Platters. It was fun, but it felt a long way from 'Heartbreak Hotel' and Elvis the Pelvis. However, The Quintones gave me my first chance to demonstrate my Elvis chops in public.

We were allowed to sing a few songs in the main school hall at an end-of-term party. By now, my schoolfriends all knew about my Elvis fixation – well, it was hard to miss! – and after The Quintones had finished, a few of them shouted out: 'Come on, Harry! Do your Elvis thing!'

Well, I didn't need asking twice! I started curling my lip, wobbling my legs, and going 'Uh-huh-huh!' as I sang 'Heartbreak Hotel'. I suppose I was like a fifties' version of *Stars in Their Eyes*!

And, if I can be forgiven for saying so, I reckon I took him off pretty well.

I was so good at being Elvis because, by now, I'd had weeks of practice. I'd spent hours in front of the mirror by the Dansette in the front room, aping his moves and singing along to *Elvis Presley*. My dad had seen me doing it and must have been quietly impressed.

I would never have dared ask my parents for a guitar like the one that Elvis had hanging around his neck so stylishly on the album sleeve. Again, I knew how much they cost, and how little money we had. But on my sixteenth birthday, on 14 October 1956, my father presented me with one.

I was *so* taken aback, flabbergasted really, when Dad gave me that guitar. He had bought it on hire purchase, which he normally totally refused to do. It was the last thing I expected, and I was so touched, but Dad said he could see how seriously I was taking singing and rock and roll.

'Harry, do you really want to do this?' he asked me.

'Yes, Dad, I do!'

'Right,' he said with a nod. 'Then you have to be as good as you can, as often as you can!'

Drawing on his days as a banjo player in India, Dad gave me my first rudimentary guitar lesson. Of course, a banjo only has four strings, so I'm not sure quite how transferable his skills actually were! But he was a game would-be teacher, and tried to show me how to play 'The Prisoner's Song'.

'Put your fingers *here*, Harry,' he said, trying to show me the C chord. 'No, not there, *here*! Now put them *here*, and that is

G. Can you play C and then G? Hmm, not quite. OK, now move your fingers *here* and *here*, and that is F!' In that first session of fiddling and fumbling on the frets, I learned my first three chords.

I wasn't exactly a very natural or gifted student and, if I am honest, I didn't apply myself very well to the guitar because I wasn't all that bothered about playing it. I just wanted to hang it around my neck and try to *look* as cool as Elvis. It was just one more visual prop in my bid to become him.

Elvis Presley released so many amazing singles through 1956 and into '57 – 'Don't Be Cruel', 'Hound Dog', 'All Shook Up', '(Let Me Be Your) Teddy Bear', 'Jailhouse Rock'. I devoured them all, as my infatuation with him continued. And, alongside it, my own desire to play rock and roll grew ever more fervent.

The Quintones naturally came to an end when I left school in 1957 and, while I was holding down a dull day job at my dad's office, I cast around for a new band. Despite my general indifference towards skiffle, I became the singer in a local skiffle group: The Dick Teague Skiffle Group. My mate, Terry Smart, was the drummer.

The guy who ran it – who, unsurprisingly, was called Dick Teague – was a skiffle purist who took it very seriously. He chose our musical repertoire: stuff like 'Rock Island Line', and 'Don't You Rock Me Daddy-o' by Lonnie Donegan, Chas McDevitt's 'Freight Train', and numbers by skiffle mainstays such as The Vipers.

I dutifully sang those songs at gigs at local social clubs and youth clubs, but they weren't really my bag. At a rehearsal, I asked Dick Teague if I could do a solo spot at our shows, singing Elvis songs like 'Heartbreak Hotel' and 'Don't Be Cruel'. I can still picture his horrified face as he shook his head!

If I'm honest, my favourite memory of The Dick Teague Skiffle Group isn't musical: it's visual. We had a band photo taken. I had an Elvis-style sweater, with a red-and-white stripe on each arm. I curled my lip for the photographer, and when I saw the resulting picture, I was delighted: *Wow! I actually look a bit like him!*

Skiffle has its place in British pop history. I've read that by the late fifties, there were as many as fifty thousand skiffle bands in Britain, banging their washboards and twanging their tea-chest basses up and down the land. But it didn't have the heart or guts of rock and roll, and it never did it for me.

Terry and I had a chat, agreed that we loved rock and roll, not skiffle, and quit The Dick Teague Skiffle Group. We recruited our old pal Norman Mitham on guitar, called ourselves The Drifters, and started rehearsing like mad, playing the stuff we really liked: Ricky Nelson, Buddy Holly and *lots and lots of Elvis.*

When Cliff Richard & The Drifters took off with 'Move It' in 1958, then we changed our name to The Shadows, I grew a little less obsessed with Elvis and hanging on his every move. *A little.* I had my own career to think about – and also, it was dawning on me that I had to find my own identity.

When I broke through, I started getting called the 'English Elvis' or the 'British answer to Elvis'. As I've always said, that second description ignored one basic fact: *Elvis was not a question.* I was secretly flattered and thrilled to get called this, but I also knew it could be a limitation for me.

When I sang my breakthrough hit 'Move It' on director Jack Good's TV show *Oh Boy!* in 1958, Jack very quickly twigged that I was basically a tribute act and made it clear to me that he didn't want an Elvis impersonator on his show. It was great advice, and I'll talk about it more when I write about 'Move It' later.

Yet even more key to me finding my own identity as a performer, and not being just an Elvis Mini-Me, was widening my musical style. Initially, this came about almost by accident. When I made my first film, *Serious Charge*, in 1959, I had no idea that I was contractually obliged to release a song from it as a single.

The song was 'Living Doll', which was a thin, pretend rock and roll song. Hank Marvin and Bruce Welch had joined The Drifters by then and thought it pretty ordinary, as I did, so Bruce took it upon himself to rearrange it as a country and western song. *Voila!* A tune, and a Number 1 hit, that parents were as likely to buy as teenagers!

Even when I was singing gentler material like that, though, and turning into Cliff Richard the family entertainer, I still hung on to my rock and roll roots. The flip side of 'Living Doll' was 'Apron Strings', a full-on rocker that was originally offered to Elvis. I insisted that we always rocked on our B-sides.

The other reason my Elvis obsession lessened a tad was that he also moved away from red-blooded rock and roll. When he started doing songs like 'Crying in the Chapel' and 'In the Ghetto', I still thought they were terrific, but they weren't the side of Elvis that had drawn me in. They weren't 'Heartbreak Hotel'.

But I still fundamentally loved him. I remember my second American tour, with The Shadows in 1962. We had a night off in New Orleans, and the band and I decided that we were going to walk down Bourbon Street, the main music street in the French Quarter, and have a drink in every bar we came to.

Well, we didn't realise quite how many bars there are on Bourbon Street! We had started early, it was a long night, and by the time we got to the fifth or sixth bar, I was distinctly wobbly on my feet! Clarence 'Frogman' Henry, the famous rhythm and blues singer and pianist, was playing in the bar.

Some kind soul from our party went up to him and told him, 'This is Cliff Richard – he sings in England!'

'Oh, really?' said Clarence. 'Come up on stage! What do you wanna do?'

I sang Elvis's 'I've Got a Woman' with him, very drunkenly and very badly. I'm glad that was a time before mobile phones and YouTube!

As an Elvis aficionado, I wasn't so keen on his Las Vegas years in the seventies. I don't know how much he really wanted to do all those shows, and it seemed like he had lost his way. He didn't look in great shape and, from what I heard, some of the performances he gave were well below his usual high standards.

I heard one Vegas recording where he forgot a lyric, burst out laughing, and was chuckling, getting the words wrong and hardly bothering to sing for the rest of the song. The crowd were cheering him, but I hated it. At his peak, Elvis was a master showman, always in control, and that was how I loved him: on top of his game.

I can't bear singers forgetting lyrics – especially when it happens to me! On one quite recent tour, I forgot the opening line to my song 'Dreamin''. It has a long intro, but I stopped my band as they were playing it, and said, 'Sorry, but can someone tell me my first line?' Everyone looked at me vacantly. No one could.

Even my backing vocalists' minds had gone blank! Then, suddenly, a woman in the front row of the audience shouted out the line: 'Four o'clock, I've been walking all night!' Everybody laughed, and clapped, and I thanked her. But I made sure it never happened again. And I *certainly* didn't like it happening to Elvis.

I famously never met Elvis. In fact, I never met him twice! The first time was right back in 1959. I went on a driving holiday to Italy with three friends, Elvis was in the US Army in West Germany at the time, and we made a spontaneous detour to Bad Nauheim on the way home to try to meet him.

We found his house and I knocked on his door. I was only eighteen and I could not have been more nervous: I thought he might be able to hear my heart thumping against my chest! When a guy answered and said Elvis wasn't home, I don't know if I was more disappointed . . . or relieved.

Our second non-encounter was far more poignant. It was in 1976, during Elvis's Vegas years, and I was in the US to promote 'Devil Woman', a single from my *I'm Nearly Famous* album. A journalist asked me, 'Why did you start making music?' and I told him the truth: it had been because of my utter veneration of Elvis.

When the interview had finished and the guy was packing his stuff away, he asked me if I was still a big Elvis fan. 'Yes, of course!' I replied. 'Oh, because I know him!' the journalist said. 'I'm going to Vegas this week. Would you like to come with me and meet him?'

I was gobsmacked. 'Wow! *Really?*'

'Yes! Come along, and I'll take a picture of the two of you together for my paper!'

I thought hard . . . and I said no. Elvis had put on a little weight, and I preferred to wait until he looked fantastic again. 'Let's wait until he is about to make his next movie, because he always slims down for those,' I said to the interviewer. 'Let's do it next time.'

Well, of course, there *wasn't* a next time. Elvis was dead just over a year later. I so dearly wish now that I had taken up that offer and gone to meet him. My advice to anyone who gets a chance to meet their hero is: *Go and do it, however they look!* Because, like me, you may never get another chance.

The legacy that Elvis Presley left on the world of rock and roll is inestimable. For me, his influence hangs over virtually every song I have included in this book. So, when the Baz Luhrmann *Elvis* movie that I mentioned earlier came out in 2022, I went to see it, keen to see if it would honour that legacy.

Well, it did . . . and it didn't. The film was beautifully made and had some truly great moments. Austin Butler was brilliant as the young Elvis and, to my surprise, even looked quite a lot like him. And yet, ultimately, I felt the movie focussed too much on his slightly difficult later years, and not enough on the power and glory of Elvis.

I wanted more on the *joy* of Elvis: the irresistible magic and magnetism that made The Drifters and me fill our live sets with his amazing songs before we had many of our own. Instead, it was basically two-and-a-half hours of the decline of Elvis, and him being duped by Colonel Tom Parker. And I thought that was a shame.

Elvis Presley was the reason I got into rock and roll and now, as my career begins to wind down, I have one big, pressing item left on my to-do list. In 2014, I sang a duet with Elvis's original vocal on 'Blue Suede Shoes' (which I will talk about next). And now, more than anything, I want to record a whole album with him.

I want to meet somebody at the top of the record label that owns all of Elvis's hits and get them to agree to release a duets album called *Elvis and Cliff*. It would be my ultimate labour of love, and I genuinely think it could sell a million. I think his fans like me, and mine *love* him: after all, I've always told them he's why I exist!

As I explained in *The Dreamer*, I even have an image for the album sleeve: it's a painting, imagining Elvis and me singing on stage together, that a Spanish artist painted for me years ago. I long to make this record – but Priscilla Presley tells me she thinks his label will never go for it. I honestly don't know why. It's *such* a pity.

Elvis Presley was *the* shaping influence on my career. That will never change. I no longer think, 'What would Elvis do?' whenever I have any big decisions to make, as I did in my earliest years. I've been through that. I stopped being the 'English Elvis' and started being me, Cliff Richard, a long time ago.

I still feel like I owe him everything, though, and I thought, just for fun, I'd collate a hit parade of my top ten Elvis songs for this book. If I'm being honest with you, it changes every week, but right here, right now, this is my chart rundown:

10. 'Mystery Train'

9. 'Let's Have a Party'

8. 'Trying to Get to You'

7. 'Blue Moon'

6. 'Don't'

5. '(Let Me Be Your) Teddy Bear'

4. 'Hound Dog'

3. 'Don't Be Cruel'

2. 'All Shook Up'

Well, I say it changes every week, but there is one placing that never really alters. That is the very last one, my chart topper:

1. 'Heartbreak Hotel'

Because, if I had never heard that song blasting out of a Citroën window in May 1956, none of this would have happened. That gawky schoolboy, Harry Webb, would never have transformed into Cliff Richard. I have many mornings when I wake up in Barbados, get up, gaze out of my bedroom window at the Caribbean, and wonder, *How the hell did I get from Cheshunt to here?*

And the answer is Elvis Presley.

THREE

'BLUE SUEDE SHOES' – CARL PERKINS

I initially assumed it was an Elvis song – I was wrong

When Elvis exploded with 'Heartbreak Hotel' in 1956, he sounded like the future – heck, he *was* the future! – but he wasn't the only great American star to appear from nowhere. *From outer space*. Elvis was the gateway into US rock and roll for so many of us, but once that gate was open, hordes of artists poured through it.

We had hardly known this music existed, but suddenly there was a tidal wave of rock and rollers crashing over us. They seemed to be coming at us non-stop, with all these brilliant songs based around those three chords* that my dad had taught me, and we lapped it all up. We couldn't get enough.

When I heard 'Blue Suede Shoes' as the opening track on my first ever album, *Elvis Presley,* I had no idea that it wasn't originally Elvis's song. In actual fact, it had been a big hit in America already

---

* If I have learned anything in my very long career, it's that you can do a lot with three chords!

for the musician who wrote it, a Tennessee-born singer, guitarist and songwriter named Carl Perkins.

I didn't hear Perkins's version until many months after Elvis's, but when I did, I thought it was terrific. Elvis's version was very similar, even down to the little ad libs in the song, but, as an impressionable teenager, I was hugely impressed that Perkins hadn't just sung the song but had *written* it, too.

From what I understand, Elvis didn't write a lot of songs, but he got an awful lot of co-writing credits! The music industry in the fifties was a bit like the Wild West, especially in America. There was a lot of exploitation and sharp practice going on, and Colonel Tom Parker, Elvis's manager, was a famously wily operator.

When Elvis was at his peak, hundreds of songwriters would beat a path to Colonel Tom's door. Elvis was selling millions of records all over the world, so all of those songwriters knew that if he sang their song, and made it a big hit, they would get hundreds of thousands of dollars.

The sole time I ever met Colonel Tom, on my first tour of America in 1960, he was gracious and charming, but, apparently, he was very different with these hopeful songwriters. Legend has it he would tell them: 'You want my boy, Elvis, to sing your song? Then he wants fifty per cent!'

This meant that Elvis would score a co-writing credit on the song, meaning that he would receive half of all the songwriting royalties, in addition to his performance royalties. It was an outrageous demand, but a lot of songwriters would swallow it because they had no option, and because they knew they would still make a mint. And they sure did.

Interestingly, one person who *didn't* fall in with Colonel Tom's demands was Dolly Parton. When her self-written song 'I Will Always Love You' was Number 1 on the US country chart in 1974, Parker met with her and said that Elvis wanted to cover the song, but he would have to have half of the publishing rights.

'Honey, it's my song!' Dolly told Colonel Parker. 'I won't do that!' And she walked out of their meeting. She later laughed that she had been upset at the time that Elvis never got to sing it, but things had worked out rather well for her: 'When Whitney Houston's version came out, I got enough money to *buy* Graceland!'*

Elvis didn't get a co-writing credit on 'Blue Suede Shoes' either, and Carl Perkins was a big deal. In the US they called him the King of Rockabilly, which was a mix of rock and roll and the wild 'hillbilly' folk and country music that was mostly coming out of the mountain regions of the American south.

That makes sense to me. Hillbilly and country *were* very influential on rock and roll, and country singers made some of the greatest early rock records. It was all tied in together – as well as the Black music/rhythm and blues element, which the very best rock and roll records had.

Carl Perkins talked about how he wrote 'Blue Suede Shoes'. He said he based it on a US nursery rhyme: 'One for the money, two for the show, three to make ready and four to go!' Apparently, that's what Americans used to say at the start of kids' races: their version of our 'On your marks, get set, go!'

That nursery-rhyme angle is interesting, because I think

---

* Dolly was joking – well, I assume so anyway! She certainly never did it!

there *is* a kind of brilliant simplicity to those early American rock and roll songs. They were just those three chords – *those sacred chords* – and a simple story laid on the top. They were *fun*, and that was the epitome of what rock and roll was about.

Johnny Cash had an interesting story about 'Blue Suede Shoes'. In his memoir, he said that he was touring America in 1955 with Elvis and Carl Perkins, and he told Perkins about a guy he had known in the army who always wore blue suede shoes when he was off duty, and warned people to be careful not to step on them.

'You should write a song about that!' Cash said.

'But I don't know anything about shoes!' Perkins answered.

When Perkins wrote and sang the song a few months later, it went racing up the *Billboard* chart to Number 2, but – to take a small detour here – he wasn't the first American rocker. There had been other artists playing rock and roll well before that, all of whom I slowly learned about in the wake of hearing Elvis.

Fats Domino had made 'The Fat Man' as far back as 1949: some music historians claim that it was the first rock and roll single. I don't know if that's true or not – *and, frankly, who does?* – but I enjoyed some of his fifties hits, such as 'Ain't That a Shame', 'Blueberry Hill' and 'I'm Walkin''.

In fact, one or two of my cousins were big into Fats Domino, which would cause a few friendly family arguments when I rode my bike over to visit them in Waltham Abbey. 'You must love Fats Domino!' they'd tell me. 'He's the greatest!' 'No, no, you're wrong!' I would reply. 'Elvis is the best!'

Bo Diddley was another extraordinary figure who I became

aware of after Elvis. When I first heard his name, I had no idea what it was: I thought maybe a 'bo diddley' was a new dance craze! In actual fact, Bo was basically a *rhythm*: later, that famous rhythm even got named after him! I also liked the fact that so many of his songs had his name in the title.

I didn't know about it at the time, but in 1963 Bo Diddley toured Britain on a bill with the Everly Brothers and Little Richard, with some obscure new group called The Rolling Stones opening up the show each night. Can you *believe* it? That is one tour I *certainly* wish I'd seen!

Some of those wild early American rock and rollers had correspondingly wild private lives. Little Willie John was certainly one of them! He had a big hit with 'Fever' in 1956 and I loved his young, confident and passionate vocal. Peggy Lee did a gentler, sweeter version of the song later, but Little Willie John was something else.

I loved it, and I didn't know for years that Little Willie John was a hard-drinking roughneck who was often in trouble with the law even before he killed a man and died in jail when he was only thirty. Goodness me! It's a ridiculous life story, but it doesn't change how great the song is . . . or stop it playing in my head.

But let's get back to 'Blue Suede Shoes'. I never met Elvis, but I once sang the song with him. Sort of! When I recorded my *Just . . . Fabulous Rock 'n' Roll* album of reinterpretations of rock classics in Nashville in 2014, I duetted on it with the original vocal that Elvis had recorded for his single, fifty-eight years earlier.

By then, I knew both versions of the song, of course. I preferred Elvis's version, but I liked the slower tempo of the Carl

Perkins original. So, I kept the mood and feel of Elvis's take, but slowed the rhythms of the song right down.

It was a weird, weird session. I made that album amid the hell of the untrue sex allegations and police investigation that wrecked my life for more than two years, when I figured I would never know 'normal' or feel happy again. But for that two minutes and six seconds of singing with Elvis, I was transported. *Lifted up*.

I remember I had my headphones on in the studio, and when Elvis's powerhouse voice first appeared in them – '*Weeee-ll, it's one for the money!*' – I was floored. It felt like he was standing next to me: I almost turned around to check! But I had to collect myself, and sing the next line: '*Two for the show!*'

I loved the whole experience and I was so pleased with the version of 'Blue Suede Shoes' that Elvis and I sang together. The fact we decided to slow his vocal down a little didn't diminish the quality of his voice, thanks to modern technology. In any case, that voice *can't* be diminished. It will always sound magnificent.

Carl Perkins never really got his dues for writing and performing 'Blue Suede Shoes'. It is one of the all-time rock and roll classics, and his version of it was genuinely terrific, but he got dwarfed by Elvis, as did so many other performers. And one other factor is that Carl Perkins was really, really unlucky.

When he had 'Blue Suede Shoes' at Number 2 in the *Billboard* charts, in 1956, he was on his way to appear on Perry Como's TV show to perform it when he was in an awful car crash. A truck driver died, and Perkins was hospitalised. While he was there, unable to promote the record, a song leapfrogged him to Number 1.

And what was that song? *'Heartbreak Hotel' by Elvis Presley!*

Carl Perkins was a bit of a one-hit wonder. After 'Blue Suede Shoes', he had no other big *Billboard* hits, although he was a regular in the US country chart. Yet he was an influential figure. In the same way that I credit Elvis for my career, Paul McCartney has said, 'If there was no Carl Perkins, there'd have been no Beatles.' It's so interesting that The Beatles were influenced by the same artists as The Shadows and me, even though we took off five years before they did.

'Blue Suede Shoes' was also recorded by Eddie Cochran, Buddy Holly and even by John Lennon and Yoko Ono (!), but ultimately, people will always think of it as an Elvis Presley song. From what I can gather, Carl Perkins was quite stoical about this. He once got asked why he thought Elvis became a superstar, and not him.

'Elvis had everything,' Perkins said. 'He had the looks, the moves, the manager and the talent. He didn't look like Mister Ed,* like a lot of us did! Elvis hit them with sideburns, flashy clothes and no ring on his finger. I had three kids!'

And there you have it. Carl Perkins gave the world a fantastic rock and roll song, but he is spot on: in music, you need the entire package. And it was Elvis Presley who had everything.

---

* *Mister Ed* was an American sitcom about a talking horse. Carl Perkins was no Elvis the Pelvis, but I think he was a tad hard on himself to say he looked like a horse!

FOUR

'LUCILLE' – LITTLE RICHARD

The rock and roller from Mars who said he liked me

I've explained that one thing I loved about rock and roll, when it first came along, was that it had an edge and an attitude that just weren't there in Frank Sinatra or Perry Como. Yet even within rock and roll, some artists were a lot more extreme than others. And nobody, I mean *nobody*, was more extreme than Little Richard.

From the very first time I heard him, on AFN, I knew this guy was different from any other rock and roller out there. He was so outrageous: *What is this?!* He was completely out on his own, a total one-off, and you either loved him or you hated him. And I absolutely loved him.

He'd apparently been making records since 1951, when he was still a teenager, but I first heard Little Richard, like everybody, when 'Tutti Frutti' was a hit in the UK in 1957. It leapt out of the radio and grabbed me by the throat! I couldn't believe that amazing yelp of a chorus: '*A-wop-bop-a-loo-bop, a-lop-bam-boom!*'

After that, I was straight down to Marsden's to hand over a shilling for almost every single he made in the mid-fifties: 'Rip It Up', 'She's Got It', 'The Girl Can't Help It'. But the one that really got to me, and whose impact stays with me even now, was 'Lucille'.

As a singer, I always listen closely to vocalists, and 'Lucille' is one of the all-time great rock and roll vocals. It's partly a squeal, partly a howl, driven and demented yet somehow also perfectly in tune. Little Richard had an amazing high range, and he sounded like the very spirit of rock and roll made flesh.

This crazy guy could have terrified some people – and I'm sure he did! – but whenever I played 'Long Tall Sally' or 'Lucille' on the Dansette at home, Mum and Dad liked it. They never said, 'Turn that racket down!' Beneath the yelling and the chaos, there was a musicality, and they enjoyed it.

Little Richard was something else. As I've said, when I first heard and saw Elvis, I wanted to *be* him. Well, I would certainly never have dared to want to be Little Richard! He was just so far out there that it was unthinkable. It would have been like wanting to live on Venus!

I could tell he was flamboyant, but I didn't realise quite how much until the first time I saw him on television, singing 'Lucille'. It was incredible. He was a small guy but so charismatic and exaggerated, big-eyed in a pompadour quiff and baggy suit, singing and hammering at a piano while he was standing up. *What the . . . ?*

He looked the complete showman in his dramatic make-up – very daring for a male artist in the fifties – but it wasn't just all show: he was clearly a formidable talent. And had been since childhood. There is footage on YouTube of Little Richard playing the piano when he was just ten years old. If you've never seen it, google it now! It's unbelievable.

I used to really envy artists who played the piano. My family background was way too humble for my parents ever to be able to afford something like piano lessons for me, but I've always admired pianists. Pianos have such a full sound. I mean, guitars are great, but there's only so much that you can do with six strings.*

Rock and roll is full of larger-than-life extroverts, and I'm sure that Little Richard's background contributed to him being such a peculiar character. He was one of twelve children born to a family in Georgia. His father was a pastor at the local church, but also ran a nightclub and sold bootleg moonshine on the side!

Little Richard used to sing in that church as a boy but then apparently got kicked out of the choir for screaming and hollering too much! He must have been really going for it, because those choirs can be wild. Believe me, there are few happier, more uplifting sounds in the world than a gospel choir singing 'Hallelujah!'

When he was little, his family wouldn't have blues, or rhythm and blues, in the house because they said it was 'the devil's music'.†

---

* The guitar has other advantages, though. I've never been a virtuoso guitarist, but when I used to do a lot of charity work in Africa and Asia years ago, at least I could just put my guitar over my shoulder and go off and play it anywhere. I mean, good luck transporting a piano to the middle of an African jungle!

† I saw a little of that attitude in the sixties. When I became a Christian, I would go and sing and speak in churches, but some of them didn't want me because they didn't trust rock and roll. Then the churches slowly realised that it's *not* the devil's music – it's just that the people who play it can sometimes be devils!

I think that attitude left an impression on him all through his life, even when he was one of the best rock and rollers in history. He went back and forth between loving what he did and feeling guilty about it.

I remember that crazy incident in 1957 when Little Richard threw all his rings off the side of a ferry on tour in Australia. He told his band he'd just had a vision of angels, and seen a fireball in the sky, and so would give up showbiz to become a preacher. His proof of this epiphany was to chuck his gold jewellery in a river!

Of course, he didn't stick to that. Little Richard didn't stick to *anything* much. He preached in churches and at evangelical events, while also taking loads of drugs ('They should call me "Lil Cocaine!"' he once said). He proclaimed that he was gay, then said that he wasn't. He was every inch as wild and impulsive as his music.

If it's OK to say this nowadays, Little Richard seemed to me to be a fascinating weirdo. He was almost the ultimate rock star of his day. He was such a strange guy, and yet I never felt as though he was dangerous to anybody else. He wasn't going to go nuts and start shooting people. He was just a crazy rock and roller.

I remember watching one television interview that he gave, back in the sixties. Little Richard was drawling away, in that camp, high-pitched, quick-talking way that he had, and he was absolutely hilarious. He seemed to be having such fun with the questions – until one particular, rather rude one.

'How does it feel to always come second to Elvis?' the interviewer asked him. Or something like that. Little Richard stared at him as if it was the most ridiculous thing he had ever heard.

'Ah am second to no man!' he declared. 'Ah. Am. The. Number. One. Man!'

It was so funny: it could have been Muhammad Ali talking! Then, towards the end of the interview, the questioner asked him which other singers he liked to listen to. Little Richard gave him a few names – then added one that stopped me dead.

'Ah like that Cliff Rich-hard, from England,' he lisped. 'Yes, that Cliff Rich-hard. I like him!'

I nearly fell off the sofa! *Little Richard mentioned my name!* It was such a thrill. Back then, after I'd become a Christian, journalists had begun dismissing me as 'Goody Two-Shoes Cliff Richard', and here was the wildest rock and roll star of all time saying he liked me! *Wow!* I was floating on air for the rest of the day.

I sang 'Lucille' on record once. Back in 1983, I made an album called *Silver* to mark my twenty-fifth anniversary in show business. Compact discs had just come in, and I needed a couple of bonus tracks to go on the CD version of the album. So – *why not?* – I decided to have a crack at 'Lucille'.

It was fantastic! I know that, due to songs like 'Living Doll' and 'Miss You Nights', people think I'm a very calm and moderate singer, but I went to town on 'Lucille'! I was yelling and screaming away like crazy, and having my own Little Richard moment. It was so much fun to record and I'm really proud of it.

Sadly, I never met him, although I could have done once. I was recording in Memphis in 2011, and somebody in the studio mentioned that Little Richard was in town and staying in a hotel nearby. As soon as I heard that, a daring thought formed in my head: *Could I go down and try to meet him? Introduce myself?*

I went back and forth on the question during the day – *Yes, I will! No, I won't!* – but I've never been one for shoving myself forward like that and, in the end, I decided not to do it. Now, of course, as with Elvis, I very much wish that I had. You have to take these rare chances when they present themselves to you.

I loved his music as a teenager and I love it now. Little Richard was one of the shaping influences of rock and roll, and yet also truly unique: there was *nobody* else like him. I'm not sure that I would necessarily believe every single word that he ever said, mind you.

Apparently, Little Richard met Elvis in 1969, and had a chat with him. Afterwards, somebody asked him what Elvis had said to him. And Little Richard said, 'Elvis told me, "Forget about me – *you* are the greatest! *You* are the greatest there has ever been!"'

Ha! It's a fantastic quote! And, if I were you, I'd take it with a sizeable pinch of salt . . .

FIVE

'SCHOOL DAY (RING! RING! GOES THE BELL)' – CHUCK BERRY

He really did deliver us from the days of old

You know, it's impossible to explain just how exciting it was to be a music-loving teenage boy in the spring of 1957. I think you had to be there! Elvis had opened those floodgates, and that tidal wave of American rock and rollers was washing right over us. It felt like there was a new star splashing down every day.

More than ever, I was glued to AFN and Luxembourg every evening and weekend. Even the stuffy old BBC Light Programme was playing rock and roll by now! And I spent so much time – not to mention so many shillings – at Marsden's that I reckon they should probably have named a listening booth after Harry Webb!

Those amazing artists just kept coming. Chuck Berry was another who blew me away as soon as I heard him. There's no question that, like Elvis and Little Richard, Chuck is one of the founding fathers of rock and roll. There is a rawness and directness to his music that thrilled me from the off, and it still does today.

Like most Brits, I first heard Chuck when 'School Day (Ring! Ring! Goes the Bell)' was his first British hit in 1957. I loved it, both for the power of the song and the fact that, for once, it actually had a lyric that I could relate to!

I was sixteen. I'd never had my baby left me, or had to move down the end of Lonely Street to Heartbreak Hotel, but I *was* still putting on my tie and blazer, picking up my satchel and trudging off to Cheshunt Secondary Modern School every day. Chuck's first line – 'Up in the mornin' and out to school' – now *that*, I related to!

Yet there was another, far more crucial line in the song. Towards the end, Chuck sings, 'Hail, hail, rock and roll! Deliver me from the days of old!' It sounded like a rallying call, a defiant statement that this new music was sweeping the old guard of crooners away. They'd had their time. *This was ours.*

Another thing that I loved about 'School Day' was that it sounded like Chuck was singing a duet with the guitar. He'd growl something and it would answer him back. That was a big influence on a lot of rock and roll to come. If I am honest, I think my first single, 'Move It', definitely borrowed that same trick.

After I heard 'School Day', I worked backwards with Chuck Berry, and found he'd had a few hits in the US before then. I managed to track them down. 'Maybellene' was tremendous, with an amazing guitar line and chorus: 'Maybellene, why can't you be true?' Again, it's that rawness and directness. It gets me every time.

A great thing, for me, about early rock and roll is that, as far as listeners were concerned, it was totally colour-blind. There was no danger of any racism towards artists from music fans, because we had no idea what colour they were. It was weeks before I saw a photo of Chuck Berry and realised, *OK, he's a Black guy*! Black or white didn't matter. We just loved the records.

Nor did we care about their backgrounds. I didn't know, for years, that Chuck was another of those early rock and rollers with very, shall we say, *eventful* lives. He did an armed robbery in his teens, and spent three years in youth prison before he even began his musical career. *Well, forget that! Listen to that guitar riff!*

It wasn't long after hearing Chuck that I quit The Dick Teague Skiffle Group and skiffle and, with Norman Mitham and Terry Smart, formed The Drifters. At our sporadic gigs in Cheshunt youth clubs and pubs, we were playing Ricky Nelson and Jerry Lee Lewis songs and, of course, *loads* of Elvis ... but nothing by Chuck Berry.

Why was this? I thought I couldn't manage the vocal! My teenage voice didn't feel raucous enough. I've always said that the greatest Black singers of blues, soul and rock and roll sound as if their vocal cords are made of concrete. At that tender age, I felt as if mine were made of cotton wool.*

Luckily, I conquered that mental block. After I had broken through, and got more confident and experienced as a singer, we began doing the odd Chuck Berry song in our live set. The Shadows and I were playing one when we toured South Africa for the second time, in 1963, and it went down an absolute storm.

---

* I don't feel like my vocal cords are made of cotton wool anymore, but I do have one song, 'Mobile Alabama School Leaving Hullabaloo', that I play live extremely sparingly. After I've sung it, I always feel as if my throat has been sandpapered – from the inside!

Chuck had written a song in 1955 called 'Thirty Days (To Come Back Home)'. It had been a hit in 1959 for an American band called Ronnie Hawkins & The Hawks, who for some obscure reason changed the title to 'Forty Days (To Come Back Home)'. We kept that new lyric when we played it.

We had no idea before we got to South Africa, but it transpired that young guys in that country had to do forty days national service in places like Mozambique, so had adopted the song as a sort of ironic anthem. They went nuts for it, and it was a highlight of the set every night of our tour.

In more recent years, I've performed a few Chuck numbers. I will never tire of singing 'Roll Over Beethoven' – what a song that is! I also love to have a good go at 'Memphis, Tennessee'. Chuck was always pretty rough-edged, and all the better for it, but that tune has a terrific melody.

Chuck's great thing was always riffs, though, and 'School Day (Ring! Ring! Goes the Bell)' was an absolute killer. A few years later, that guitar rhythm was to show up, virtually unaltered but with new words, rebranded as 'No Particular Place to Go'. Ah, well! Chuck's not the first, or last, rock and roller to recycle the odd riff!

In his later years, Chuck Berry got a reputation for being what the Americans call 'ornery'. He became known for being very money-motivated, and notorious for refusing to go on stage for his shows until the concert promoters had paid him his fee upfront, in full – in cash!

Well, you know what? I think that's entirely understandable.

Chuck Berry is just one of the many early Black bluesmen and rock and roll stars who were ripped off very badly by white managers, promoters and record company owners. He got paid in buttons for his brilliance, and he had every right to feel aggrieved.

I remember once seeing some amazing video footage. Chuck was in the wings at a concert and the guy on stage was saying, 'Now, we have a very special guest!' Chuck was shaking his head and saying, 'Nuh-uh – not until I've got my money!' He wouldn't go on until someone ran up to him with an envelope of cash.

The rip-offs were a shameful episode in rock and roll history, and it wasn't just Chuck who suffered at the hands of exploitative music industry bosses. Over the years, I've had a few encounters with, and come to know, Dionne Warwick, one of the most talented and brilliant soul singers we've ever seen.

Dionne has had hit after hit after hit for sixty years. She had two of the greatest songwriters in the canon, Burt Bacharach and Hal David, writing a conveyor belt of tunes such as 'Walk On By', 'I Say a Little Prayer' and 'I'll Never Fall in Love Again' for her. And yet, somehow, ten years ago, Dionne Warwick went bankrupt.

How could that happen? Well, it was down to mismanagement of her business affairs. I can only guess exactly what happened, but it shook me. *Good grief! If Dionne Warwick can't make a living from music, what chance has anybody else got?!* And, in his early years, I gather that Chuck Berry got into a worse financial situation than Dionne, despite his success.

It's an utter disgrace. I'm no politician, so I'm not going to start talking about the payment of historical reparations, but there's no doubt we white people have a lot to answer for. You and I can't be punished for the sins of our grandfathers, but the fact that Chuck Berry got treated as badly as he did ... well, shame on them.

Luckily, there was a happy ending to Chuck's story. He may have been exploited back in the day, but he more than made up for it in his later years. When he died in 2017, aged ninety, he left an estate of $50m. *Well, good for him!* And a lot of it was because he wrote his own songs. The writing is where the money is.

One funny thing about Chuck Berry is that anyone who was a child in Britain in the early seventies will have grown up knowing him for his Number 1 hit, 'My Ding-a-Ling'. It was a lewd novelty song, not written by Chuck, full of innuendos about his 'silver bells hanging on a string' and him being 'caught playing with my ding-a-ling'.

Now, I have nothing against novelty records as such. Paul McCartney had 'The Frog Chorus'; David Bowie had 'The Laughing Gnome'. Hey, even I had my cover of 'Living Doll' with the guys from *The Young Ones*!* But 'My Ding-a-Ling' isn't my favourite Chuck Berry song. In fact, it's not in my top 100 Chuck Berry songs!

His music blew me away in Cheshunt in 1957 and it does exactly the same now. When I recorded my *Just ... Fabulous Rock*

---

* I was so wary about doing that charity record in 1986. I told Rik Mayall and the other guys, 'Look, I've spent *years* building my image. Please don't start swearing all over the place and trash it!' They didn't: they were as good as gold and extremely professional.

'n' Roll album of rock and roll classics in 2014, I included no fewer than three Chuck Berry songs: 'Sweet Little Sixteen', 'Roll Over Beethoven' and 'Memphis, Tennessee'. And, believe it or not, even Elvis only got two!

Yeah. 'Hail, hail, rock and roll!' indeed. Chuck Berry was a genius.

SIX

'ROCK AROUND THE CLOCK' – BILL HALEY & HIS COMETS

The first rocker I saw live – we'll always have Edmonton!

The thrills and spills kept coming fast in that spring of 1957. By now, I had spent nearly a year sculpting my hair into a quiff and discovering all of the amazing new American rock and roll stars who were changing the world around me. Now, I was finally going to get a chance to see one in the flesh. *Live.*

I first heard Bill Haley & His Comets' 'Rock Around the Clock' on AFN in 1954. It was re-released in 1955, and became the first rock and roll record to top the charts in both America and Britain but, at the time, I didn't find it remotely as seismic or life-changing as I did Elvis, a year later I just thought it was fun.

I had just turned fourteen when it first came out, so I was a bit young fully to embrace rock and roll, but I can remember loving the song and throwing myself about to it whenever I heard it. That's one important element of early rock and roll that shouldn't be overlooked. It always made you want to get up and *dance*.

I still remember one end-of-term school dance in the big hall where they played 'Rock Around the Clock' *so* many times and everyone was up and jiving. My sister Donna and I jived to it at home. I'd be jumping about, waggling my hips, spinning Donna around and sliding her through my legs. As I say, such fun!

Some people saw a lot more meaning in 'Rock Around the Clock'. It gained a fresh significance, and even began getting called 'an anthem for rebellious youth', when it played under the opening credits of a major movie, *Blackboard Jungle*, starring that brilliant American actor, Sidney Poitier.

Blackboard Jungle was set in an inner-city American high school full of delinquent pupils getting into anti-social behaviour, violence and crime. Glenn Ford starred as an idealistic English teacher, who tries to pull these kids back onto the straight and narrow but gets disrespected, abused and even beaten up by them.

I went to see the film when it came out and I thought it was brilliant. It was a serious movie, with a message about social deprivation and inequality, and it was another chance to hear that great Bill Haley song! But I was horrified by the wave of aggro that followed in the film's wake.

Kids watching *Blackboard Jungle* were getting swept up and carried away by the movie, and replicating what they saw on the screen. There were a lot of stories in the newspapers about adolescents smashing up picture houses, ripping out the seats, and vandalising shops and cars when they got out of the cinemas.

If I'm honest, I was disgusted by this. It seemed pointless and stupid to me. Yes, it was a great movie, and an important one, but what was the thinking behind copying it? These kids doing the damage weren't from deprived American inner cities: in fact, most of them came from well-off families in the Home Counties!

There were suddenly a lot of rebels without a cause, to quote another famous, well-known film from the same time, and it baffled me. It was the same as when Elvis first came along. People in some quarters were scared of rock and roll and saw it as rebel music, with Elvis as its frightening figurehead.

Even when I broke through with 'Move It', I was depicted to a certain degree as a rebel, making music to stir things up and threaten society. *Well, excuse me!* I had never heard anything so ridiculous in my life! I was playing rock and roll because of Elvis, and for kicks, and I had absolutely no desire whatsoever to rebel.

In any case, what did I have to rebel against? I wasn't upset about my upbringing. I loved and respected my mum and dad. They were fantastic with my sisters and me. They never had much cash, but they always found my weekly thruppenny-bit pocket money. What was I supposed to hate about that?

No, I hated the hooliganism that sprang up around *Blackboard Jungle*, and I hated it even more at a couple of 1959 gigs with The Drifters in London when yobbish Teddy Boys threw missiles at us on stage and trashed the venues. They just ruined the shows for everybody else. And *why*? As I keep saying, rock and roll was, and is, supposed to be *fun*!

So, I loved jumping around to 'Rock Around the Clock' when it first came out, but it never remotely rearranged my mind, or my whole life, in the way that Elvis was to do. Even so, when I heard that Bill Haley & His Comets were to play just a few miles down the road from me in 1957, I just *had* to see them.

Until that point, American rock and rollers had seemed mystical, even mythical figures to me, an alluring combination of amazing music over a crystal radio and occasional photographs in newspapers and magazines. Now, I had the chance to see one in real life. In the flesh. In *Edmonton*.

Bill Haley & His Comets were to play the Regal Theatre in Edmonton in north London, just five miles from Cheshunt, on Sunday, 3 March 1957. As soon as we heard this jaw-dropping news, my friends and I began grouping in huddles in the school playground to hatch a plan. There was no way we were going to miss it!

The tickets were going on sale a few weeks before the show. Norman Mitham, Terry Smart and I, with two or three other mates, decided to take no chances. That crucial Monday morning, we set our alarms for 4am and met up to get the bus to Edmonton to be at the venue before the ticket office opened.

When we got to the Regal before 6am, we discovered we weren't the only people with that idea! The queue of eager rock and roll fans already stretched from the front door of the venue down the street and around the corner. It took three hours to inch our way to the front. All that were left were seats in the balcony.

We were all wearing our Cheshunt Secondary Modern uniforms, because we had planned to go straight into school, but by the time we'd got the tickets, we'd missed assembly and figured it was too late. One of the lads had keys to his house and his parents were out at work, so we went there and hung out all day playing records.

The perfect plan, huh? Well, not quite! We got rumbled. To this day, I have no idea who it was, but somebody or other saw us queuing outside the Regal in our blazers and ties and snitched on us to the headmaster. When we got to school the next morning, we got called into his office for a dressing-down.

By now, I was a prefect, but he took my badge off me for a couple of months. I was a bit upset about this. I'm not sure why: being a prefect basically just meant spending your breaks ticking off younger kids for running down corridors! There were no real perks. But I guess it had a certain status, which I liked.

Well, it was worth it to see my first ever rock and roll show! I was counting down the days until 3 March. When it finally came around, I donned my drainpipe trousers – because those were days well before jeans! – and we were all in the Regal two hours before Bill Haley was due on stage.

I could not have been more excited. The atmosphere was electric. If I could have got my hand into the pockets of my skin-tight trousers, I think I would have been pinching myself. *Wow! I am about to see a proper American rock and roller! They actually exist! Is this really happening?*

It was, and when Bill Haley & His Comets strode on stage and launched into 'Razzle Dazzle' – *'On your mark! Get set! Now, ready, go!'* – every single person jumped up out of their seats. The noise was deafening. Everybody was leaping up and down so much that I was sure the balcony was shaking under our feet.

Everybody was cheering, and some of the girls were scream-ing. This was funny, in a way. Bill Haley was thirty-one by now – *ancient!* – and a portly, chubby-chopped guy. Girls were in a frenzy over a man who looked like a friendly uncle. I mean, no disrespect to him, but nobody was ever going to call him Bill the Pelvis!

Bill had a few moves at the mic, and the guitarist was swaying away, but the real star of the night was the double-bass player. He spun around as he plucked at it, then threw himself on the floor and played it lying down! When they played 'Rock Around the Clock', the place erupted. They must have heard it in Cheshunt.

What a night! I'll never forget it. I had heard quite a few great songs and artists by now, but Bill Haley & His Comets in Edmon-ton brought rock and roll right into my own life. Brought it alive for me. I left buzzing with excitement, with my ears ringing, and my mind even more made up than it already was:

Yep. That is exactly what I want to do with my life!

There was one more repercussion at school from my unchar-acteristic, accidental one-day truancy to buy my concert ticket. My English teacher, Jay Norris, was an inspirational figure and some-one I respected a lot. It had been Miss Norris who gave my friends and me the classroom to rehearse The Quintones after school.

Despite this, Miss Norris was horrified at me taking a day off to buy a ticket, and losing my prefect's badge. She was a cultured woman but it was classic generation-gap stuff: she just didn't 'get' rock and roll.

'What a stupid thing to do, Harry!' she chided me. 'In ten years, you won't even remember Bill Haley!'

Well, she was wrong on that one! Jay Norris and I kept in touch after I left school, and on 3 March 1967, ten years to the day after the Edmonton gig, I drove from London to Cheshunt with a box of chocolates for her. I knocked on her door. When she opened it, I handed her the chocolates and said 'Bill Haley!'*

Bill Haley had a handful more mid-fifties classic rock and roll hits, such as 'Shake, Rattle and Roll' and 'See You Later, Alligator' I remember buying one of his early 10-inch albums and loving songs like 'Dim, Dim the Lights'. I'd like to play those songs live again, today, in a contemporary style. I think they deserve it.

As we got to the end of the fifties, though, Bill Haley & His Comets fell away. The hits dried up and Bill faded into relative obscurity, as had Carl Perkins. Why did it happen? I always find it so hard to know – except that maybe, like Carl, he was another one who didn't have *everything* in the way that Elvis did.

From the sixties on, Bill Haley's only chart action, either here or in America, came whenever his record label re-released 'Rock Around the Clock' for an anniversary or a TV advert tie-in. Still, I guess if you have to be known for one song above all others, what a great song to be known for!

I've been fortunate enough to be invited twice onto *Desert Island Discs*, the BBC's long-running radio interview show that casts you away on a desert island and asks you to choose eight records to take with you. I was only twenty when I first went on, in 1960, to be grilled by its genteel host, Roy Plomley.

---

* I'm still in touch with Jay, who, at the time of writing, is 102 years old and still going strong. Maybe I'll send her a copy of *A Head Full of Music* to show her that I *still* remember Bill Haley, sixty-six years on!

I was still a callow youth but, somehow, I managed to sound far cooler and more confident than I felt inside. I obviously chose 'Heartbreak Hotel' as one of my eight songs. But when, at the end of the show, Mr Plomley asked me to select one disc to save if all the rest got swept away by the waves, I didn't pick Elvis.

I picked 'Rock Around the Clock' by Bill Haley & His Comets.

For me, this song will forever summon up that magical night in Edmonton, and my first rock and roll gig. It will always remind me of jiving with Donna in our humble council house. And it will forever conjure up an *innocence* that I fear we have largely lost nowadays, both from music and from life.

And, you know what? I miss it.

SEVEN

'TWENTY FLIGHT ROCK'
– EDDIE COCHRAN

A fun hit that I first heard in the local flicks

There were two cinemas in Waltham Cross. The Embassy was the smarter one: a lovely Art Deco building that boasted a balcony, an organ and even a café. The Regent, right over the road from it, was a more basic place, to say the least, and went by the rather unflattering local nickname of 'the fleapit'.*

When I was a teenager, whatever little pocket money I had left after I had spent most of it at Marsden's generally went on trips to the pictures. And the Embassy was where, in 1957, I went to see a movie called *The Girl Can't Help It*, starring one of the hotshot Hollywood bombshells of the time, Jayne Mansfield.

Oddly enough, I was to meet Jayne Mansfield just two years later, when I was a naïve young rock star encountering all sorts of unlikely people in TV studios. She was lovely and friendly. But in 1957 she was one more sexy cinema goddess, as beautiful

---

* Cheshunt also had a cinema, the Central, which I went to occasionally as a little kid. It had the even more unflattering nickname of 'the bug hutch'.

and distant as Marilyn Monroe or my personal favourite, Brigitte Bardot.

The Girl Can't Help It was a musical comedy in which Jayne played Jerri Jordan, a woman being forced into a singing career against her will, and it was a big deal for rock and roll fans. This was because the movie had a great soundtrack and cameo appearances by Little Richard, Gene Vincent . . . and this guy. Eddie Cochran.

Halfway through the film, Jerri Jordan's mobster boyfriend phones her up and orders her to switch on the television to watch a star whose charisma and clever moves she should try to emulate on stage. Jerri runs across the room, turns on the set, and gazes avidly as Eddie Cochran performs 'Twenty Flight Rock'.

And it *is* quite a performance. Handsome in a sharp pink jacket and with his hair coaxed into a perfect quiff, Cochran hunches over his guitar, jumps from foot to foot and waggles his knees as he fires out the catchy song. Fixing the camera with a piercing stare, he looks every inch the stylish rock and roller. Like Elvis, it was a very *physical* performance.

It was a thrill for me to watch because I already knew a bit about Eddie Cochran. I'd bought a couple of his singles. He'd had a hit early in 1957 with 'Sittin' in the Balcony', a song about a subject any teenage boy could relate to: taking a girl to the pictures, and sitting in the back row to try to get a kiss and a cuddle!

He followed that up with another great song called 'Mean When I'm Mad', and I was off to Marsden's to get his debut album, *Singin' to My Baby*, at the end of the year. But when he sang

'Twenty Flight Rock' in the movie, and then released it as a single, I thought it was the best thing that he had done.

'Twenty Flight Rock' is such a fun and *funny* song. I think that is definitely an understated factor about early rock and roll: just how funny some of the lyrics could be. If the rhythm gets you jumping around the room, and the words put a smile on your face, that's a pretty irresistible combination!

'Twenty Flight Rock' is a story song, about a young guy who goes around to visit his girlfriend on a Saturday night, hoping for a dance and to 'hold her tight'. But her apartment is right up on the twentieth floor, and when he arrives at her building, he hits a major snag: 'The elevator's broken down!'

Well, our lovelorn hero starts the long ascent up twenty flights of stairs. It gets tougher and tougher. By the twelfth floor, he's 'startin' to drag'; by the time he reaches the fifteenth, he's 'a-ready to sag'. When he finally gets to the top, and his girl's flat, he's totally wiped out: 'I'm too tired to rock!'

It's a song that requires a twinkle in the eye as you sing it, and Eddie certainly had that, especially in the movie! The lyrics were suggestive but it was a gentle, sweet humour, rather than anything too over-the-top. It's simple, harmless fun, suffused with that sense of innocence that I miss today.*

'Twenty Flight Rock' is very much a rock and roll song, but

---

* It's certainly a long way from some of today's rap stars, with their sexually explicit lyrics, denigrating women and insulting them as 'hos'. I wouldn't have that music, or those guys, in my house. I wouldn't even have them in my garage!

the humour and the comic narrative are suggestive of country music. As I've already said, country singers made some of the best early rock and roll records. And a great song will always lend itself to any genre.

By the time *The Girl Can't Help It* and 'Twenty Flight Rock' came out, Norman, Terry and I had started playing local gigs as The Drifters. We stuck the song into our live set straight away. It was easy to learn – those three chords again! – and I always looked forward to singing it. It was a highlight of our shows.

Eddie Cochran was an amazing talent. There was a definite Elvis influence, both in his vocal and his stage moves, but he was hardly unique in that: let's face it, we were *all* stealing from Elvis, me more than most! And where he actually outdid Elvis was that, as well as a great performer, he was a brilliant songwriter.

Eddie was only two years older than me. He co-wrote 'Twenty Flight Rock' when he was just seventeen, and over the next two years, he was to write or co-write more rock and roll classics: 'C'mon Everybody', 'Somethin' Else', 'Three Steps to Heaven'. All penned by someone so young? *I ask you!* It's extraordinary!

I admired Eddie Cochran's talent and always listened out for his new songs. After I had my career breakthrough and became a recording artist myself, I viewed him as my competition: after all, we were both aiming for the same chart places. And I even got to meet him once. Well, sort of.

By the end of the fifties, I began to appear nearly every year at the big *NME* Poll Winners Party. The winners were voted for by the magazine's readers. In 1960, it was at Wembley Empire Pool, and I got named 'Best British Male Singer' for the second year in a row. Elvis always won 'Best World Male Singer', and quite right, too!

The *NME* Poll Winners Party was such a big deal that, in February 1960, I flew home from my first American tour *just for one night* to appear at the ceremony and receive my prize. (That wasn't all I did that night: I was then rushed to Oxford Street to headline a live TV show, *Sunday Night at the London Palladium*! Crazy schedule, huh?)

I was excited about flying in for the *NME* party, but also pretty exhausted and a bit jet-lagged. So, I watched through a personal haze as Billy Fury sang a number, Gene Vincent gave a characteristically eccentric performance . . . and Eddie Cochran did a brilliant, intense version of 'C'mon Everybody' that got the fans screaming.

It was worth flying back from America for one night, though, when I walked on stage to get my award and triggered a wall of noise so loud that it almost knocked me backwards. 'Screams galore greeted the appearance of Cliff Richard,' *NME* later reported. When I was young, that was my favourite sound in the world.

Backstage at Wembley, I mentioned to one of the organisers that I was an Eddie Cochran fan. 'Oh, his dressing room is just down the corridor!' the guy answered. 'Would you like to meet him? I'm sure he won't mind!'

'Sure!' I replied. 'Why not?'

My escort led me on the short walk down the corridor. Eddie Cochran's dressing room door was open, so we walked straight in.

Eddie was sitting with his back to the door, his feet on a table, holding a guitar and with a small entourage of girls and general hangers-on around him.

'Eddie, hi, this is Cliff Richard!' the *NME* guy said. 'He'd like to say hello!'

Eddie Cochran stayed sitting down, but glanced over his shoulder at me. Our eyes met for a millisecond. 'Oh, hi there!' he mumbled, then looked down again and returned to strumming on his guitar and chatting to the girls. So, that was that. I turned around and walked back to my dressing room.

It was hardly the effusive, fulsome welcome that Jayne Mansfield had given me! But I didn't mind too much. We all have days when we don't feel like meeting new people, and I reckoned I would forgive Eddie Cochran anything, so long as those terrific songs kept coming.

Sadly, they didn't. One of the unfortunate themes of this book, alongside the wild lives that some early rock and rollers led, is the tragic ways in which many of them met their ends. Eddie Cochran never made it back to America. Just six weeks after that awards gig, at the age of twenty-one, he was dead.

It's a truly awful story. Eddie was in Britain on a co-headline tour with Gene Vincent. Gene was another artist that I liked, especially his first album, *Bluejean Bop!*, and his big hit, 'Be-Bop-a-Lula'. That was a song that really knocked me out when I first heard it.*

---

* It still does. I've never sung a whole lot of falsetto, but I did a falsetto version of 'Be-Bop-a-Lula' on tour a few years ago. I loved it. A great song can take anything that you throw at it!

Eddie Cochran hadn't wanted to come over for that 1960 UK tour. He had been good friends with Buddy Holly and Ritchie Valens, who had died in that terrible plane crash in America in 1959 (which I'll talk about later). It had really freaked Eddie out, and made him worry that he might also die on the road.

Apparently, Eddie had told his fiancée, Sharon, that he wouldn't tour anymore after that tragedy, and would stay in the studio to concentrate on writing songs and making records. Yet he needed money to support them in the meantime, so had reluctantly accepted the offer to tour Britain.

The last night of the tour was at Bristol Hippodrome on 16 April. After the show, Eddie, Sharon and Gene Vincent got a taxi back to London in the early hours to get ready to fly home to America. The taxi driver, who was only nineteen years old, was speeding, and smashed his car into a concrete lamppost in Chippenham.

Sharon later said that as the car crashed, Eddie flung himself over her in the back seat to try to protect her from the impact. She and Gene Vincent were hurt, and Eddie Cochran was flung out of the car and smashed his head against the road. He never regained consciousness, and died the next day.

By now, rock and roll was such big news that the television and newspapers were covering it, as well as music magazines, so Eddie Cochran's death was all over the papers for days. I couldn't believe it. The Shadows and I were shocked as we took it in: *Oh, my God! Eddie Cochran! Dead, in Britain! How can it be?!*

We didn't know Eddie personally, so it wasn't like we were losing a friend, but it still felt a huge loss because he was such an amazing songwriter and artist. He'd achieved so much already, in his short life: who knows what he would have done, had he lived on? I think he'd have become one of the true greats.

It's a testament to Eddie Cochran that so many incredible artists have covered the songs he wrote and recorded in that short life. Just google it! It's an unbelievable list: The Rolling Stones, The Beatles, Jimi Hendrix, The Beach Boys, Tom Petty, Bruce Springsteen, Rod Stewart, The Who, David Bowie, U2, Led Zeppelin . . . *

Eddie Cochran dying so young was an unmitigated tragedy. The only consolation for us, as fans, was that he never got a chance to tarnish his legend. James Dean was famously fond of saying, 'Live fast, die young and leave a good-looking corpse.' In many ways, it's a fitting epitaph for Eddie.

James Dean is a great comparison. The two coolest young American actors in the fifties were him and Tony Curtis. As the years went by, Tony grew old, gained weight, lost his looks and his hair, and made some ropey TV shows. He aged, as we all do. James Dean? He lived fast, died young and stayed good-looking.

Eddie Cochran is the same. Unlike Elvis, he never got to make a series of not-great movies† or do cabaret in Vegas. He'll always be that hip young dude in *The Girl Can't Help It*, his eyes twinkling, climbing the stairs to the twentieth floor, only to get there 'too tired to rock'. And that image will live on forever.

---

* I'm informed that Sid Vicious, from the Sex Pistols, also had a hit with a version of 'Somethin' Else'. I've never heard that, and I hope I never will!
† I'm not such an Elvis buff that I won't admit he made some terrible movies. I will always love *Jailhouse Rock*, *Loving You* and *King Creole*, but, yep, he was in a few failures as well!

EIGHT

'GREAT BALLS OF FIRE'
– JERRY LEE LEWIS

The in-your-face classic that I've sung to a future king

There are some people, some artists, in this book who always feel to me like the very epitome of rock and roll. Everything about them seems to embody the most exciting music there has ever been. Elvis is like that, so are Little Richard and Chuck Berry . . . and, right up there with the best of them, we have Jerry Lee Lewis.

They called him 'The Killer' and do you know what? They may just have had a point! Jerry Lee was a human firework who could explode, in any direction, with no warning. He was a true wild man, on stage and off, and one of the most compelling performers I've ever been lucky enough to witness. And to meet.

He burst into my life, like so many artists in this book, in 1957. I could hardly believe my ears when I heard 'Whole Lotta Shakin' Goin' On' blasting out of our new radio, which Dad had just bought. What grabbed my attention from the first second was his berserk hammering at the piano, like he bore it a personal grudge.

Then, a few months later, when 'Great Balls of Fire' came along – *Wow!* Was it possible to sound as frantic, as possessed, as this in a song? Was it *legal*? Jerry Lee howled, yowled and at one point appeared to be almost *yodelling* over a beat that sounded like it was itself on fire. No question: he was the real deal!

Jerry Lee Lewis was totally in your face from day one, and I loved that. He was a wild-sounding singer but that wildness had a shape. He yelled and screamed a little like Little Richard, but where Richard was a loose cannon, Jerry Lee always seemed that crucial bit more in control. He knew what he was doing.

Norman, Terry and I went mad for Jerry Lee and we added 'Great Balls of Fire' to The Drifters' set list. We didn't have a piano and, even if we did, none of us could have played it, but the song worked on just guitar, and I loved letting loose on the vocals. For those two-and-a-bit minutes, I could be a wild man, too.

By early 1958, a local guy, John Foster, had started managing The Drifters. He told us Jerry Lee Lewis was coming over to play the UK, and got us tickets. It would be only my second live American rock and roll show, after Bill Haley, and I was super-excited. But Jerry Lee's visit was not to be a happy one.

When he flew in to Heathrow, that May, to play a month-long tour, a few journalists were waiting to greet him. He had a very young-looking woman with him, Myra Gale Brown, who said she was his wife. The surprised reporters asked Jerry Lee how old she was. He told them that she was fifteen. *But she wasn't.*

When the journalists got back to their newsrooms, they did a bit of rooting around and discovered that Myra Gale Brown wasn't fifteen: she was *thirteen*. She was also Jerry Lee's second cousin. And, to cap it all off, apparently, he hadn't even divorced his previous (second) wife before marrying her!

Well, Fleet Street sprang straight into action. Jerry Lee Lewis was immediately Public Enemy Number One, and on all the front pages. Fans were publicly ripping up the tickets they'd bought to see him. Some protestors even went to picket outside his concerts.

It seems extraordinary, and wrong, to modern sensibilities, but to this day, I reckon Jerry Lee probably didn't get what all the fuss was about. In his part of the American Deep South, marrying young cousins was probably not all that unusual! But perceptions were very different here. A furore was swirling around him and his first show, at my local haunt the Edmonton Regal, was apparently pretty empty.

So was his second. John Foster had got us tickets to see him at the Gaumont State, in Kilburn, on 25 May. It was an enormous venue, with a capacity of four thousand, but when we got inside, there must have been less than two hundred people there. *Uh-oh! This is awful! What's he going to do?*

We were assuming he would pull the show, but we decided to stick around and see. We could sit anywhere we wanted in the empty venue, and we twigged that Jerry Lee's piano was on the left side of the stage, so we plonked ourselves in seats on that side, about six rows from the front, and waited hopefully.

I am so glad that we did. Jerry Lee Lewis must have been in a defiant mood about all the grief he was getting, and ready to fight back, because he came out in a cool, snazzy jacket and he played to that empty room as if it were packed with four thousand people cheering him to the rafters. It remains one of the greatest shows I've ever seen.

Jerry Lee was absolutely fantastic. He sat at his piano stool, and twitched and squirmed as if it had electric shocks going through it. He hammered at the keys as if they had done him wrong, then kicked away the stool and jived and twisted as he played, as if he was dancing with the piano. I couldn't take my eyes off him.

It's great to hear rock and roll records, but you can always learn something new about an artist when you see them live, and I learned that Jerry Lee Lewis was a force of nature. A true genius. The songs sounded exactly like they did on the records, but his performance took them to another level.*

His uncle was playing guitar – Jerry Lee clearly believed in keeping it in the family! – but this show was only about one man. In front of a tiny audience, with the whole world outside on his back, Jerry Lee Lewis looked like he was having the time of his life. As I say, he looked like the spirt of rock and roll incarnate.

Later, press reports said that some songs were 'greeted with boos'. *Rubbish!* Even though there were only two hundred of us, the crowd were clapping along with the music and cheering him on. And when Jerry Lee grinned and fired into 'Great Balls of Fire', we all lost our minds. *What a night!*

And it wasn't over yet. For us, anyway. As Jerry Lee Lewis took his final bow and vanished into the wings, John Foster went

---

* Back then, when you just had a voice, guitar, bass and drums (and, here, piano), it was easy to make stage shows sound like the record. Nowadays, there is so much technology used in the studio that it's a very different story.

down to the front and spoke to a bored-looking security guard (he hadn't exactly had a lot to do!). The guy nodded, and John came back to our seats, grinning.

'OK, lads!' he said. 'Are you ready? We're going back to meet Jerry Lee!'

What?! To this day, I have no idea how John pulled that one off. He wasn't a smooth music business operator, with lots of contacts. When we'd met him, he was driving a lorry in a local sewage works. But John had the gift of the gab, and I guess that has always opened doors.

I hardly had time to think, or to mentally prepare myself. The security guy led us through a door, behind a curtain, and down a brightly lit backstage corridor. We came to a door, he knocked on it, and an American voice said, 'Come in!' And when we walked in, there was Jerry Lee Lewis.

He was drenched in sweat, and he was still wearing his fancy stage jacket, but he was smiling and looked friendly. John Foster went straight over to him. 'Hello, Mr Lewis!' he said. 'This is my band, The Drifters. This is Cliff. They're going to . . . well, we don't know *what* they're going to do yet, but they wanted to meet you!'

Jerry Lee smiled and waved us over. 'Ah'm pleased to meet you boys!' he said. 'Did y'all enjoy the show?' And, as I stood there, I could see his mouth moving, and I could hear the words, but I felt as if I were in a dream. My head was in a whirl.

I was seventeen years old, and I was standing in a backstage dressing room talking to Jerry Lee Lewis. *Oh, my gosh! Jerry Lee Lewis! You're a rock and roll god! I've got all your records at home, and*

I play them all the time! You're fantastic! Gulp! I just tried to be normal and join in the conversation.

Luckily, Jerry Lee made that easy. He was charm itself. He talked as if we were all equals, *rock and rollers together*, rather than one superstar and three overawed kids. I can't really remember what we talked about (it wasn't his wife!). I think, with all the hassle he was getting, he was just pleased to see some friendly faces.

It was such a thrill to be standing there with Jerry Lee Lewis. Our brief encounter came to an end, and as we were about to leave, he asked, 'Say, do y'all want a photograph?' *Didn't we just!* John Foster whipped out a little box camera. *Snap!* Sixty-five years on, that photo remains a prized possession.

We floated home in a daze – but the writing was on the wall for Jerry Lee Lewis and his tour. He played one more London show, the following night, but he never even made it out of the capital. The outrage grew too loud, a lot of venues pulled the plug on him, and he flew home with his teenage bride within the week.

That scandal killed Jerry Lee Lewis's rock and roll career. Back in the US, radio stations stopped playing him, and his record company, Sun Records – Elvis's first label – stopped promoting him. He had no option but to give up making rock and roll records, and turned instead to country music.

Over the years, I heard a few of those country records here and there. I could tell that some of them were really good, but they never grabbed me by the throat in the way that his first manic singles had. They just didn't give me the same buzz as when he was a full-on rock and roller.

Even when Jerry Lee Lewis switched to country, he still had mad adventures! He debuted at the Grand Ole Opry in Nashville in 1973. It's the cathedral of country music, and doesn't allow rock songs, but Jerry Lee ignored all of the rules, swore his head off, and played 'Great Balls of Fire' and 'Whole Lotta Shakin' Goin' On'!*

I also read a story recently, in a vintage rock magazine, about Jerry Lee turning up at Graceland one night in 1976, at 2.30am, drunk, carrying a gun and demanding to see Elvis. Elvis, understandably, told his security not to let him in. Instead, Jerry Lee was hauled off down to the local police station and arrested.

Yet, when I read that kind of story, I always think, *Is that what really happened?* There may well be a grain of truth in it, but newspapers and magazines twist and exaggerate stories so much that it gets lost. It's happened to me *so* many times, over the years. So, I tend to take everything with a pinch of salt.

For me, Jerry Lee Lewis will always be one of the kingpins of rock and roll. The Killer was a musical magician and 'Great Balls of Fire' will always be his most triumphant, transcendent trick. Why, it can even make future kings dance!

What do I mean? Well, let me explain . . .

Growing up in a fairly impecunious family in the fifties, I obviously never did anything as exotic and well-heeled as go skiing. In fact, it wasn't until the year I turned fifty, 1990, that

---

* I was lucky enough to play the Grand Ole Opry in 2013, when I was in Nashville recording an album. I didn't swear my head off, or sing 'Great Balls of Fire' – I was just excited because Elvis had once played there.

some friends of mine persuaded me to go along with them to Lech, Austria, on a skiing holiday and give it a try.

Well, I loved it from day one! It's such a healthy, enjoyable sport, and surprisingly easy to pick up. I had a bit of catching up to do: there were kids there of three or four, skiing down the baby slopes between their grandparents' legs! They had nearly fifty years on me, but I did my best to make up for lost time.

A little gang of us began going back to Lech, usually once a year. There was my friend Charles Haswell and his wife, Sue; composer Simon May and his wife, Rosie; and a couple of DJs: Mike Read from Radio One, and Graham Dene from Capital Radio. We'd ski until late afternoon, and then hit the courts to play tennis.

One year in the early nineties, Princess Diana was also in Lech with William and Harry, who were about twelve and ten. They were staying in the same hotel as us but had to keep their room curtains closed all day long because of the paparazzi outside with their lenses trained on their windows. It was horrible to see what they were having to deal with.

I had met the Princess of Wales a few times, at royal events or at Wimbledon. One morning in the Lech hotel, she came up to me in the lobby. Mike Read and I would sometimes take our guitars down to the hotel bar for a good old sing-song on Friday evenings, and Diana had got wind of this.

'Cliff, I hear that you sing on Friday nights?' she asked me.

'Yes,' I said.

'I see. Could you do it for my boys?'

'Of course!' I replied. 'Why don't you join us after dinner tonight?'

'Could it be *before* dinner?' Diana requested, with that world-famous coy smile. So, after skiing, Mike and I collected our guitars and went to our usual corner of the bar.

We played for the two princes for about twenty-five minutes. I fondly thought they were enjoying it, but it seemed that I was wrong because, as Mike and I were doing 'Summer Holiday', I caught a glimpse of young Harry as I was singing. He was yawning his head off and looking bored stupid.

Mike had spotted him as well, so we looked at each other, smiled, and stopped playing. 'Excuse me, Harry,' I said. 'Is there anything you would rather hear?'

'Yes!' he said, cheering up instantly. 'Do you know "Great Balls of Fire"?'

Well, that surprised me! 'Yes, we know it,' I replied. 'But how do *you* know it?'

'Oh, Mummy plays it to us *all the time*!'

Mike and I started playing Jerry Lee Lewis's greatest tune and the two princes started dancing. They could not have been more different! William stood up and shifted demurely from foot to foot. He was moving in time to the music, but he carefully kept his cool and his dignity.

Harry was a different story! He was going crazy and leaping around the bar like Jerry Lee himself, interspersed with some very creditable attempts at a Michael Jackson moonwalk. He was really going for it, and Diana, Mike and I were laughing our heads off. There was a young rock and roller if ever I saw one!

Honestly, Jerry Lee Lewis could make *anyone* dance, from Teddy Boys in the fifties to royal princes forty years later! I doubt

I will still be alive when William comes to the throne, but if I am, and he asks me to do a Royal Command Performance, I'll say to him: 'I did one for you once before – do you remember?'*

Jerry Lee Lewis was rock and roll from his fingertips to his toes. He didn't 'live fast, die young and leave a good-looking corpse'. Far from it: he married seven times, had six children and died in 2022 at the ripe old age of eighty-seven. And I'll *never* forget him rocking an empty theatre in Kilburn as if his very life depended on it.

What a showman.

---

* Somehow, I don't think he will.

NINE

'STOOD UP' – RICKY NELSON

A 1958 smash for a man far too handsome for my liking

Ever since Dad had given me my guitar, and gently coaxed me through the three chords of 'The Prisoner's Song', I had airily assumed those chords were all I'd ever need. I had mastered them, and could cover any rock and roll hit from the charts with them. They were second nature to me by now:

> *First finger on the first fret of the second string, second finger on the second fret of the fourth string, third finger on the third fret of the fifth string: that's the C chord.*
>
> *Index finger on the first fret of the first and second strings, second finger on the second fret of the third string, third finger on the third fret of the fifth string, and the fourth finger on the third fret of the fourth string: that's the F chord.*
>
> *Keep those fingers on the same strings and slide them all up to the third fret . . . voila! The G chord.*

I knew I was a very basic guitar player, but at least I thought I knew *all* of the basics. Then, in the late spring of 1958, I heard a terrific song that absolutely blew my socks off. But one thing bothered me about it: *Huh? What's that extra chord? Rock and roll has a fourth chord? I didn't know that!*

For what it's worth, it was A minor.

The song was 'Poor Little Fool' and it was by Ricky Nelson. Ricky was a bit of an unusual case. He was the same age as me, but had been a superstar child actor in the US. From the age of eight, he'd starred in a hugely popular radio, and later TV, sitcom, *The Adventures of Ozzie and Harriet*. He had made his first movie when he was just twelve.

The Adventures of Ozzie and Harriet was about Ricky's real-life family: his father and mother, Ozzie and Harriet Nelson, were both well-known actors in America. I suppose the show was a fifties' version of *The Osbournes*! But because the series wasn't shown in Britain, nobody here knew anything about it, or about Ricky.

Off the back of the show, Ricky had forged a successful music career in America. Very successful, in fact! Some people had called him the first 'teen idol'* and his debut album, *Ricky*, had reached Number 1 in the *Billboard* chart in 1957. Not bad for a kid who was still only seventeen years old, huh?

Ricky hadn't had any hits in Britain but I'd heard a couple of his singles on AFN: 'A Teenager's Romance' and 'Be-Bop Baby'. I quite liked them, without thinking they were anything out of the

---

* Personally, I'm not sure that is true. I think the first teen idol would have been Elvis – or even Frank Sinatra, with his bobby-soxers.

ordinary. I could take them or leave them. But then he put out a song that I liked far more than those: 'Stood Up'.

'Stood Up' was a classic rock and roll song. It had a smart double-bass thrum and handclaps which powered it along, and Ricky's voice, over his jaunty guitar strum, was so cool and controlled that you could almost *hear* his top lip curl. It became his first hit in Britain, and I did my bit by buying it as soon as it came out.

Despite its jauntiness, 'Stood Up' was another heartbreak song. 'I've been waiting ever since eight,' Ricky sighed, as it opened. 'Guess my baby's got another date.' Then he swooped straight into the chorus: 'Stood up! Broken-hearted! Again.' The simplicity and directness were the song's appeal, along with the fabulous guitar solo.

It was definitely the main theme of early rock and roll songs: people falling in love, or falling out of love, or getting dumped and being heartbroken. Those are the main preoccupations of teenagers, when they're a mess of hormones. And I guess teenagers loved buying records that sang about how they felt.

Those rock and roll songs all had something to say and yet, personally, although I paid attention to the lyrics, they were never the big thing for me. It was all about the tune, and the voice. I never tried to figure out *why* I liked something: I either liked it, or I didn't. And I liked 'Stood Up' very, very much. Norman Mitham and I learned how to play it. I liked how the guitar solo was a melody on its own. We added it to The Drifters' growing repertoire, and started playing it at every local gig we did.

It didn't take us long to play! In common with every early

rock and roll single, 'Stood Up' was short. *Very* short. It was over in less than two minutes: one minute and fifty-seven seconds, to be precise. Some hits were even briefer than that. Elvis's '(Let's Have a) Party' was less than one-and-a-half minutes.

I gather this was partly because of the technology. The old shellac 10" singles that played at 78rpm could only hold a maximum of three minutes' music per side. But I think there was an advantage to this limitation. It made the songs punchy, direct, and gave them a kind of purity. There was no time for messing about!

Because we hadn't seen *The Adventures of Ozzie and Harriet* in Britain, I had no clue what Ricky Nelson looked like. When I finally saw a photograph of him, I couldn't believe it. *Are you kidding me? This is ridiculous!* The guy looked totally amazing. All at once, I understood why he'd become a teen idol in America.

Ricky had jet-black hair and striking blue eyes, like Elvis. It was the combination I'd always craved, rather than my own brown hair and hazel eyes. I mean, I didn't think I was *too* bad-looking, but I had quite a round face as a teenager. And here was Ricky Nelson, with cheekbones sharp enough to strike a match on. *Huh!*

'Stood Up' also sounded great because Ricky had a colossal guitarist in his band. James Burton was a maestro, and made everything he played sound untouchable. There is a real knack to being a great rock and roll guitarist: I've certainly never had it, but I admire people who have!

I remember meeting James once, in the sixties, and asking him how much time he got to do his incredible solos on Ricky Nelson records. James looked at me and laughed.

'Ha! I never got *no* time!' he said. 'They'd just say: "OK, here's the song. Start playing in C. Oh, by the way, see those twelve bars there? Play a solo!"'

What a talent! James was to go on to play in Elvis's band, when he was in Las Vegas at the end of his career. And Elvis certainly would not have any old hack playing for him! He always insisted on the best, and James was one of the very best rock and roll guitarists. He was certainly a big influence on Hank Marvin.

Ricky Nelson seemed to have everything – looks, talent, charisma, a great band – but his musical career didn't last. He blew my mind with that A minor chord in 'Poor Little Fool', and then there were a couple more at the very start of the sixties: 'Travelin' Man' and a cover of a Gene Pitney song, 'Hello Mary Lou'.

But then his songs charted lower and lower. When the famous mid-sixties British Invasion saw bands such as The Beatles, Rolling Stones, Kinks and Dave Clark Five break America, some established US rock and roll artists became seen as old hat and forgotten. Ricky Nelson was one of them. I think that was a shame.

It seemed like the world had moved on from Ricky Nelson, and I probably half-forgot about him myself. But he made a comeback in 1972 with a really striking tune called 'Garden Party'. It was a country song, really, with a haunting melody and a lovely chorus, and it got him back in the game in America.

It felt good to have Ricky back, and when he toured Britain, early in 1972, Bruce Welch and I went to see him at the Royal Albert Hall. That was *such* a strange gig. We went along eager to hear 'Poor Little Fool' and 'Travelin' Man' and, most of all, 'Stood Up' – and he just didn't play them.

Ricky had shortened his name to Rick Nelson by then, formed a band called The Stone Canyon Band, and was playing mellow country rock. It was as if he was embarrassed about his early rock and roll career and had disowned it. They say to give the public what it wants, but Ricky, sorry, *Rick*, certainly didn't do it that night.

He played nearly all new songs, and I wanted to like them, but I'm afraid they just didn't do it for me. Halfway through the show, Bruce leaned over to me and whispered, 'Another rock star's career dies!' And, sorry to say, Bruce was right. As he normally is on these things.

It breaks my heart writing this . . . Ricky is another rock and roller who met a tragic end. It was a plane crash. On New Year's Eve 1985, he was in a small propeller aircraft on his way to play a gig in Dallas. The plane had technical problems, burst into flames and had to make a crash-landing. All of the passengers died. He was only forty-five.

Ricky Nelson may not have had the long career he merited, but when I came to reinterpret my favourite fifties tunes on *The Fabulous Rock 'n' Roll Songbook* in 2013, 'Stood Up' was one of the very first songs I chose to include. I will always be grateful to Ricky for that, and for 'Poor Little Fool' . . . which taught me A minor.

TEN

'MOVE IT' – CLIFF RICHARD & THE DRIFTERS

The song that launched my career – and it was written on a bus

After I had heard so much great rock and roll music, by 1958 I decided it was time to start making some myself!

After I had quit Dick Teague's skiffle band, The Drifters had been making some progress. Norman, Terry and I rehearsed at my home every chance we got, and we'd even done our first live concert, in March 1958, at the local badminton club where I played with my dad.* We went down pretty well, if I say so myself.

The pace picked up a little when we got ourselves a manager. It's a story that I told in *The Dreamer* and, again, I never tire of telling: after a gig at the now-long-gone Five Horseshoes pub in Hoddesdon, near to Cheshunt, a lanky guy wandered up as we packed our gear away, and announced to me, 'I can make you a star!'

---

* Dad and I had recently won their father/son doubles competition!

The guy's name was John Foster, and he wasn't exactly Lew Grade: his job was driving a lorry in the local sewage works. But he did say one thing that excited us: he knew a man called Tom Littlewood, who booked the acts at the 2i's coffee bar in London, and he told us he could get us a gig there.

It's hard to explain nowadays just what a big deal the 2i's was. This coffee bar had a downstairs gig venue that some of the biggest names in the nascent British pop scene had played. Tommy Steele and Terry Dene, the nearest things that the UK had to rock and rollers at that point, had both been discovered playing there.

If I'm honest, I wasn't a huge fan of Tommy* or Terry. Their music kicked things off here, but it sounded a bit too *English* (i.e. non-American) for my liking. But I knew how crucial a gig at the 2i's could be for aspiring rock and rollers. John fixed up a Saturday afternoon audition with Tom Littlewood for us a week or two later.

We got the Green Line bus to London and couldn't have been more excited to be walking around buzzing Soho, our guitars around our necks! Our audition went well and Tom even asked us to come back and play a few songs that night. We went down OK, so he booked us in to do a full week of shows at the club.

That week was exhilarating and pretty eventful! We rocked the cellar with our Elvis, Ricky Nelson and Eddie Cochran covers, and had a couple of interesting chance encounters. One night, a

---

* Of course, Tommy Steele later found his niche in musical theatre, and was brilliant at it.

girl called Jan Vane collared us after we had finished playing. Jan was in the 2i's celebrating her sixteenth birthday.

She told us she thought we were great and she'd like to start a fan club for us. It cracked us up! 'The only "fans" we have are our families!' I told her. 'We're only just starting. But, sure, feel free, if you want to!'

Well, Jan didn't know what she was getting herself into! Within two years, that fan club was to be the biggest in Britain, with hundreds of thousands of members. She ran it for donkey's years! Yet, with all respect to the lovely Jan, another of our encounters at the 2i's was to be even more significant for us.

One evening, a smart young guy with a quiff came up and introduced himself. He was a couple of years older than us, and his name was Ian Samwell. Ian said that he was on leave from the RAF, where he was just finishing his national service, and in his spare time he was playing the guitar in a skiffle band.

Ian was like me: his heart was with rock and roll, not skiffle. He asked if we might need another guitarist. We asked him to bring his guitar down the next day and play to us. When he did, he was clearly a lot more skilled than Norman *or* me! Ian was in – in fact, he played his first gig as a Drifter that night.

That 2i's week also saw me change my name. It wasn't my idea – in fact, I'd never even thought of it. But a nightclub owner from Ripley, in Derbyshire, called Harry Greatorex wandered into the cellar, looking for bands to book for his club. He liked the look of us, and offered us a gig.

There was one stipulation, though. Harry didn't want just to hire The Drifters. In those days, the trend was for bands to have their singer's name upfront – Bill Haley & His Comets; Dion & The Belmonts – and Mr Greatorex wanted us to do the same. 'What's your name, son?' he asked me.

'Harry Webb.'

'OK, so you're Harry Webb & The Drifters.'

Nooooh! As soon as it left his lips, it felt wrong to me. I'd never really liked my first name. 'Harry' sounded ordinary, boring, square and, most important of all, *not rock and roll.* 'I don't want to do that!' I said, quickly.

'Well, you need a singer's name, or you can't play my club!'

'We'll be back shortly, Mr Greatorex!' said John Foster. 'Just wait here, please!' And we decamped to a pub around the corner to rename me.

We ran through a few ideas – Russ Clifford? Rich Clifford? Cliff Russard? – but none of them felt right. Somebody suggested 'Cliff Richards' and I mulled it over as I sipped my beer. I loved 'Cliff' straight away. It sounded like a cliff made of rock (a Cliff made of rock and roll?) but 'Richards' wasn't quite there . . .

Our newest member, Ian Samwell, who had only been in the band for two days, came to the rescue. 'Why not take the "s" off Richards, and be Cliff Richard?' he said. 'Interviewers will say "Cliff Richards" by mistake and you can correct them. They'll have to say your name twice, which means everyone will remember it!'

Ha! What a master plan, huh? So, 'Cliff Richard' it was. Harry Greatorex was pleased, and slapped 'Cliff Richard & The Drifters' on posters when we played his club in Derbyshire a few weeks later. For my part, I took to my new name straight away.

I have to say, for a lorry driver, John Foster was proving surprisingly adept at band management. He got us a couple of unpaid gigs at teenager clubs at the Gaumont in Shepherd's Bush. At the second one, excited kids screamed at us and chased me down the street! I had to hide in a public toilet! A policeman escorted me out.

Wow! Things were suddenly happening, and they seemed to be happening even faster when John booked us into a tiny recording studio – a recording cupboard, really – above HMV in Oxford Street to make a demo. It cost us £5 to record Elvis's 'Lawdy Miss Clawdy' and 'Breathless' by Jerry Lee Lewis.

John gave the tape to a showbiz agent, George Ganjou, who played it to Norrie Paramor, head of A&R at EMI record label Columbia. Norrie asked us to come in to audition, liked our spirited run-throughs of Elvis and Jerry Lee, and made an offer: his label would release a single by us. Of his choosing.

The single Norrie gave us was 'Schoolboy Crush': an upbeat, jaunty little number that had been an American hit the year before for a country singer called Bobby Helms.* I could not have been more thrilled about the chance to make a record – but, if I'm honest, I was pretty lukewarm towards the song.

When The Drifters was just Norman, Terry and me, we'd never given a thought to *where songs come from*. We just heard hits we liked on the radio and learned to play them. We had never

---

* Bobby Helms's main claim to fame was that, at Christmas 1957, he'd become the first artist to release, and have a hit with, 'Jingle Bell Rock'. Sixty-five years later, I recorded it for my *Christmas with Cliff* album. You can't keep a good song down!

read the names of the songwriters on singles, or tried to write any ourselves. It just never occurred to us.

This was to change, dramatically, now Ian Samwell had joined the band. Ian used to get the Green Line 751 bus from his home in London Colney to my house in Cheshunt to rehearse with us. One fateful day, he turned up at my door looking animated, and holding not just his guitar but also a few scraps of paper.

'Hey, guess what?' he said. 'I just started writing a song on the bus! I'm calling it "Move It"!'

We went through to the living room, and Ian plugged his guitar into our little Selmer amp. He had only written the bare bones of the song. It didn't really have an intro yet: it was just a riff, a verse and a chorus. But he played us what he had, and I absolutely loved it from the second I heard it.

As soon as Ian played the riff – '*Dah-dah-dah-dah, dah-dah-dah dah-dah-dah!*' – I got excited. It sounded raw, primal and fantastic. It sounded like . . . *a proper rock and roll song*! Only it hadn't been written by Chuck Berry in America! It had been written by . . . one of us, on the 751 to Cheshunt!

Ian didn't have the full lyrics yet, but he already had a few words: 'C'mon, pretty baby, let's move it and groove it!' They fitted the riff perfectly, like a hand in a glove. Ian had finished playing inside a minute. He looked at us, and shrugged. 'I dunno. What do you think?' he asked.

'I think it's fantastic!' I replied. 'Did you *really* write it on the Green Line?'

'Yep.'

Ian, Norman, Terry and I spent that afternoon working on 'Move It' and trying to lick it into shape. To my ears, it sounded better every time we played it. It felt incredible to be playing an original song for the first time. And there was one very important person that I wanted to hear it, straight away.

John Foster phoned up Norrie Paramor and asked if we could see him again to play him something. We were still tweaking our new baby on the Green Line to London. It was coming together, but it still only had one verse and a chorus. It was far from finished.

When we got to Norrie's offices, I found it nerve-racking to play our own creation to him. I found it hard even to look at him as I was singing it. But I needn't have worried. Norrie liked 'Move It' and said that we could record it as the B-side of our debut single, 'Schoolboy Crush'.

'But it's only half a song at the moment, Mr Paramor!' I said, surprised.

'Oh, that doesn't matter!' said Norrie. 'We'll put a guitar solo in, and then we'll just do the whole thing again!'

Norrie initially wanted an orchestra to play 'Move It' and me to sing over the top, but I felt strongly that it was a rock and roll song that needed a rock and roll band to play it. Norrie relented, but still wasn't sure we had the musical ability to do it properly. He explained that he was going to hire two session guys to help us.

So, Cliff Richard & The Drifters had two temporary extra men when we came to record it – but we were also one original member down. Norman Mitham's guitar skills weren't up to the level of Ian Samwell's. With me strumming away as well, we didn't really need Norman in the band, and we went our separate ways.

It was a tough call to make because I'd known Norman since school. We'd always hung out together, he'd been with me in Waltham Cross when I first heard Elvis, and he'd been a founder member of The Drifters. But the music had to come first. I couldn't be sentimental. I'm just pleased that our friendship survived.

We recorded 'Move It', not long after we'd first played it to Norrie, on a Sunday afternoon in EMI's studio in St John's Wood, northwest London. It was a slick, intimidating complex unlike anything we'd seen before. It was certainly nothing like the cupboard over the HMV store where we'd made our demo!

Norrie was to produce the single himself. He certainly cut quite a dash in the studio! We'd only seen him looking like a sober and suited businessman before, but he rocked up in Abbey Road in a Hawaiian shirt and Bermuda shorts. He was still in holiday mode, having recently got back from Morocco.

Norrie introduced us to the session men. Ernie Shear was a small Scottish guy in horn-rimmed specs. He usually played the banjo in one of Norrie's groups, The Big Ben Banjo Band, but was to play guitar with us that day. Frank Clarke was a tall, broad, good-looking double-bass player.

Ernie and Frank were in their late twenties or early thirties. They were friendly to us, but probably thought us teenage rock and roll kids were a bit of a novelty. We had never met them, but I was glad they were there: I couldn't *imagine* how Ian, Terry and I could do 'Move It' justice on our own.

And when Norrie got behind the production desk, the green light went on, and we began playing, I saw at once how right Norrie had been to bring them in. We recorded 'Schoolboy Crush' first and I instantly realised that I was playing with the big boys now. With real musicians. These guys knew exactly what they were doing.

Then we turned to 'Move It', which at this stage still didn't even have an intro. Well, that was before Ernie Shear seemed to pull one from thin air. He glanced at Ian's notes for the song, asked, 'What if I go, "*Do-do-do-do, do-do-do?*"' and fired out this brilliant noise. It was perfect: just what the tune needed.

Frank Clarke got a great rhythmic throb going on the bass to power us along, and Ian Samwell was cranking out that killer riff. *Wow! Amazing!* I was strumming at my guitar as well, as I sang . . . until Norrie's voice came over my headphones, telling me to put my guitar down: 'We don't need it, Cliff.'

Huh! Charming!

I'm joking! I didn't mind. I wanted whatever was best for the song. But I was so used to holding my guitar as I sang that it felt a bit weird to sing without it. A few minutes later, Norrie came back on my headphones and told me to pick my guitar up again if it helped me with my vocals – but not to play it!*

Terry, Ian and I may have been wet behind the ears and new to a studio, but the experienced guys we were with were bang on

---

* I tried to obey Norrie, but I got so into the music that I couldn't help having a couple of crafty strums. So, my guitar playing may well be somewhere on 'Move It' – you'd just have to listen very, very hard to hear it!

the ball. Unbelievable as it is, we recorded 'Move It' in just two takes. After our second run-through, Norrie said, 'Yes, that's a good take. That will do.' And that was that!

It was all done and dusted in no more than forty-five minutes and we headed to the production room and gathered eagerly around Norrie's console for the playback. *It sounded sensational.* Ian, Terry and I were staring at each other in glee: *Wow! Did we just do that? Is that really our own song?*

It's always strange to hear your own voice, and I couldn't believe that it was my singing coming out of the huge studio speakers. I couldn't believe . . . *how good it sounded*. On the Tube, and the Green Line bus back to Cheshunt, I was on cloud nine. We had just made a rock and roll record. *Our own* rock and roll record.

The recording of 'Move It' had gone incredibly well, but Norrie had still chosen 'Schoolboy Crush' as the A-side of our first single. I'd still been a schoolboy only a year earlier, so I guess he thought it was apt. It wouldn't have been my choice, but I wouldn't have dared suggest an alternative plan to the mighty Mr Paramor.

Thankfully, somebody else who was about to get inextricably involved in my story was a lot more confident – and a lot more powerful.

Jack Good was a young TV producer who had launched the BBC's pop show *Six-Five Special* in 1957, and was now working on a similar, imminent show for ITV called *Oh Boy!* He also did some pop writing, notably as a columnist on music magazine *Disc*, and got given a copy of our debut single.

Jack was indifferent towards 'Schoolboy Crush' but absolutely loved 'Move It' and went to town about it in his *Disc* column. He compared it to Elvis (*Goodness me! I think I need to sit down!*) and Jerry Lee Lewis, and raved that it was the handiwork of 'a 17-year-old boy from Cheshunt . . . the mind just boggles!'

Jack Good could not have been more positive about Cliff Richard & The Drifters, but he also did something even more important than write nice things about us in a magazine. He booked us to appear on the first episode of *Oh Boy!*

This appearance came with one major stipulation. 'I like this band, but if they are coming on my show, they are *not* playing "Schoolboy Crush",' he informed Norrie Paramor. '"Move It" is their best song. They are doing that, or nothing.' Norrie was no fool, and he wasn't going to lose a precious TV slot. He agreed.

Crikey! I could not believe that we were going to go on the telly – and play our own song! It was mind-boggling, impossible to take in, but Jack Good made sure that we didn't get carried away and were focussed on the task in hand. In fact, he worked us to within an inch of our lives.

The show was to be live from the Hackney Empire and we had to prepare for it for a full week in a rehearsal room in nearby Islington. Jack may have liked our debut single (or, at least, one side of it) but he also knew we were novices. So, he had a good, hard look at our act . . . and he didn't like some of what he saw.

Jack Good twigged pretty much straight away that, at that point, I was basically an Elvis Presley tribute act. Well, he didn't want an Elvis impersonator on his show, a fact that he made clear to me in very direct language.

'Look, you're *not* Elvis Presley,' he told me. 'You may want to be, but you're not. So, you can shave those sideburns off, for a start! And put down your guitar. You don't need it, so just concentrate on your singing!'

My first reaction was horror – *Oh, no! My sideburns! My guitar!* – and yet I didn't argue with him. Jack Good clearly knew television, and music, inside-out, plus he had charisma, and a drive and conviction that were very compelling. I could tell at once that he knew what he was doing. In short, I trusted him.

In any case, his feedback to me wasn't all negative. Over that week in Islington, Jack gave me detailed, step-by-step instructions on how I should move on stage; how I should sing; how I should dance; how I should *stand.* He gave an awkward 17-year-old boy a crash course in how to become a rock and roll star.

'Cliff, hold your left shoulder with your right hand when you sing this line,' Jack would say. 'Look straight into the camera lens. For this part, keep your feet still but turn your body sideways. Now, run across the stage, from this side to that. Look up to the balconies. *Concentrate – and don't try to be Elvis!'*

It was a lot to take in, but I was an enthusiastic student and very keen to learn. That week in Islington was gruelling, and I could not have been more nervous before *Oh Boy!* debuted on 13 September 1958. But it went well, and when I saw the show back, I realised that everything Jack had taught me had worked.

He had shown me how to be a performer. He had shown me how to find me.

That first television appearance altered everything for me. The day after we played 'Move It' on *Oh Boy!* I was public property. I couldn't walk down the street without people – well, girls! – running up to me wanting a chat, an autograph and a kiss on the cheek. My whole life changed overnight.

How did I feel about it? *What do you think?!* I absolutely loved it! It felt like – no, it *was* – everything I had wanted, ever since I had heard Elvis, discovered rock and roll, and fallen in love with the idea of being a singer. As I said in my memoir, I had a dream, and that dream came true. And now I was ready to live it.

For a few days after *Oh Boy!* my record company was still saying that 'Schoolboy Crush' was the A-side of the single. It didn't last. 'Move It' was the song everyone was going crazy for, and Norrie Paramor bowed to the inevitable: 'OK, let's flip it over!' *Ta-da!* 'Move It' was now the A-side.

I'd never have dared ask him directly to do it, but I was so pleased when he did. If 'Schoolboy Crush' had been my first hit, I would have been seen as just one more covers artist. Instead, Cliff Richard & The Drifters had arrived doing fresh, brand-new material. And it set the tone for what was to follow.

I'll never forget seeing – and holding – my first copy of 'Move It'. The centre label was green, with white lettering on it, and it came in a plain black sleeve. And, you know, it's remarkable: even sixty-five years on, I can still remember the catalogue number. I don't even need to check. It was 45-DB 4178.*

'Move It' was the record that made me. I'll talk later in this

---

* You could buy 'Move It' on 78rpm 10" shellac *or* 45rpm 7" vinyl. It's a sign of how long ago it came out that stereo recordings (or 'stereo sound' as it was still known then) were still new-fangled technology. I saw copies of 'Move It' where the sleeve said: 'ALSO AVAILABLE IN STEREO!'

book about how it rose and rose up the hit parade, week after week, coming to rest at Number 2. But its importance is bound up in far more than mere chart positions. It's still, even today, acknowledged to be the first British rock and roll single.

It's an amazing thing to have on my career CV, and as my legacy. I've never seen its claim to that status challenged or disputed. When John Lennon famously said 'before Cliff and "Move It", there was nothing worth listening to in British music', I felt incredibly moved and proud. *How could I not?* What a compliment!

Yes, 'Move It' was the first original British rock and roll song, written by a Brit and sung by a Brit. And nothing, and nobody, can ever take that away from me.*

There's a funny P.S. to the story of 'Move It'. Almost forty years later, in 1995, Hank Marvin was recording an album of my songs called *Hank Plays Cliff*. He asked me to sing 'Move It' with him on the record, and we had an idea: 'Shall we finally add that second verse that we never got around to doing at the time?'

We managed to track down Ian Samwell, who was by then living in California. Ian loved the idea, and wrote a second verse, including the line 'Fireflies in the night, and bullfrogs croaking' (well, as I say, he *was* living in California!). Hank and I had a load of fun recording this new, longer version for his album.

Bruce Welch has always been a musical purist and he's never liked me singing this second verse. 'It's wrong, because "Move It" didn't have that verse when it was a hit!' he complains.

---

* *Just let them try!*

'Brucie,' I reply, 'it was always *meant* to have a second verse. We just got rushed and didn't have time to do it!'

I have played 'Move It' at virtually every show I've done since 1958. Occasionally, I wonder if I should give it a rest every now and then. I remember, many years ago, putting a band together for an American tour, and mentioning in rehearsal that I was thinking of leaving 'Move It' off the set list.

Well, the band were *horrified*! 'Oh no, Cliff!' they said. 'We've *got* to do "Move It"! We really want to play it – and it wouldn't be a Cliff Richard show without it!'

And, you know what? I think they're right. I'll carry on playing 'Move It' live until the day that I get bored of playing it, or the fans don't want to hear it anymore. And I think that I might know exactly when that will be.

Never.

ELEVEN
'A TEENAGER IN LOVE'
– MARTY WILDE

My 'rival' that I'm still friends with, sixty-five years later

I may have released the first British rock and roll single in the autumn of 1958, but I certainly wasn't the only British rock and roll singer. No, the rise of Elvis and the American rockers had given birth to loads of British artists who were as driven as me to emulate the sounds, and the attitudes, beaming across the Atlantic.

When The Drifters and I started going on Jack Good's *Oh Boy!*, we found ourselves in the midst of a whole heap of young British rock and roll singers. They became both our friends and our competitors: our rivals for valuable TV airtime and chart positions. And foremost among them, from the off, was Marty Wilde.

Marty was a year older than me and a little bit ahead of me. He'd released his first single, 'Honeycomb', with his band, The Wildcats, in 1957, then two more in the first half of 1958. None of them had been hits – but it was a different story in June 1958 when he released 'Endless Sleep'.

'Endless Sleep' was a cover of a recent US hit by an American rockabilly singer called Jody Reynolds. It was a big, lush, romantic song, with a sad but ambiguous lyric (was the singer's girl dead? Had she drowned?) and a twangy guitar. I liked it, and it shot up the UK hit parade and into the top five.

This meant that Marty Wilde was more established than me when I joined *Oh Boy!* and he headlined early shows over me. But 'Move It' went down well on my first appearance, and as it became a hit, Jack Good began to alternate Marty and me as the programme headliners. One week, Marty; the next week, me.

Marty Wilde thus immediately became my rival – but, luckily, there was no edge to that rivalry. Off camera, our relationship was terrific. We would hang out in our dressing rooms, talking about our favourite American stars and comparing thoughts on their latest songs. He was a cool guy.

Jack would sometimes get artists to sing together. One week, he told Marty and me, plus another Brit rock and roller, Dickie Pride, to do a number together: The Coasters' 'Three Cool Cats'. We lined up in front of the camera and harmonised sweetly through that neat Leiber and Stoller song.

It seemed to go well, but when I saw the recording, years later, I was horrified: *Oh, no! Why did they let me on TV looking like that?!* Marty looked like an absolute cool cat, as he always did, and Dickie Pride looked fine, but I looked like an utter slob: a greaseball! Jack Good was happy with it, but I hated it when I saw it.

Marty and I ticked along quite nicely, alternating the weekly headline slots on *Oh Boy!* I have to admit that I enjoyed the shows most when The Drifters and I topped the bill – and then, suddenly we were doing that nearly every week, because Marty vanished off the programme. And it was all down to his manager.

Marty was managed by a man called Larry Parnes: a maverick and influential figure in early British rock and roll. He was an extremely driven young London entrepreneur with a reputation for being very money-motivated. In fact, I can remember the newspapers used to call him Mr Parnes, Shillings and Pence!

Parnes was still only in his late twenties when we did *Oh Boy!* but he had already amassed an impressive stable of young rock and rollers. He would sometimes drop in on rehearsals to check that his acts were all OK. I must admit, some weeks he seemed to be managing everybody on the show, except for me!

Parnes had started off managing Tommy Steele, and then signed up a young guy called . . . *wait for it* . . . Reg Patterson! Well, let's face it, Reg Patterson is an even more rubbish name for a rock and roller than Harry Webb, so Parnes quickly renamed him Marty Wilde. In fact, renaming his artists was quite a Parnes trait.

He loved giving them tough, dramatic names. So, a singer named Ron Wycherly turned into Billy Fury, Richard Kneller was renamed Dickie Pride and Roy Taylor became Vince Eager. Ray Howard became Duffy Power and John Askew turned into Johnny Gentle. A guy called Clive Powell became Georgie Fame.*

I think Larry Parnes probably thought I was still a young

---

* Not everyone went along with Larry Parnes's renaming plans. Joe Brown refused to become Elmer Twitch. I think I'm with Joe on that one!

upstart next to the more established Marty Wilde, and he took exception to Jack Good giving us an equal number of billings and headline slots on *Oh Boy!* Larry told Jack he had to scale down my appearances and focus more on his man, Marty.

Well, Jack Good wasn't having *that*! As I'd learned first-hand, Jack was a genius control freak. *Oh Boy!* was his baby, and he wasn't going to take any interference from lippy artist managers! He told Larry Parnes either to mind his own business or sling his hook. And Parnes did the latter. He pulled Marty Wilde off the show.

The row was a load of nonsense over nothing, really, but it certainly benefited Cliff Richard & The Drifters, because we got a lot more top billings while Marty wasn't around. And, next time I saw Marty, he was as friendly as ever. There were no hard feelings. Why should there be? It had all been nothing to do with us.

Marty Wilde had some more hits over the next year or two. In 1959, he covered 'Donna' by Ritchie Valens, not long after Ritchie had died in that plane crash with Buddy Holly. And then, that summer, he reached Number 2 with the song that I have chosen for this book: 'A Teenager in Love'.

Like most of Marty's hits, 'A Teenager in Love' was a cover, in this case of a recent US hit by a New York doo-wop/rock and roll band, Dion & The Belmonts. Well, let me tell you, The Drifters and I *loved* Dion & The Belmonts! We had listened avidly to such previous hits as 'I Wonder Why' and 'No One Knows' on AFN.

Dion & The Belmonts had such beautiful harmonies and, if

I'm honest, I maybe liked their original version of 'Teenager in Love' *slightly* more than I did Marty's cover. But Marty's version was tremendous as well. When it got to Number 2 in the charts, I thought that it deserved it.

Of course, Marty Wilde wasn't the only British rock and roller The Drifters and I met on *Oh Boy!* For a year, it was the main television platform for music stars, and every record company and manager going was desperate to get their artists on the show. It gave me a chance to have a good close look at our competitors.

Billy Fury was the same age as me, and came on *Oh Boy!* when he released his first single, 'Maybe Tomorrow', early in 1959. Billy looked great, and he had that fierce surname, courtesy of Larry Parnes, but the main thing I remember about Billy in those early days is just how *shy* he was.

He was a good performer, but when he got offstage, he hardly said a word. If you caught his eye, he'd smile at you then look down. The Dallas Boys, who did all the backing vocals on the show, often commented to me how quiet Billy was. The Vernon Girls, the all-female group who were on most weeks, said the same.

That was OK. It wasn't rudeness, or trying to be cool: he was just shy. Billy Fury was a good guy and I liked him a lot. And I enjoyed some of his hits as he got more established, such as 'Halfway to Paradise' and 'Jealousy'.

Adam Faith also came on the show now and then. I was on speaking terms with Adam, and we had no animosity between us, but he was probably my fiercest musical rival. We were both very competitive people (I'm afraid I still am!) and we kept a very close eye on each other's songs and chart placings.

Adam broke through with that big Number 1, 'What Do You Want?' in the autumn of 1959, and suddenly he was everywhere. I liked it, and his follow-up 'Poor Me', but that little vocal hiccup that he did when he sang sounded *very* familiar! I think he borrowed it from Buddy Holly.

I must say, Adam was a great-looking guy, with those sparkling blue eyes and razor-sharp cheekbones. He always looked more like an actor than a real rock and roller to me, which is how his career panned out. In the seventies, he stopped making records and began doing TV series like *Budgie*, playing a wide boy, and starring in movies like David Essex's *Stardust*.

One singer that I really liked on *Oh Boy!* was Vince Eager. He was always friendly backstage, and seemed to be a priority for Larry Parnes, but he never had a big hit, and instead ended up playing clubs and doing West End plays. Vince and I used to send Christmas cards, but we lost touch years ago. I hope he's doing well.

But let's get back to Marty Wilde. He had further hits in 1959, such as 'Sea of Love', which I thought was a great song, but then his record sales hit a slump as we moved into the sixties. He had one last Top 10 hurrah in 1961 with 'Rubber Ball', and then that was pretty much it, charts-wise, for Marty.

That seems bizarre to me. When I look back at me singing 'Move It' and Marty singing 'Endless Sleep', I think Marty was a far more *mature* singer than me. He seemed to be comfortable with his voice from the off, whereas it took me ages to find my best singing voice. It took me years to *let go*; to *free myself*.

I remember once, in those early days, my dad telling me that I should 'sing harder, like Little Richard!' It quite upset me at the time. But he was right: my young voice was undeveloped. I think Dad would have loved to hear me nowadays, when I not only go wild on certain songs, but even sing falsetto.

I met Marty Wilde again at the end of 2022. I was in London, and Bruce Welch and Brian Bennett took me along, as their guest, to the Society of Distinguished Songwriters (SODS)* awards. Now, *I've* never been a distinguished songwriter, but I admire the people who are. Without them, we singers are nothing.

It was such a fun evening. I walked in with Bruce and Brian, and the first person we met was Terry Britten, who wrote 'Devil Woman' and many other hits for me. Then I saw Mitch Murray, who co-wrote 'Goodbye Sam, Hello Samantha'. And, as I moved into the main hall, I saw Marty Wilde, sitting at the same table I was on.

We had a great chat, like we always do. We reminisced about the fifties; about Jack Good; about *Oh Boy!* I reminded him of the two of us singing The Coasters' 'Three Cool Cats' with Dickie Pride, and me looking like a greasy slob! *That* made Marty laugh! 'I don't think you did, Cliff,' he said, politely.

Marty still performs, and he was doing a few numbers at the end of the SODS awards. I had to leave early, as I needed to catch a flight the next morning, but I would have loved to have stayed and watched him. Marty might even have asked me up on stage to do a song with him. *That* would have been fun.

---

* That name makes me laugh – we *are* all a bunch of old sods, nowadays!

It would have reminded me of those old times . . . and yet whenever I think back on those long-gone *Oh Boy!* days, something baffles me. Not to put too fine a point on it, it's this: why am I the last of that first wave of British rock and rollers still standing? *Why am I still here?*

Marty Wilde had two or three years of success at the start of the rock and roll era, then he saw his chart fortunes fade. So did Tommy Steele and Terry Dene. So did Billy Fury, Adam Faith, Dickie Pride, Vince Eager and the whole of Larry Parnes's stable of young starlets. So, why am *I* still going, sixty-five years later?

It's the question I've been asked more than any other in recent years. It's a very good question, and my answer is this: *I haven't got a clue.* I've no idea. I've just carried on, day by day, doing what I'm doing. I've hung in there and kept going, and, well, here we are!

I mean, think about it! I used to be in chart battles with Elvis and with Marty Wilde. In the eighties, I was in chart battles with Marty's *daughter*, Kim. And now, into *my* eighties, I'm in chart battles with a whole generation of new performers who weren't even born when I was *forty years* into my career.

The fifties' newspaper headlines used to shout It's Elvis Vs Cliff For Number One! At the end of 2022, when I released my Christmas album, they were saying It's Cliff Vs Stormzy! I was fighting for Number 1 against Stormzy and Bruno Mars – and, believe it or not, I somehow saw them both off.*

---

* I didn't quite get Christmas Number 1 album. Taylor Swift released her record a week before Christmas, and beat me by a few hundred sales. But Taylor is just about the biggest artist in the world right now. There's no shame in losing to her!

I will always think fondly of Marty, and Adam, and Billy, and Vince, and all of the other guys from the *Oh Boy!* days. Ultimately, though, the only answer to 'Why am I still here?' is 'Why does it matter? I AM!' Maybe it's down to hard work. Maybe it's just luck. But, whatever it is, I hope it helps me to stick around for a while longer yet . . .

TWELVE
'WHEN' – THE KALIN TWINS

They may be one-hit wonders, but what a hit!

When I look closely at *A Head Full of Music*, some of the artists in here burned bright for a few years and then saw their stars fall away. Others have had wonderful, decades-long careers (nearly as long as mine!). By contrast, The Kalin Twins were, with all respect to them, essentially one-hit wonders.

But what a hit it was.

In the summer of 1958, two American twin brothers named Hal and Herbie Kalin released a song called 'When'. It was a sweet, melodic tune, with a hint of doo-wop, and it shot up the UK hit parade and spent five weeks at Number 1. For a few weeks, you couldn't get away from it, and nor did you want to.

When I saw them on TV, The Kalin Twins were smart, preppy guys who smiled and snapped their fingers as they crooned the song. It reminded me of a hit from the year before, 'Little Darlin'' by The Diamonds, which I had also really liked. Both songs had great harmonies and, well, as I said earlier, I *do* love a good harmony!

That '58 summer, The Kalin Twins were hot property, so when we were told we were going on tour with them after 'Move It' came out, I thought, *Wow!* It might have seemed an odd match, because the Kalins weren't really rock and roll at all, but I was excited to tour with an act who were a) famous and b) *American.*

It also felt a great time to take Cliff Richard & The Drifters out on tour, because we had just undergone a major line-up change. We had added two musicians who would help to reshape the band's sound and, over the next few years, become hugely influential, and household names in their own right.

After Norman Mitham left The Drifters, Ian Samwell switched to largely playing bass. This left us a lead guitarist down. Our first manager, John Foster, set out to rectify this, and went back to where it had all begun for us – the 2i's coffee bar in Soho – to try to scout out a new recruit.

John had arranged to meet a guitarist named Tony Sheridan, who had played with Gene Vincent on tour (and was later to play with The Beatles in Hamburg). But Tony didn't show up, for whatever reason, and instead John fell into conversation with a couple of friendly Geordies named Hank Marvin and Bruce Welch.

Hank and Bruce were old school pals who had moved from the Northeast down to London a few weeks earlier to try to launch music careers. Hank was as much a fan of Buddy Holly as I was of

Elvis (well, if that is possible!): he had even started wearing big dark-rimmed glasses to look more like his idol.*

Bruce was working in the 2i's at the time, manning the orange-juice machine, and Hank was hanging out with him. Hank had his guitar with him and played a couple of tunes for John – Buddy Holly, obviously! He was note-perfect. John was blown away and asked if he would come to meet me and play on our tour.

'Aye, OK,' said Hank. 'But only if my mate can come, as well.'

John came back raving to me that Hank looked like Buddy Holly and sounded like James Burton. I have to say, that sounded promising! So, I was excited, a day or two later, when Hank and Bruce turned up at my council house in Cheshunt. They plugged their guitars into our weedy Selmer amps and, with Ian Samwell and Terry Smart, we all ran through a few songs such as Elvis's 'Baby I Don't Care', Fats Domino's 'Blueberry Hill' . . . and, of course, 'Move It'.

Wow! Hank and Bruce sounded absolutely fantastic! Their musicianship was a big step up on anybody else in that room. Just as importantly, they were both really funny guys and I liked them a lot. We asked them to join The Drifters and come on tour with us. I couldn't have been more delighted when they said yes.

It felt like a major piece had fallen into place. Now for

---

* Hank didn't need a Larry Parnes to change his name for him: he did it himself, from his birth name of Brian Rankin. In later years, of course, 'Hank Marvin' got used as Cockney rhyming slang for 'starving'. Did Hank mind that? He *loved* it!

another one: my clothes for the tour. I'd always been fascinated by what rock and roll stars *looked* like, as well as what they sounded like, so John Foster took me to a tailor in Soho to sort out my wardrobe to take on the road.

Looking back, it was quite the outfit! I chose a bright pink jacket, black drainpipe trousers, a black shirt, a pink tie and luminous pink socks. I could not have been prouder of my gear at the time – but I do wonder, now, if I was the first bad-taste dresser in Britain!

Of course, it wasn't to be *only* The Kalin Twins and Cliff Richard & The Drifters on that British tour. Things were very different in those days. Tours were made up to be entertainment packages, or travelling variety shows. There was to be quite the range of different acts on the road with us.

There was a singing duo called The Most Brothers. They weren't real brothers, but one of them was Mickie Most,* who went on to be a famous record producer. Eddie Calvert, a trumpeter, had had a couple of British Number 1s in the early fifties, including 'Oh, Mein Papa'. There was even a jazz trio: The Londonaires.

We artists were to travel from show to show in a coach, and met up outside London Planetarium in Baker Street on 5 October 1958. It felt a bit like a very exciting school trip (after all, I *was* only seventeen!). All of the other artists were chummy from the off, and The Kalin Twins were particularly friendly.

Hal and Herbie were in their mid-twenties by then. They were twins, but not identical ones, so, happily, I could easily tell

---

* Mickey had something in common with Bruce: he'd worked at the 2i's. But where Bruce was on the orange-juice machine, Mickey was a singing waiter!

Sammy Davis Jr. 'I might as well give up and retire now!' I said, when I saw his stage show in London in 1961. 'How can I compete with *that*?'

My hero, and the man I wanted to *be*: Elvis Presley, forever the King.

Below: the first album I ever bought.

Carl Perkins wrote 'Blue Suede Shoes' but said he never got as big as Elvis because he looked like Mr Ed, the talking horse!

Jerry Lee Lewis, Carl Perkins, Elvis and Johnny Cash as 'The Million Dollar Quartet' at an all-night jam session at Sun Studios in 1956. Wow! What would I have given to be there!

Little Richard: so far
out that I'm sure he
came from Venus.

Raw, raucous and
always rocking: Chuck
Berry delivered us from
the days of old.

Bill Haley & His Comets in London in 1957, on the first rock and roll tour that I ever saw. Check out the saxophonist and the double bass player!

Eddie Cochran rocks the 1960 *NME* Poll Winners Party at Wembley that I flew home from my US tour to attend. And guess what? That's future Shadows man Brian Bennett on drums!

I hope that piano's insured! The Killer, Jerry Lee Lewis, ripping it up: still one of the greatest performers I've ever seen.

'Oh, come on! *Nobody* can be that handsome!' Ricky Nelson, a brooding teen idol.

Making a racket with The Drifters in my mum and dad's front room, early 1959: Hank Marvin, Tony 'The Baron' Meehan, me and Bruce Welch.

We took turns to headline and, sometimes, we even performed together: on *Oh Boy!* with my friend Marty Wilde on New Year's Day 1959.

Herbie and Hal, two friendly, smart, all-American guys: The Kalin Twins. 'When?' Well, as you ask, it was 1959!

He could even make spectacles look cool. The great Buddy Holly with his Crickets: Jerry Allison and Joe B. Maudlin. They wrote 'Peggy Sue' after Jerry's girlfriend dumped him!

Me, hoping a fight doesn't break out! The Everly Brothers didn't always get on well in day-to-day life …

… but on stage, Phil and Don were always in perfect harmony.

them apart. And they were utterly charming, as Americans can be, in a totally natural, sincere way. Fame certainly hadn't gone to their heads. They couldn't have been more approachable.

The first night of the tour was in Hanley, near Stoke-on-Trent. The format of the evening was that each act played for twenty minutes. Cliff Richard & The Drifters were given the slot right before the headliners, The Kalin Twins, which I thought was good for us. I hadn't yet realised just *how* good.

I'll never forget that opening night in Hanley. The venue was crammed and sold out, mainly with teenagers. They listened quietly and clapped politely during sets by The Londonaires, Eddie Calvert and The Most Brothers. And when Cliff Richard & The Drifters came on, they completely lost their minds.

The fans were screaming at a volume I'd only ever heard before on Elvis concert footage from America. The racket nearly blew my ears off! It was as much as I could do to hear myself sing, over the white wall of noise and the shrill screaming of hundreds of girls: 'Cliff! Cliff! We love you, Cliff!'

Wow! What 17-year-old boy wouldn't enjoy *that*, eh? We came offstage buzzing and stared at each other, in shock, in the dressing room. When I went back out later, and watched a little of The Kalin Twins' set from the side of the stage, they didn't seem to be having the same impact.

That was to become the major theme of the tour. Cliff Richard & The Drifters were a hard act to follow. The addition of Hank on guitar, and Bruce on rhythm guitar, had taken us to a whole other level. We sounded sleek, powerful and dangerous: like a proper rock and roll band. We sounded *American*.

It was my name the girls were shouting, and yet I felt like they were screaming for all of us. Hank and Bruce both looked great and were so charismatic on guitar that it was impossible not to get carried away. It was the tour that started the trend that, for years, the girls came to our shows for me, and the boys for Hank.

By now, I'd also got some pretty wild stage moves, which had been drilled into me by Jack Good. After the first night or two, I realised that a waggle of my knees, a thrust of my hips, or clutching my shoulder would drive the crowd's noise levels right through the roof. I would do it, and then thrill to the screams.

The Drifters saw what I was doing to maximise the hysteria and encouraged me. Bruce was particularly naughty. I remember one night he sidled up to me while he was playing his guitar. 'Go on, Cliff, go for it!' he said, over the din. 'Send them mad! Let's have a right ruckus in here tonight!'

I guess we were good to watch, and to listen to, and I think that's why we even gained an extra band member during the tour . . . without trying! Jet Harris was playing bass with The Most Brothers, but not really enjoying their gentle, sedate songs. One day, he came up to us in our dressing room.

'I love watching you guys every night,' he said. 'Do you mind if I join you?' Jet looked terrific, with his dyed blond hair, and was a great player, so we said 'Sure!' He ramped our performance up yet another notch. The screams got even louder.

During the tour, 'Move It' was racing up the singles chart. John Foster would get a call from our agent: 'It's Number Seven this week!' On my eighteenth birthday, it got to Number 4.

Waiting for the weekly chart placing added to the excitement of what was already a totally unbelievable experience.

*Could we get to Number 1?!**

The tour was going brilliantly for us, then . . . but for The Kalin Twins, it was a whole different story. They were two easy-going crooners, playing mild music, and they were very good at it, but they were having to follow a full-on, frenzied, rock and roll band. Plus, the crowd only knew one of their songs. It was a real struggle for them.

Some nights, when Hal and Herbie went on, the crowd was still chanting, 'We want Cliff! We want Cliff!' They'd have to wait until the fans had calmed down before they could get started. The poor guys were doing their best, and it wasn't their fault, but they were on a hiding to nothing.

The Kalin Twins played castanets during 'When', which went down well, and they had a couple of other smart songs, such as 'Three O'Clock Thrill' and 'Forget Me Not'. But there was no getting around the fact that, after us, their set felt like an anticlimax. I'd see fans filing out of the venue before the end.

It was obviously a problem the Kalins were aware of. Half-way through the tour, their manager took me to one side. 'Cliff, you and your band are going down so well that it's impossible for us to follow you,' he said. 'Could we switch the bill around, please, so that you play earlier in the night?'

---

* 'Move It' didn't make Number 1, in the end. It finally came to rest at Number 2, below Connie Francis and 'Stupid Cupid'. It was certainly a great song to lose out to – but, in my heart, I still feel that 'Move It' deserved to top the chart.

It was a fair question, and a reasonable request, but *I didn't for one second think of agreeing to it*. I knew how much good the tour was doing Cliff Richard & The Drifters. The newspaper headlines were saying: KALIN TWINS CAN'T FOLLOW OUR BOY CLIFF! Why on earth would I throw *that* away?

'No,' I said. 'I'm sorry, but it's the perfect place on the bill for us. We're staying there.' I didn't even bother to ask the rest of the band, or John Foster, what they thought. The Kalin Twins' manager was as charming and gracious as his act, and he didn't try to persuade me. He just said, 'OK, fair enough,' and left it there.

I guess you may be thinking this doesn't sound like the 'Goody Two-Shoes Cliff Richard' people have been led to believe I am. But that's never *really* been me. I've always been very driven in my career, and will do whatever's needed to boost it, even if it means being hard sometimes. The music always comes first.

Even so, I did always feel a little guilty about how I behaved towards The Kalin Twins in 1958. They were lovely guys who didn't deserve such a harrowing tour. *Your conscience won't always let you rest*. So, when I got the opportunity to make it up to them, more than thirty years later, I jumped at the chance.

In 1989, I staged a huge extravaganza at Wembley Stadium called The Event. It was a celebration of my three decades in music, from 'Move It' and *Oh Boy!* right through to the present day. I wanted to incorporate, and acknowledge, all of the landmarks of my career . . . and that, of course, included the Kalin Twins tour.

I asked my management if they could track down the Kalins in America and ask them to appear as my special guests. That was no easy task. Hal and Herbie never did manage to find that elusive follow-up to 'When'. They had got disillusioned in the early sixties, given up on music, and gone back to college.

They'd done straight day jobs and concentrated on raising their families ever since, except for occasionally playing small, local club gigs in the US. To all intents and purposes, their performing career was behind them. They certainly weren't expecting Cliff Richard to call them, asking them to play a stadium in London!

Well, I'm *so* glad that I did. When they flew over, Hal and Herbie were still as charming and friendly as they were back in 1958. They had aged, of course, but I recognised them as soon as I saw them. It was so good to see them again, and the years just fell away.

They greeted me with a gift. Hal and Herbie had dug out the castanets that they'd played on the 'When' single and on the 1958 tour, fixed them up (they'd seen a bit of wear and tear!) and presented them to me. It was a small but incredibly thoughtful present. I felt very moved.

I instigated a conversation with the Kalins. 'Look,' I began, 'I feel embarrassed to talk to you about this, but I'm sorry I was so nasty and thoughtless on our tour, years ago, refusing to move down the bill.' And their reply was predictably gracious.

'Please, don't worry about it!' Hal said. 'It's absolutely fine. We couldn't follow you, because you were getting such an incredible reaction, but we understood exactly why you wouldn't switch – and we still do. It's all good. We're just so grateful to be asked to this show now, and so thrilled to be part of it.'

They were, too. The Event had by now grown to two nights at Wembley, and it's hard to imagine what it must have felt like for The Kalin Twins, having given up music and virtually retired, to be walking out in front of 72,000 people! But they went down well, and 'When' triggered a joyous crowd sing-a-long.

The Kalin Twins were, without question, two of the nicest people I have ever met in my very long career in rock and roll. I'm so pleased that our history together had that happy ending . . . and I will always treasure those castanets.

I'm not a big fan of online music-streaming sites – I think they pay artists and songwriters dreadfully – but they have their uses. I recently looked up The Kalin Twins on one of the main ones. Their big song, 'When', has had three-and-a-half million plays. Their second most popular tune, 'Sweet Sugar Lips', has had 36,000. *One per cent as many.*

They were one-hit wonders . . . *so what*? If 'When' *is* The Kalin Twins' sole legacy, it is still one to be very proud of. And I'm very proud to have known them.

THIRTEEN

'PEGGY SUE' – BUDDY HOLLY

An all-time great who perished on the saddest day in rock and roll history

I suppose some people may feel the great Buddy Holly should really have appeared earlier in this book. After all, I was into him as early as 1957! But unfortunately, Buddy – and Ritchie Valens – will forever be associated in everyone's mind with 3 February 1959, and the terrible events of what they call The Day the Music Died.

Buddy Holly was a colossus of early rock and roll. For me, he is up there with Elvis, Little Richard, Jerry Lee Lewis and Chuck Berry as one of the giants who invented this magnificent music in the first place. It's still extraordinary to me just how much Buddy achieved, before his life was tragically cut short.

I first became aware of Buddy Holly – like all of Britain – in 1957, when he released 'That'll Be the Day'. Suddenly, there was this great catchy, attitudinal rock and roll song bursting out of AFN and climbing up the chart to Number 1. Let me tell you, I was straight down to Marsden's on my bike to buy that one!

Then, a little while later, this came along: 'Peggy Sue'. *What a fab track!* The way the guitar and the drums hit the same racing beat and stay there throughout; the urgent thrust of the melody; Buddy's yearning vocal: 'If you knew Peggy Sue, then you know why I feel blue . . .' *Yeah!* This was rock and roll craftsmanship at its peak!*

It's always hard to explain exactly why you love a song. Some of them just have this special, intrinsic magic, and 'Peggy Sue' is one of them. It's utterly timeless. You could re-record it today, in a slick studio with contemporary production, and it would sound totally modern. It would still have its lustre; its *shine*.

The story of how it was written is very endearing. A girl called Peggy Sue Gerron was the girlfriend of Jerry Allison, the drummer in Buddy's band, The Crickets. The couple split up. Jerry went to a rehearsal broken-hearted, and he and Buddy wrote a song about how he felt: 'I love you gal and I need you, Peggy Sue!'

Well, Jerry and Peggy Sue got back together, and she didn't even know the song existed until she went to a Buddy Holly & The Crickets concert and heard them play it. It didn't get quite the reaction from her that Jerry was hoping for: 'I was so embar-rassed, I could have died!' she told him afterwards.†

Buddy Holly was in that first wave of rock and rollers but he seemed unique from the start. He had his own distinctive style.

---

* You want to know how much I love this song? When I had my place in Portugal, I used to keep chickens, and I called one of them Pecky Sue.
† Sadly, there is no happy ending to this romantic tale: Jerry and Peggy Sue married in 1958, but divorced six years later.

He invented his own way of singing: I was fascinated by those little vocal hiccups he would introduce, which, as I said earlier, I'm certain that Adam Faith picked up on when he got started.

Maybe I love Buddy so much because he had an Elvis epiphany, like me! When he was nineteen, Buddy was playing country and western in his home town of Lubbock, Texas. He was half of a musical duo called Buddy and Bob and, in 1955, they supported Elvis when he came to town on tour.

Well, Buddy was so smitten with Elvis that he dropped the country side of things straight away and switched to full-on rock and roll. It's a story that confirms my core instinct: there are so many founding fathers of rock and roll, but Elvis is the one who gave it a look, a sound and an attitude. The one who *shaped* it.

Buddy Holly might have loved Elvis, but when I first saw a photo of him, I realised that he certainly didn't look like him. With his big glasses and slightly goofy smile, Buddy almost looked a bit geeky. But the truth is that he was one cool character – and those glasses became as much his visual signature as Elvis's curled lip.

I have never worn glasses on stage. I first needed them when I was aged ten, and having trouble seeing the blackboard at school, but I would always take them off before Cliff Richard & The Drifters did a show. Why? Well, I just always had this idea in my head: *I'm a rock and roll singer! I can't wear glasses!*

I don't know whether it's vanity or simply habit but I still do the same thing today. If you ever see me out and about, I will almost certainly have my specs on. There are thousands of photos out there of me in glasses. And yet, when it comes to showtime, they stay in the dressing room. That's just me.

Hank is a totally different story. He needed spectacles when he was a kid, and he loved rock and roll, and it really encouraged him when Buddy Holly came along, singing his amazing songs while wearing big glasses. * What with the guitar and the specs, it's no surprise that Hank fell in love with Buddy and his music. Hank now plays amazing Django Reinhardt-style 'gypsy jazz' music – but he will always love Buddy.

After 'Peggy Sue' was a hit, Buddy and his band released their debut album, *The "Chirping" Crickets*. I bought it as soon as it came out and there were *so* many great songs on it. The opener, 'Oh, Boy!', was terrific. 'You've Got Love', which was co-written by Roy Orbison; 'Not Fade Away', a fantastic song . . .

And the cover of the album was almost as interesting. It was Buddy and the band lined up, in suits and red ties, holding their guitars. Buddy was holding a brown-and-black Stratocaster that just looked *so* cool! When Hank joined The Drifters, he used to ogle that sleeve, and that guitar, like a kid looking in a toy shop window!

In 1959, I wrote off to Fender in America and bought a Stratocaster for Hank to play in The Drifters. It was the first one they had ever exported to Britain. I guess I assumed it would be brown, like Buddy's, but when it arrived it was a pink-y red. That was fine by me – it meant that it matched my favourite stage suit!

---

* Buddy's spectacles have had quite the influence! Elton John has admitted that when he was thirteen, he started wearing specs to look like him – even though he didn't need glasses!

Hank was already a fantastic guitarist and he became an absolute virtuoso on that Stratocaster. He's been called 'the first British guitar hero' and so many famous guitarists have admitted to being influenced by him: Eric Clapton, Mark Knopfler, Peter Frampton, Jeff Beck, Peter Green, Brian May, Neil Young. The list goes on. And Hank first picked up that guitar because of Buddy Holly (my only claim to fame is that I paid for it!).

Buddy Holly & The Crickets toured Britain in 1958. It sounds unbelievable now, but they did more than fifty shows in twenty-five days. That is a *massive* amount of singing! I couldn't begin to do that today. Whenever I tour, I try to have a day off after each show, to give my voice a change to rest and recover.*

I didn't see that 1958 tour, to my bitter regret, but apparently Mick Jagger and Keith Richards did. Mick has said that Keith took a lot of his original guitar stylings from Buddy Holly. When they started The Rolling Stones, their first big UK hit, in 1964, was a cover of 'Not Fade Away'.

Although I didn't go to a show, I did get to see Buddy Holly & The Crickets while they were over in 1958. They did a turn on *Sunday Night at the London Palladium*, which back then was the biggest entertainment show on British TV. I was glued to it. They did 'That'll Be the Day', 'Oh, Boy!' and 'Peggy Sue' and they were amazing.

Well, I was to learn that it was all the *more* amazing as Buddy

---

* The only modern performer who can sing as much as that is Bruce Springsteen. He does these three- or even four-hour shows, and sounds as good at the end as at the beginning. Then he goes again the next day. He must have concrete vocal cords, like those great Black blues singers!

was fighting a dental emergency! A year later, when I had begun my musical career, I had an agent, David, who had worked with Buddy Holly on that tour. I mentioned to him how much I had enjoyed the *Sunday Night at the London Palladium* appearance.

'Ha! Well, Buddy had a tooth stuck in with chewing gum!' he said.

'Pardon?'

David laughed. 'He broke a tooth before the Palladium show and he didn't know what to do. No dentists were open on a Sunday, so I bought some chewing gum, told Buddy to chew it and then stuck the tooth back in place with it. I warned him to make sure he didn't eat anything backstage!'

What a fantastic story! Buddy Holly was to have a few more cool hits in 1958, such as 'Maybe Baby' and 'Rave On'. But then his brilliant career was cut short horribly early . . . along with that of a precocious young talent who had barely even had a chance to get started. His name was Ritchie Valens.

I first heard Ritchie, like all the great American rock and rollers, on Luxembourg and AFN. He had his first hit in 1958, when he was just seventeen (as I was to do, later that year) with a neat rock and roll tune called 'Come On, Let's Go'. But it was his follow-up song that really, really did it for me.

'Donna' was a plaintive, heartfelt ballad, set to gorgeous plucked guitars and swooning backing vocals. It was incredibly simple in its style and composition, yet sounded heartfelt and bereft: 'I love that girl! Donna, where can you be?' Any teenage lad who'd been dumped could empathise with poor, brooding Ritchie!

And the incredible thing was that he had written it himself!

Ritchie's high-school sweetheart was a girl named Donna Ludwig, and he had written this wonderful song about her! He was just a seventeen-year-old American boy, writing a sweet song for his girlfriend and seeing it become an enormous hit.

I bought it, and when I flipped the single over, the B-side was just as tremendous. Ritchie's parents were both Mexican and he had arranged a traditional Mexican folk song, 'La Bamba', in a rock and roll style. It could have been cheesy, but it had me jumping around. The young guy's talent was phenomenal!

Really, Ritchie Valens had promise to burn. He would probably have become the next truly great rock and roll star. But that promise was cut short, along with that of Buddy Holly, on that fateful date, 3 February 1959, that, as I say, people always insist on calling The Day the Music Died.

It is, for me, the most heart-breaking tale in the history of rock and roll. Buddy and Ritchie were out on tour in the US with Dion & The Belmonts and The Big Bopper.* It was deep mid-winter and they were travelling through sub-zero temperatures in battered old school buses. Their heating kept breaking down.

The agents who planned the tour had badly messed up. Buddy and the other guys were calling it 'the tour from hell'. They were driving for ten hours a day, with no days off. It was so cold on Buddy's bus that his drummer got frostbite in his toes. Many of the musicians caught colds or flu and had to miss shows.

After they played a show in Clear Lake, Iowa, Buddy Holly

---

* I loved The Big Bopper's smash hit and signature tune, 'Chantilly Lace'. When I did The Event at Wembley in 1989, I sang it with the girls who used to dance on *Oh Boy!*

had had enough. He couldn't face another hideous 300-mile bus ride the next day, and chartered a six-seater propellor plane, or prop plane, to fly them to their next date in Minnesota. Then they all set about deciding who should go on the plane.

Waylon Jennings, Buddy's bassist, was down to fly, but gave up his seat to The Big Bopper, who had a bad case of flu. When Buddy learned that Waylon was not to fly, he said, 'I hope your damn bus freezes up!' 'Well, I hope your plane crashes!' Waylon joked back. Those words were to haunt the poor guy forever.

Buddy's guitarist, Tommy Allsup, was also due to be on the plane. He agreed to toss a coin for his seat with Ritchie Valens. Somebody at the Clear Lake show tossed the coin for them, and Ritchie won. Witnesses said that Ritchie laughed: 'That's the first time I've ever won anything in my life!'

The pilot of the small plane was only twenty-one, and took off after midnight into a windy, snowy sky with low visibility. The aircraft crashed a few minutes later, only six miles from the airport. The three famous passengers – The Big Bopper, Ritchie Valens and Buddy Holly – were thrown from the plane and died instantly.

It was such an awful event, with so many levels of tragedy. I read later that Buddy Holly's wife of six months, Maria, was pregnant, and shortly after hearing the dreadful news, she miscarried. I tell you, even now, more than sixty years on, thinking about that terrible night brings a tear to my eye.*

---

* The Shadows – as The Drifters had by then become – and I met Buddy's widow, Maria, and his parents when we played Lubbock, Texas, on our first American tour in 1960. His mother said they found watching us very moving because Hank, in his big glasses on stage, looked just like Buddy. Hank found that very moving, too.

The Drifters and I heard the news in London. We had played a gig the previous night, at the Lyceum on the Strand, that had been disrupted by hooligans. Teddy Boys had ripped out the seats and thrown coins, bottles and glasses at us. We had had to cut the show short for everybody's safety.

We were still grumbling about those thugs the next morning – but that all got put into perspective, and forgotten, when we saw the headlines on the newspaper sellers' boards. BUDDY HOLLY AND RITCHIE VALENS DEAD. *How could this be?* It's no exaggeration to say we were in a state of shock for days afterwards.

We had never met Buddy, nor Ritchie, and yet it felt as if we had lost friends – or, maybe, *comrades*. We knew their deaths were just so bad for rock and roll. Hank was particularly cut up: after all, Buddy Holly was his hero. I guess he suffered the same loss as I was to feel when Elvis died in 1977.

Just one week after the plane crash, The Drifters and I recorded my debut album, *Cliff*, at Abbey Road Studio Two. It was basically a live album: over two nights, the band and I simply played our normal live set, in front of an invited audience of fans. Norrie Paramor recorded it and turned it into an album.

We included Buddy Holly's 'That'll Be the Day' and Ritchie Valens's 'Donna'. We didn't do it because they had just passed away. Those two songs were always in our set list, so we had already planned to do them. But it made them painfully poignant for me to sing. I guess our versions served as our tributes.

There was so much mourning when Buddy Holly and Ritchie Valens died – rightly so! Everybody listened to their tunes and bought their records. A month after the disaster, Buddy had a posthumous Number 1 in Britain with 'It Doesn't Matter Anymore'. It stayed at the top of the chart for three weeks.

Buddy Holly and Ritchie Valens were only able to release one album each in their short lifetimes. Music *didn't* die on 3 February 1959. Not really. As they say, *rock and roll will never die*. It will go on long after I have gone. What *did* happen was that we lost two of the brightest talents that rock and roll has ever seen.

And I, and many others, still miss them.

FOURTEEN

'LET IT BE ME'
– THE EVERLY BROTHERS

The warring brothers who were in perfect harmony on record

The first wave of rock and roll was a broad church. Not everything had to be full-on, raucous and wild. Alongside Elvis, and Little Richard, and Jerry Lee Lewis, we had other artists who took a gentler, more melodic approach to making truly unbelievable music – and foremost among them were The Everly Brothers.

If you love harmonies as I do, then The Everly Brothers are untouchable. The way those two brothers, Don and Phil, blended and melded their sumptuous voices was unsurpassable. Don had this deep, resonant baritone, and Phil this smooth tenor croon, and when you put them together . . . well, it was beyond anything I had ever dreamed of.

Don and Phil had always kept it in the family! When they first started out, in Iowa back in the late forties, they apparently sang with their parents, Ike and Margaret Everly, as The Everly Family.

They had moved to Tennessee by the time they became The Everly Brothers in 1956, when Don was nineteen and Phil seventeen.

They got lucky when they secured a deal and their record company hooked them up with a husband-and-wife songwriting team: Felice and Boudleaux Bryant. That duo had initially written country songs but went on to pen hits for Buddy Holly, Roy Orbison, Jerry Lee Lewis and even Simon & Garfunkel.

The Bryants wrote the first song that I ever heard by The Everly Brothers, and it blew me away. I was sixteen years old, it was the start of 1957, and the song was 'Bye Bye Love'. *What a swoon!* When the Everlys followed it up later that year with 'Wake Up, Little Susie',* it showed that first gem had been no one-off.

I was absolutely *transfixed* by The Everly Brothers. They sounded magical. I had never heard such immaculate harmonies. I don't know whether or not the voices were so well matched because they were brothers, but they just seemed to dovetail naturally. Honestly, they sounded like liquid honey.

After The Everly Brothers had arrived, their beautiful hits just kept coming. 'All I Have to Do is Dream' gave me goose bumps the first time I heard it, and was a Number 1 in 1958. Its follow-up, 'Bird Dog', was more rock and roll, and found Don and Phil trading lines as they told the song's story. I thought it was amazing.

The Drifters and I quickly began covering Everly Brothers' songs in our set. We got the hang of them pretty well. All of their

---

* Sixty-five years on from first hearing it, I sang 'Wake Up, Little Susie' with my backing vocalists, David and Tim, on my last tour, in 2022. That made it a little different as it added a third harmony. I will never tire of singing it.

songs were in two-part harmonies, so Bruce would harmonise the high parts with me, and Hank the low ones. I'd pick up my guitar, and we'd all strum together.

As Cliff Richard & The Drifters took off, I would still always listen out eagerly for new Everly Brothers songs. In the summer of 1959, '(Till) I Kissed You' was a joy. Then, towards the end of that year, they released the song that I have selected for *A Head Full of Music* – 'Let It Be Me'.

'Let It Be Me' was apparently originally a French song called 'Je t'appartiens', but The Everly Brothers made it totally their own. It was a pledge of devotion to a true love: 'I bless the day I found you'. Don and Phil's harmonies were so sheer, so precise, that it literally sounded like one voice. Truly breathtaking.

'Let It Be Me' is a song that could be sung by a man to a woman, or a woman to a man ... *or by anybody to a person that they love*. It could be sung a cappella at a wedding, or even a funeral. I wanted to sing it at my dear friend Olivia Newton-John's funeral but, sadly, it wasn't possible. I'll talk more about that later.

At their peak, The Everly Brothers were one of those rare acts whose quality just never drops. They began the sixties with one of their all-time classics, written by Don: 'Cathy's Clown'. To be honest, I'm afraid it's one of those songs where words fail me when I try to describe it. The harmonies seem to drip pure gold.*

---

* More than half a century later, I sang 'Cathy's Clown' on my *Just . . . Fabulous Rock 'n' Roll* album, and it was *still* a thrill to harmonise on. I'd have loved to hear Phil and Don cover my song 'Miss You Nights'. They would have been wonderful.

The Everly Brothers' fortunes dipped in America in the sixties. The record industry can treat even its biggest and best stars horribly, and they fell out with their music publisher. He blocked them from singing any more Felice and Boudleaux Bryant songs. They weren't even allowed to record some tunes they had written themselves!

Yet even while they floundered in the States, The Everly Brothers kept having hits in Britain. I met them at one of their London shows in the mid-sixties. I had a shock. Before the show, somebody told me Don and Phil were getting on so badly that they arrived at their gigs separately and had separate dressing rooms!

What? I couldn't believe what I was being told. How could they work together if they were at odds like that? Surely the guy was exaggerating! I watched the show like a hawk for signs of tension between them, but there were none. The two brothers were slick and totally professional.

Indeed, the harmonies were so clear, and so precise, that it was like listening to their records. The songs sounded as exquisite as ever. I also loved that they were both playing jumbo Gibson acoustic guitars. I bought one of those myself in 1959, and I still have it, and sometimes play it, today.*

However, when I went backstage to meet the Everlys after the show, they *were* in separate dressing rooms. *Uh-oh!* I had to visit first Don and then Phil. Happily, they agreed to get together

---

* I'm advised my jumbo Gibson is worth a fortune now, both for its antiquity and my history with it. I'm told not to travel with it in case it gets dropped and breaks – even though I keep it in a case that is so tough that I think I could drop it off the Empire State Building and it wouldn't break!

for a photograph with me. I still have it. I'm standing between them, looking rather wary. Maybe I was afraid a fight might break out!

This enmity between The Everly Brothers clearly continued, because in 1973 they split with two farewell concerts in California. They were a disaster. On the first night, Phil smashed his guitar on the stage and strode off, leaving Don to finish the show on his own. Don played the second gig, on the following night, solo. 'The Everly Brothers died ten years ago,' he told the crowd.

Phil and Don began solo careers, and in 1981 I got to perform with Phil. *Talk about a dream come true!* I was on a tour where I was playing a lot of classic rock and roll hits, and my management reached out to Phil to duet with me on a song at Hammersmith Odeon. I couldn't have been more excited when he agreed.

Phil flew in especially for the show, which was on 1 May, and we did a little joke on stage about how little time he'd had to recover from the flight.

'How do you feel?' I asked him. 'Are you over the jet-lag?'

'I feel fine,' Phil replied. 'And I just want to wish you all a Merry Christmas!'

We sang a 1960 Everly Brothers song, 'When Will I Be Loved', and harmonising with Phil felt phenomenal. Even more magical than I hoped it would. Then, in 1983, I duetted with Phil on a pop-rock number, 'She Means Nothing to Me', for one of his solo albums. We had a Top 10 hit with it in Britain.*

---

* The original appeared on his *Phil Everly* album, but I also remixed it, with louder vocals, for my *The Rock Connection* album in 1984.

In 1983, Phil and Don appeared finally to have patched up their differences. They re-formed The Everly Brothers, with two huge comeback gigs at the Royal Albert Hall. Sadly, I was out of the country and I couldn't make it along to see them, but I was so pleased that they were back, and finally seemed to be getting on again.

The Everlys re-forming was such big news for me – and for others! Paul McCartney wrote a comeback single for them, 'On the Wings of a Nightingale'. He later made a comment proving, once again, that The Beatles had the same musical heroes as I do. 'When John and I started to write songs,' he said, 'I was Phil and he was Don.'

I was fortunate enough to be able to perform with Phil Everly one more time. In 1994, I was playing ten nights at Wembley Arena, as part of my *The Hit List* tour. Through our record labels, Phil and I arranged for him to join me on stage to duet on a number that we could release as a live single.

We deliberately kept this plan secret, so when I announced to the crowd, 'Please welcome . . . Mr Phil Everly!' the roar almost took Wembley's roof off! We crooned one of the Everlys' stone-cold classics, 'All I Have to Do is Dream'. I was delighted when it was a Top 20 hit. That's rare for a live record!

The great thing about having a few encounters with Phil Everly over the years – apart from harmonising with one of the best harmonisers in musical history! – was that I got a chance to explain to him how much the music he made with his brother had meant to me. Such opportunities are rare, and must be grasped.

'Phil, my band and I cut our teeth on Everly Brothers music!' I told him. 'We just loved the way you guys sing. The Everly

Brothers were how, and *why*, we learned to do harmonies. Can I be honest with you? I'm really just a frustrated one-man harmony group!'*

'Aw, shucks!' Phil said.

Phil Everly passed away in 2014. Had he and Don mended their troubled relationship by then? Well, yes and no. Don Everly famously didn't go to his brother's funeral, but he was to explain that it wasn't because he was still angry with him. He just feared he would find it too emotional.

In an interview after Phil died, Don admitted they had a 'difficult life' together. He said some of it was down to politics, of all things: Don was a staunch Democrat, and Phil was an arch Republican. But Don also revealed that he kept a little urn of Phil's ashes in his home and said, 'Good morning!' to them every day.

It's so ironic, don't you think? That two brothers, riven by sibling rivalry offstage, could make such sweet music together? Don was to die in 2021. Astonishingly, Margaret Everly, the mum they had first started singing with, outlasted both her sons. She also died in 2021, at the grand age of 102.

The Everly Brothers' musical genius will stay with me forever. I'd like to do one last tribute to them. I don't have many items left on my music wish list now, but, as well as my longed-for album of Elvis duets, I'd *love* to make a record of Everlys songs, celebrating their golden harmonies.

Tony Rivers, the king of harmonies, who worked on my

---

* That love of harmonies has stayed with me for my entire life. Sometimes, in the studio, I sing my own backing harmonies: or sing them, then get a couple of guys and a girl to double-track exactly what I have just done.

albums in the seventies and eighties, says he'll help me. I'd like to multi-track vocals like Queen, or Enya, used to. I'd sing the lead, with layers of voices stacked up behind me. I have this instinct that it could sound fantastic.

Will it ever happen? Well, if I close my eyes and wish hard enough, maybe I can *will* it into being. *Because, all I have to do is dream . . .*

FIFTEEN

'TREASURE OF LOVE' – CLYDE McPHATTER

The greatest soul singer that you may never have heard of

In 1959, Cliff Richard & The Drifters had to change our name. In fact, we found out that it wasn't *our* name at all. We had unwittingly been borrowing it from some other people, and now they wanted it back, thank you very much!

We had arrived at calling ourselves The Drifters by a roundabout route. I had originally thought of 'The Planets', but worried that it sounded too much like Bill Haley's Comets. I'd then looked up 'planet' in a dictionary and found the phrase 'cosmic drifter'. 'Cosmic' sounded a bit OTT* so we settled on 'Drifters'.

After 'Move It' and 'Living Doll' were huge hits for us in Britain, our record label wanted to start putting out Cliff Richard & The Drifters records in America. But then Norrie Paramor

---

* A few years later, in the far-out, psychedelic sixties, 'Cosmic' might have fitted in fine! But that music was never really my thing.

received a legal cease-and-desist letter. It appeared that if we were to do so, it would be a breach of copyright.

A very good band called The Drifters already existed in America, and had done so since 1953. They had been originally founded by a great soul, and rock and roll, singer who had since gone solo and whom, coincidentally, we were very soon to meet. His name was Clyde McPhatter.

For now, though, we were in need of a new name, and it was Jet Harris and Hank who came up with one. They went for a pint, and Jet said, 'Let's call ourselves The Shadows – because we're always in Cliff's shadow!' *Hmm.* I wasn't *totally* sure about that, but . . . *whatever.* It was a great name, so The Shadows it was.

The forced name change was a minor inconvenience but, luckily, Cliff Richard & The Drifters, sorry, The Shadows, had far too many exciting things going on at the time to worry about it for very long. Because we were about to do something beyond our wildest dreams. We were about to go to America.

Ever since I'd heard Elvis blaring out of that Citroën window, America had been an almost mythical place for me: a promised land. It was the crucible, the homeland, of all of the great rock and roll music that had been thrilling me every day for three years now. To actually *go* there . . . *wow! Was it really going to happen?*

It was. The Shadows and I flew into New York City in January 1960 to play an American tour. We were to appear on a mixed bill of artists that would be like a more illustrious version of the UK tour we'd done with The Kalin Twins. When we landed at

Idlewild Airport,* we still didn't know who else was on the bill with us.

And when we found out, we couldn't believe it.

Headlining the show was Frankie Avalon, who was then probably the biggest teen idol in America. There were soul giants Sammy Turner and The Isley Brothers, doo-wop band The Crests, instrumentalists Johnny & The Hurricanes, US teenage rock and rollers Bobby Rydell and Freddy Cannon . . . and the former (US, original) Drifters' singer, Clyde McPhatter.

And we had to match up to this competition, night after night! Blimey! No pressure, then!

We had a couple of days to acclimatise before the tour began. The Shadows and I walked around New York, cricking our necks gazing up at the skyscrapers, and thrilling at the noise, the bustle, the accents, the landmarks . . . everything. *Thrilling at being in America*. But, as I remember, what impressed us most were the cars.

New York was full of these giant Cadillacs and Chevrolets and Thunderbirds and Oldsmobiles, honking their horns furiously as they inched through the snarled-up Manhattan traffic. *Cor! We'd never seen anything like that in Cheshunt!* It began my love affair with American automobiles that was to last for decades.

As soon as I got back from America, I got rid of the little Sunbeam Alpine I'd been pottering around in and bought a Ford Thunderbird. I later traded that in for a Cadillac, and then a

---

* It has long since been renamed JFK.

Corvette Stingray. Today, of course, those big cars are written off as selfish gas-guzzlers. But we didn't know about global warming back then.

I thought I was the bee's knees in my black Cadillac, with its super-cool fins. I can remember once, in London, stopping at a red light. A Ford Anglia pulled up next to me. It wasn't even as long as the Cadillac's bonnet (or, strictly speaking, hood)! The guys in the Anglia all glanced over at me. I could see the thought bubbles over their heads:

Just look at that berk! Who does he think he is, driving that?*

Back in the US, after a couple of days in New York we got driven to Canada to begin the tour. The promoters were calling it The Biggest Show of Stars for 1960. They had promo posters made with all of the American stars' names on. And at the bottom was a pink flash with information about a special bonus artist:

EXTRA ADDED ATTRACTION: ENGLAND'S NO. 1
SINGING SENSATION, CLIFF RICHARDS!

Cliff Richards! Honestly, I ask you! How did I react to it? I sighed, smiled, rolled my eyes to myself, and thought, *OK, here we go again*! Because it wasn't the first time that that had happened. Nor would it be the last!

The tour was to travel around America on two Greyhound

---

* I bought a car phone for that Cadillac, when they were a new thing. My first call was to my mum. She picked up, and I said, 'Hi, Mum, I'm just leaving London, on my way to you.' 'Are you in a phone box?' she asked, 'No, I'm in my car!' I said, proudly. There was a pause, then: 'Oh, Cliff, stop being so *silly*!'

buses (I'll explain *why* there were two in the next chapter – it was *not* a good reason). The US stars were all friendly on the drive from New York to Montreal but, sitting quietly in my seat as the American landscapes flashed by, I got a serious attack of the nerves.

This was a lot to take in. Just two years before, I'd been a schoolboy in Cheshunt. Now I was in the home of rock and roll, *in America*, with a bus full of artists who, in my eyes, were superstars, on my way to play sold-out shows to thousands of fans in nearly every major US city. Talk about intimidating! *Could I do it?*

The nerves reached their peak on the first night, when I was standing behind the plush curtains in the wings of the beautiful Forum de Montréal Theatre. As I prepared to go on, I heard thousands of kids screaming. Nobody was around me. I bent double, put my hands on my knees . . . and threw up all over the floor.

Yuk! Oh, my God! I didn't know what to do. I was about to go on – I could hardly run off looking for a mop! Instead, to my shame, I have to confess that I simply left the puddle of sick there and ran on stage when the MC shouted, 'Ladies and gentlemen, all the way from England – Cliff Richard & The Shadows!'

Despite my initial terror, our set went incredibly well. I was buzzing afterwards, but still too mortified to tell anyone from the venue that I had puked behind their nice stage curtains. I did confess to The Shadows, though. They all laughed – 'Oh, Cliff!' – then admitted that, yeah, they'd all been pretty nervous, too.

My nerves soon dissipated, though, because night after night, The Shadows and I were going down *unbelievably* well. Each artist only had a twenty-minute slot, so we were doing the same five-song set every night:

- 'Forty Days (To Come Back Home)' – the Chuck Berry song
- 'A Voice in the Wilderness' – from the soundtrack of a movie I had made, *Expresso Bongo*
- 'My Babe' – a cover of a US blues hit by Little Walter
- 'Living Doll'
- 'Whole Lotta Shakin' Goin' On' – the great Jerry Lee Lewis, of course

Looking back at that list now, it feels bizarre to me that I didn't sing 'Move It' – just about the only tour when I haven't done so! But I guess the promoters didn't want us doing too many of our own songs that the crowd wouldn't know, and 'Living Doll' had been a minor hit in America, reaching Number 30.

Well, the promoters didn't need to worry – and nor did I! The crowds went crazy for us every single night. The screaming was deafening. My stage moves got the same wild reaction as they did in Britain. There were the same yells: 'Cliff! Cliff! Oh, Cliff, we love you!' It really felt like America was falling for us.*

It was beyond anything we had dared to hope for. There were three acts on that crowded bill that brought the house down

---

* It didn't. I was to tour in America two or three more times, but never broke big there – my record label just never seemed to want to put the resources behind me. But at least now, in my later years, it means that I can walk around there with blessed anonymity!

at every show. We were one of them. US teen idol Bobby Rydell, who I will talk about later, was another one. And the third was Clyde McPhatter.

Clyde was an incredible singer. He had first emerged in the early fifties in an R&B group called Billy Ward & His Dominoes, a vocal quintet who also sang doo-wop (so, a rather more successful Quintones!). Clyde's pure tenor gained them a big following, and cool hits such as 'Do Something for Me'.

Sadly, Clyde got a rough deal from the guy who ran the group, Billy Ward. Even when The Dominoes were one of the biggest R&B groups in America, Clyde had to survive on a pittance of a wage. 'I'd be on a block where everybody knew my records,' he told one journalist, 'and I wouldn't be able to afford a Coca-Cola!'

Clyde left The Dominoes in 1953 and formed The Drifters for legendary Atlantic Records founder Ahmet Ertegun. However, he then got conscripted into the US Army, like Elvis, and quit The Drifters in the mid-fifties. Then, in 1956, he had a huge solo American hit with a song called 'Treasure of Love'.

I loved 'Treasure of Love' the second that I heard it wafting out of our radio in Cheshunt. It hung around a stark, almost staccato guitar strum, yet it sounded *so* rich and alluring. The backing voices could have been from a gospel tune, which was apt because, over them, Clyde McPhatter sang like an angel.

'Treasure of Love' remains one of my favourite songs of all time. *Easily*. It has these powerful lines that pull you in close. 'A treasure of love is not very far,' it promises would-be lovers. 'It glows like fire, and it shines like a star.' And Clyde breathes them out so beautifully that you believe every word he sings.

For me, it's another great example of rock and roll being colour-blind for its listeners. If you didn't know, Clyde could easily be a white man. And, who cares *what* colour he is? He has so much soul because he *feels* the song so keenly. He seems to inhabit every note of it: to *live* in the textures of the song.*

Clyde McPhatter was already a soul (and rock and roll) icon by The Biggest Show of Stars for 1960 tour, and The Shadows and I were just starting out. Yet I spent more time on that tour with him than I did with any other artist. I was in and out of his dressing room and chatting with him all the time.

Clyde was a lovely, quiet and gentle man. He knew about my band starting out as The Drifters and having to change our name to The Shadows. It was nothing to do with him: he'd left the original Drifters a full four years before our little band began in Cheshunt. And he couldn't have cared less about the fuss. *Phew!*

We could have been beneath him but he gave us his time, listened to us play and encouraged us. He shared his stories from being right there at the birth of rock and roll and R&B. He was far too modest to tell us that Jackie Wilson, who had replaced him in Billy Ward & His Dominoes, based his singing style on Clyde.

Clyde McPhatter never remotely got the praise and the acclaim that he deserved. Some musical historians say he was an inspiration for Ben E. King and Smokey Robinson. He should

---

* I think the *emotion* you put into a song is what matters, not technique or style. Once, on TV, I met up with The Three Degrees. They asked, 'Do you want us to show you how to sing soul?' But I gratefully declined their kind offer. I needed to feel how to sing it my own way.

have been up there with the very greats of Black American music. But . . . it never worked out that way.

Sadly, Clyde's career went off the rails, and so did he. In the sixties, he moved between different record labels but scored few hits. He earned a reputation for being 'difficult' and for being a heavy drinker. He even moved to England at the end of the decade, and sang with a club band called ICE.

Apparently, once he returned to America, Clyde did cameo appearances in rock and roll revival tours, but essentially became something of a recluse, blaming his fans for 'deserting' him. Tragically, he was only thirty-nine when he died in 1972, from heart, liver and kidney failure brought on by alcohol abuse.

It's so awful. And inexplicable to me, because I remember that kind, wise, cool soul singer who was happy to hang out in 1960. Clyde McPhatter got a very rough deal. If he'd been lucky enough to find an American Norrie Paramor to look after him, he'd have become the musical superstar that he really should have been.

I sang 'Treasure of Love' on my 1983 album, *Dressed for the Occasion*, recorded live at the Albert Hall with the London Philharmonic Orchestra. With their massed strings and orchestration, it was more lavish than Clyde's sweet original – but I just hoped that, if he were still alive, he'd have thought I'd done it justice.

Because I was standing on the shoulders of a giant.

SIXTEEN

'ALWAYS' – SAMMY TURNER

And here's another under-celebrated great American soul singer

It's well known that the United States in the fifties was riven by racism. They still had segregation in parts of the South. Rock and roll may have sounded colour-blind to me, listening to it coming out of the radio in Cheshunt, but for the artists actually making the music in America, the reality was very different.

There are many examples. On that first American tour, as I said, we were playing Chuck Berry's 'Thirty Days (To Come Back Home)' every night. Or, rather, we were playing 'Forty Days (To Come Back Home)', the cover of Chuck's song by Ronnie Hawkins & The Hawks, which had been a minor US hit in 1959.

Well, Ronnie Hawkins was a white guy and his original band, The Blackhawks, had all been Black. They had met so much prejudice, and had so much trouble getting gigs, in the South in the early fifties that, after the group disbanded, Ronnie had to replace them with an all-white band, which he renamed The Hawks.

Pretty grim, huh? But you would assume that, by the time Cliff Richard & The Shadows hit the States, at the start of a bright new decade, for The Biggest Shows of Stars for 1960, that kind of racism and bigotry would have been a long time dead and gone.

Sadly, you would be wrong.

When we got into New York in January 1960, the tour promoters showed us all onto two buses. The bill was split almost fifty-fifty between white and Black artists, which was great . . . but we were not allowed to travel together. There was a white-skinned bus and a Black-skinned bus.

'You guys, on this bus!' the drivers told a group of us. 'And you others, on the other one!' So, it was Frankie Avalon, Bobby Rydell, Freddy Cannon, Johnny & The Hurricanes, The Shadows and me on one coach; Clyde McPhatter, Sammy Turner and The Isley Brothers on the other.

The white bus. And the Black bus. *

More than sixty years on, it sounds preposterous, right? *Obscene.* And it *was.* But I was an overawed teenager, keeping my head down, and none of the older stars questioned it. It was presented to us in a totally matter-of-fact way: *this is how it is.* And all of the Black artists quietly accepted it. I guess they were used to it.

It was utterly ridiculous, but the great thing was that once we got off the buses, The Biggest Show of Stars for 1960 *was* completely colour-blind. The promoters wouldn't let us travel together but they couldn't segregate us backstage. And all of the artists, of whatever colour, hung out together all of the time.

---

* The Crests, the racially mixed doo-wop group, had to separate to travel.

As well as being in and out of Clyde McPhatter's dressing room, I'd also drop in on Sammy Turner and The Isley Brothers. So would everybody else. The funny thing was, we never said anything to each other about the separate buses. There was no need. We knew it was simply a load of nonsense, and just ignored it.*

We all chatted like friends, which we soon were. It was a tremendous example of a very strong belief that I have: no matter *what* kind of divided or troubled society rock and roll comes out of, it is always non-racist, because music fans don't care about colour. They didn't then and they don't now. It's all about the music.

It made me think about things a little differently, and definitely a bit harder, though. At one show, I was in Clyde McPhatter's dressing-room, nattering away, when Clyde said, 'Well, I have to get made up now!'

'Oh, do you get made up?' I asked him.

'Sure!' And Clyde showed me how he applied powder to make his face look a little lighter. *Now, why should he have to do that?* I have no idea if it was Clyde's choice, or a dictum from the promoter. But given the daft hoo-ha over the buses, I wouldn't be surprised if it were the latter.

Either way, Clyde applied his make-up a lot more skilfully than The Shadows and I did. We really hadn't got the hang of it. We'd slather this orange make-up all over our faces, to try to look

---

* I was to have a comparable experience when The Shadows and I went to South Africa for the first time in 1961 and witnessed the evils of apartheid at first hand. After that first tour, we insisted that we be allowed to play to racially mixed audiences on all our subsequent visits.

tanned, but then it would end at our chins, and our necks would be totally white. We may have looked a little odd.

I was glad that everybody on The Biggest Show of Stars for 1960 was getting on so well, because there was another Black artist on the bill that I was desperate to meet. I had loved Sammy Turner's voice ever since I had first heard it on AFN and Luxembourg, a year or so earlier.

I'd heard Sammy singing a bluesy, slightly jazzy version of the old English folk song 'Lavender Blue', which was a smash for him in America – his biggest, in fact. But the tune that had really made me prick my ears up was a single that was a hit in Britain in the summer of 1959. The song was called 'Always'.

'Always' was a standard, really. It had been written by the composer Irving Berlin in 1925 for his partner, Elin, who became his second wife the following year. The original sounded very much of its time: a mellow, symphonic swoon, like something your grandparents might listen to on a Sunday. Well, Sammy Turner was about to change all *that*.

Sammy was a smooth R&B/soul singer and, working with the producers Leiber and Stoller, he turned 'Always' into a pure soul nugget. His molten voice was to die for, but there was so much more to the song than that. He made a slightly dated musical period piece sound sharp and contemporary.

Sammy Turner's 'Always' had a hip, pulsing double-bass rhythm that urged it along, but also a fantastic, jaunty brass section that came in at a rakish angle. It made a terrific musical base for Sammy to unleash his golden tonsils and croon Irving Berlin's devoted words: 'I'll be loving you, always, with a love that's true . . .'

The song wasn't rock and roll in sound, but it certainly was in *spirit*. At the same time, something about its exotic beat reminded me of the very first song in this book, from before the dawn of rock and roll: Sammy Davis Jr's 'In a Persian Market'. It's a tune that almost defies analysis. But it doesn't defy enjoyment.

Let me tell you, I'd have *loved* Cliff Richard & The Shadows to have a chance to record and release 'Always'. It was a pretty good consolation, though, to get to hear Sammy Turner sing it, live in America, night after night. That tour had so many 'pinch-me' moments. Here was one of them.

Sammy Turner was in his late twenties by then, and had served in the Korean War as a US paratrooper. He was very much a man while, in truth, The Shadows and I were still boys. Yet when we nervously introduced ourselves, he could not have been more gallant, or welcoming. He was a perfect gentleman.

I can still remember every single word, note and inflection of 'Always'. I could sing it for you now, with no rehearsal! When I staged The Event at Wembley in 1989, it was the third song that I sang to those 72,000 fans. Those two concerts were so special, yet singing 'Always' remains a stand-out moment in my mind.

Given his phenomenal voice and talent, it's a total mystery to me that Sammy Turner's career fell away after 'Always'. He had one more small American hit with 'Paradise', in 1960, and then after that . . . nothing. Even when he signed to Tamla Motown, Berry Gordy couldn't work his magic for him.

Well, I guess there are some consolations to careers that don't reach superstar heights. Unlike many artists in this book, Sammy Turner never lost his way in life; never crashed and burned; never died young and beautiful. As I write, he is still alive, aged ninety-one, and I'm sure he is still a perfect gentleman. A great man.

If Sammy Turner was a classy, smooth soul star on that American tour, The Isley Brothers were totally different. *They. Were. Incredible!* They were three friendly, approachable brothers named Ronald, Rudolph and O'Kelly (who went as 'Kelly') and they were one of the best live acts I'd ever seen. Maybe *the* best.

The Isley Brothers were human dynamos on stage. Three slim, handsome young guys, they would line up in their shiny jackets, drainpipes and bowties, and jive, shimmy and gyrate. Ronald would do the splits while he was singing! They were in perpetual motion, and your wide eyes could not keep up with them.

Wow! What will they do next? Ronald, Rudolph and Kelly would jerk, spin and jitterbug at such a speed that you wondered how they didn't keel over. I mean, talk about having rhythm! They went down pretty well each night but, visually, they topped us all. They were consummate showmen.

I was only to find out later that The Isley Brothers had had a tragic history. With a fourth brother, Vernon, they had started out in the early fifties, singing gospel in churches across America. When Vernon was knocked off his bike and killed when he was thirteen, the remaining siblings were heartbroken and stopped performing.

They had restarted in 1957, with Ronald now their lead singer. They moved from their hometown of Cincinnati to New York, got a record deal, and switched from gospel to singing doo-wop and rock and roll. In 1959, they wrote their first song together, and it was their debut American hit. It was called 'Shout'.

'Weee-ll, you know you make me want to shout . . . !'

The Isley Brothers doing 'Shout' was a highlight every single night of The Biggest Show of Stars for 1960. Ronald would unleash this . . . *thunderbolt* of a voice, and Rudolph and Kelly would sing perfect backing vocals and dance like demons. I was surprised that the three of them didn't leave scorch marks on the stage.*

It's a sign of how well singles used to sell that 'Shout' only got to Number 47 in the US chart, but sold more than a million copies. *A million copies!* Can you believe it? Today, some weeks you only need to sell 25,000 to get to Number 1 in Britain. *Huh!* And people wonder why I don't like streaming services!

The whole experience of listening to music has changed nowadays. I used to love listening to vinyl records, or CDs, with friends, and then everyone discussing them together and giving their opinions. Today, it's all about MP3 files and headphones. Well, *it is what it is*. All we artists can do is try to roll with it.

The Isley Brothers' version of 'Shout' didn't chart in Britain. I can only assume that it didn't get the radio play it should have. (It was, however, a huge hit for Lulu in 1964. I thought that Lulu's version was tremendous, too. She has always been a soulful singer, and I love how she can belt songs out.)

I liked 'Shout' a lot, but in 1962 The Isley Brothers released a song with a curiously similar title that I loved even more: 'Twist and Shout'. They didn't write it themselves – it had originally been a non-hit for an American group called The Top Notes – but, goodness me, they certainly made it their own!

---

* There is footage on YouTube of The Isley Brothers singing 'Shout' and dancing in 1960. Have a look. It will be the happiest three minutes you spend today.

I thought 'Twist and Shout' was extraordinary the very first time I heard it, back in 1962. It's such a huge, larger-than-life number, full of vitality and attitude: I would defy *anybody* not to like it. Plus, Ronald Isley's vocal performance is simply phenomenal. As the song grows wilder and wilder, so does he.

I knew 'Twist and Shout' was wonderful but, at that time, it wasn't a song that I would have dared to try to sing with The Shadows. I'll freely admit that I thought, *Wow! I'd never be able to sing like that!* Whereas, nowadays, I reckon it doesn't matter *how* much like the original you sound, as long as you attack a song with vim and gusto.

'Twist and Shout' only got to Number 17 in the US for The Isley Brothers. Two years later, of course, it was an absolute smash for The Beatles in America, where it went to Number 1 on the *Cashbox* chart. And, I must admit, at the time that bugged me a little.

I had nothing against The Beatles for covering it, and I thought their version was perfectly fine. It was just that I thought The Isleys weren't getting the credit they were due. I remember my sisters saying to me, 'Isn't this Beatles song great?' And I replied, 'It's *not* a Beatles song . . . have you heard The Isley Brothers' version?'*

I've heard other versions of 'Twist and Shout'. A rap duo called Salt-N-Pepa did it in the eighties. A reggae group, Chaka Demus & Pliers, had a Number 1 with it in 1993. Like all terrific songs, it can

---

* The Beatles weren't even the first British band to release 'Twist and Shout' as a single. Brian Poole & The Tremeloes had had a Number 4 hit with it here in 1963.

translate to many genres of music . . . but I don't, personally, believe any version has ever come near to The Isley Brothers'.

You know what else I love about The Isley Brothers? They have had a career like mine – in terms of longevity, anyway! They've just rolled on and on and on. Over almost seventy years (!), they have sold eighteen million records in America, and have had hits in the *Billboard* Hot 100 in six different decades.*

That's not the whole story. The Isley Brothers have also been inducted into the Rock and Roll Hall of Fame, got their own star on the Hollywood Rockwalk in Los Angeles, and received a Grammy Lifetime Achievement Award. Happily, the days of having to travel on segregated tour buses are a long way behind them (and us).

They have had line-up changes over the years, of course. Seven different Isley brothers (and brothers-in-law, apparently) have been in the band over the years, and many have passed on. But, at the time of writing, Ronald is still there, at eighty-two, with his younger brother Ernie, a mere stripling of seventy-one.

In fact, a quick glance at iTunes tells me that The Isley Brothers released a brand-new album, *Make Me Say It Again, Girl*, late in 2022, with guest appearances by Beyoncé, Earth, Wind & Fire and Snoop Dogg! *Blimey!* Do you know what? I think I might even get that, and see what it's like.

Why? Because the only thing that's better than great old music . . . is great new music.

---

* I'm so proud of being the only artist to have had, in Britain, Top 5 albums in eight consecutive decades, so I know how The Isley Brothers must feel! These records are not easy to achieve!

SEVENTEEN

'SWAY' — BOBBY RYDELL

A teen idol who was so cool that he had a school named after him

Fame is a fickle mistress. In pop and rock, you can never predict for sure which songs and shows will go down well with the public. Sometimes you get artists, or performances, which seem certain to drive the fans wild. And then, for whatever reason, they just don't happen.

Frankie Avalon was an obvious choice to headline our 1960 US tour. At the time, he was the biggest teen idol in America. He was only four weeks older than me, but he'd been having hits in the US since 1957. In 1959, 'Venus' had been Number 1 for five weeks, and he'd ended the year on top of their chart with 'Why'.

I liked both of those songs, so on our tour I piled into the stage wings with the other acts to watch Frankie's set. Yet it was odd. Frankie was a smart, handsome guy, and he smiled and crooned, 'Hey, Venus! Oh, Venus!' nicely enough, but . . . *it just wasn't cooking*, as we say. And it was the same story night after night.

Frankie just didn't trigger the hysteria I thought he would. It's hard to say why. Maybe he was too static, after acts such as The Isley Brothers, and The Shadows and me, had been rocking and rolling around the stage? The fans clapped, but a lot left before the end, as had happened to The Kalin Twins on our UK tour.

In fact, after seeming on top of the world when we began The Biggest Show of Stars for 1960, Frankie Avalon was never to have another US Top 10 hit. He was a nice guy but, for some reason, he and I hardly hung out or spoke to each other the whole tour long. It wasn't deliberate. It was just how it worked out.

Bobby Rydell? Now, *he* was a different matter! Bobby had also been a bit of a child prodigy. He'd been in a US telly show called *TV Teen Club* when he was eight – *eight!* – and then drummed in rock and roll bands in his teens. He'd even been in a youthful band with Frankie Avalon, called Rocco & The Saints.

But Bobby's career really took off when he got a solo record deal in 1959. He had a US hit with 'Kissin' Time', then a Top 10 smash with 'We Got Love'. His debut album, also called *We Got Love*, sold a million copies. And while we were out on tour, he was Number 2 in the American chart with 'Wild One'.

And Bobby Rydell absolutely *killed it* on The Biggest Show of Stars for 1960! He went down a storm every single night. As I said, Clyde McPhatter raised the roof, as did we. Then, the same girls who'd been yelling, 'I love you, Cliff!' at me began screaming, 'I love you, Bobby!' Ha! Some people have no loyalty!

I'm joking, of course! With his dimples and perfect quiff, Bobby looked terrific on stage, and was a slick performer. I loved watching him. What was amazing was that he was even younger than me: still only seventeen. *That* was a new one for me! Up till then, I'd assumed that *everybody* in music was older than me!

Because Bobby and I were the youngest people on the tour, we maybe gravitated towards each other. We'd hang out backstage, and sometimes sat together on the tour bus as it pulled through the dark night to the next city. In fact, a lot of the social life on that tour happened at night, on those buses.

We'd all still be on a high from the shows, and those night drives through the ever-changing landscapes felt like yet another exciting element of our great American adventure. We would all be chattering away animatedly, then the bus would stop in the early hours and we'd pile into an all-night diner.*

Bobby Rydell and I had a lot in common. We were both teenagers who'd been catapulted to fame, and suddenly had girls screaming at us. You'd have thought we'd have talked a lot about that, and compared notes . . . but we didn't. Mostly, our bus chats were about music and the artists we loved.

I remember being very impressed that Bobby could play drums. He told me he'd been a singing drummer in some bands. I gather that when singers play Las Vegas, audiences like it if they can also drum. Bobby did Vegas in his later years, so I bet that talent stood him in good stead.

I liked Bobby Rydell, and because we'd got on so well in America, I followed his career when I got back home. He had a

---

* It was very easy to get carried away in those diners, and order burger and chips at two in the morning, or coffee with half-milk, half-cream, or beer – and I did! When I got home from America, I weighed myself. *Gulp! Twelve-and-a-half stone!* I had to go on a crash diet. I've never been that heavy since.

couple of hits in Britain, later in 1960. They weren't what you'd call rock and roll, but they were still terrific.

He sang a big, smoochy, romantic ballad called 'Volare'. You heard it a lot around that time. It had been a hit in Britain in 1958 for a guy called Domenico Modugno, who'd sung it for Italy in the Eurovision Song Contest.* Then that great crooner Dean Martin had a hit with it later the same year.

But I liked Bobby Rydell's follow-up even more. It's still one of my favourite songs of all time. It was called 'Sway', and I thought that it was absolutely phenomenal.

'Sway' was such a gem of a song. It began with swinging bossa nova rhythms and parps of brass, then in came Bobby's voice, sounding rich and resonant: 'When marimba rhythms start to play, dance with me . . .' It had lustrous strings, cherubic backing vocals, a killer beat . . . in fact, it had pretty much everything!

Apparently, 'Sway' had been written by two Mexican composers in 1953. So, in a way, I guess Bobby and his producers were doing the same thing as with 'Volare': taking an exotic, foreign song and anglicising it. Well, it worked. It was a dream of a song, and a big hit on both sides of the Atlantic.

I liked getting into songs like 'Sway', which weren't classic rock and roll, and they also shaped the way that my career was about to go. Norrie Paramor always paid attention to what was

---

* I also have my own chequered history in the Eurovision Song Contest, of course – I came second in 1968 with 'Congratulations', and third in 1973 with 'Power to All Our Friends'. But that's a different story . . . or two different stories . . .

happening in the charts – well, it was his job! – and he was keen to widen my appeal beyond just teenagers.

That was why Norrie had started getting me to make albums like 1959's *Cliff Sings*. It was new territory for me. Half of the tracks were rock and roll songs, with The Shadows. The other half was me singing songs by such venerable composers as George and Ira Gershwin, with the Norrie Paramor Orchestra.

Was I selling out rock and roll? Not at all! Sure, I wanted to sell as many records as I could, but I'd always loved playing different kinds of music – don't forget, I went from 'Move It' to 'Living Doll'! So, I enjoyed both rocking out with The Shadows on 'Blue Suede Shoes' *and* crooning 'As Time Goes By' with Norrie's orchestra.

I like to mix it up. I always have done.

I suppose, by now, I was taking the same journey as Bobby Rydell, from being a teen idol to becoming a more mature artist. I was certainly realising that what they call the great American songbook holds many classic tunes that are going to be around forever. And that I would dearly love to sing those tunes.*

The interesting thing is that I probably ended up making that transition slightly more successfully than dear old Bobby. With a few exceptions, after 'Volare' and 'Sway' his singles all seemed to come to rest lower and lower in the US chart. He only really had one further big hit: 'Forget Him', a cool, romantic rock and roll number in late 1963.

---

* Rod Stewart realised the same thing, of course, which is why he released no fewer than five albums in his *Great American Songbook* series. And, really, those classic tunes, and Rod's stupendous voice – what's not to love?

I suppose that Bobby was another all-American star who got swept away by the musical British invasion of his country in the mid-sixties. I still think that is a real shame, especially as at least one of the bands in the vanguard of that invasion were huge fans of his.

Acknowledging his influence, Paul McCartney was to admit that The Beatles were such big Bobby Rydell fans that they had based 'She Loves You', with its musical call-and-response structure, on one of his songs. It's funny: I would never have linked those two artists, but now I can *totally* see the connection.

As his record sales fell away, Bobby Rydell made TV shows, and played Vegas and club gigs. He always continued to tour. Right up until his death in 2022, he was part of a singing package tour called The Golden Boys, with Frankie Avalon and another late-fifties teen idol, Fabian Forte.

Fabian was an interesting character. Back in the day, he used to go by just his first name. He was originally spotted by a record company scout in the street in Philadelphia in 1957, just because he was so good-looking! He was only fourteen, and started recording while he was still in school.

Fabian had a handful of US hits, including, in 1959, 'Tiger' and 'Turn Me Loose'. I once sang 'Turn Me Loose' on *Oh Boy!* and the TV viewers thought I was wearing a pyjama jacket! It was actually a striped shirt, which I had fondly thought looked very stylish. *Huh! So much for trying to be flash!*

Looking back, you know, it's the weirdest thing. I had the time of my young life on that The Biggest Show of Stars for 1960 tour, with Clyde McPhatter, and Sammy Turner, and The Isley

Brothers, and Bobby Rydell. We became a little gang. Then the tour ended . . . and we went separate ways, and never saw each other again.

Why was that? Well, for one thing, it was a lot harder to keep in touch in those days. Today, you can send somebody an email, or message them on social media, or pull a phone smaller than a cigarette packet out of your pocket and text them. They will read it within a minute. As they say, we live in a global village.

Back in 1960, life was different. To keep in touch with someone in another part of the world, you'd have to make a prohibitively expensive international phone call (if you even had a phone, that is!). Or, you'd have to sit down, write a letter, post it, and wait weeks for a reply. *And how many teenagers want to do that?*

We were in the flush of youth, people like Bobby Rydell and me, and we thought the thrills, and the adventures, would never end. If we thought about it at all, we just assumed that we'd see each other again, some point further down the line. But then, life takes over, and other things happen. You move on.

Instead of staying in close touch, you lose contact, and you just catch occasional, chance glimpses of one another as the years go by. And that happened for me, with these guys, courtesy of one of the biggest musical films of the seventies.

When my close friend Olivia Newton-John became a global superstar in *Grease* in 1978, I couldn't have been more delighted for her. For one reason or another, I didn't get around to seeing the movie for a while – for twenty years, in fact! But when I finally *did*, a couple of things about it seemed very familiar.

There was Frankie Avalon as Teen Angel, middle-aged but

still trim, clad head-to-toe in white, strolling down from heaven to croon a funny song called 'Beauty School Dropout'. And what was the name of the school where Olivia, as Sandy, and John Travolta, as Danny, studied, played, sang, danced and fell in love?

It was Rydell High School – named after Bobby Rydell. Now *that* is what you call a musical legacy!

EIGHTEEN

'YOU SEND ME' – SAM COOKE

A flawed soul giant with a perfect voice

I've never put a big barrier in my head between rock and roll and soul music. I see them as two sides of the same coin. When I first started hearing them, *thrilling* to them, back in the fifties, they seemed to have so much in common, and I still feel the same. I love listening to rock and roll *and* soul. I love singing them both.

Out on The Biggest Show of Stars for 1960 tour, I had the privilege of hearing great rock and roll *and* great soul music, live, night after night after night. Yet one of my best, and my strongest, memories of my first excursion to America, a fond recollection which will never fade, came on one of our rare nights off.

I've no idea where we were. Those great American cities all passed by in one big, mesmerising blur. If this is Thursday, it must be . . . Chicago? Detroit? *'Er, Hank, do you know where we are?'* But on a rare free night, I was flicking through a local paper in the hotel when an advert on the entertainment pages leapt out at me:

TONIGHT, FOR ONE NIGHT ONLY: SAM COOKE!

Sam Cooke?! Really? Yes, please!

I had been listening to Sam for three years or so by now, on record, and couldn't get enough. His voice mesmerised me every time I heard it. I ran to find our tour manager, he made a couple of phone calls and, a few hours later, The Shadows and I were in a packed theatre and *very* excited.

Sam Cooke had got me from the moment that he opened his mouth on his debut, self-written single, 'You Send Me'. It had been a US Number 1 in December 1957, which meant it was never off AFN. It had been a lesser hit in Britain as well, and I had headed down to Marsden's the very first time that I heard it.

'You Send Me' is a song that is truly timeless, a burst of rapture, with a gorgeous languid rhythm and cooing backing vocals. Yet, ultimately, it's all about Sam's voice. His delicious, earnest, pitch-perfect croon seems to emanate right from his heart – from his, yeah, *soul*. How could *anyone* be that gifted?

Sam Cooke had this remarkable vocal range and it sounded utterly effortless. His mastery was absolute. You listen to some singers straining for a note and worry for them: *Will they make it?* That was never in doubt with Sam. He was so serene as he eased through his songs, rocking or not, that you just went with him.

In truth, his records sounded so immaculate, so perfect, that as The Shadows and I waited for him in that theatre, I wondered if he'd be able to reproduce it in front of us. Singing in a studio is one thing. Singing live, maybe through dodgy acoustics, is another. Then Sam Cooke strolled on stage and put all of my fears to rest.

He was so hip, so charismatic, that he captivated the crowd from the second that he appeared. He was wearing a fabulous suit, and incredibly good-looking: the girls all started screaming the second he appeared. Then he opened his mouth ... and sounded just as wonderful as on his records.

'*Oh, you-oo-oo-oo, send me ...*'

The crowd was 80 per cent Black, and everybody was into him. Sam was an unbelievable performer. I couldn't take my eyes off him. He walked around the whole stage and played to everybody in the place. He lay on his back to sing 'Blue Moon', and his sleek baritone never even wavered. *Huh? How does he DO that?*

In the cab back to the hotel after that extraordinary show, I was in a daze. I just couldn't wait to tell the other guys on the tour what I had seen; what they had missed! Even now, I still remember how great Sam Cooke was that night. And after that, every time he had a new song out, I was all ears.

For all his vocal purity, Sam was also a versatile performer. He could dream up, and bring to life, a sweet soul nugget such as 'Only Sixteen', which he wrote for the singer Lou Rawls's stepsister. Or he could write, and reel off, a prime piece of rock and roll like 'Twistin' the Night Away'. They both came naturally to Sam.

Another self-written Sam Cooke song I loved was 'Chain Gang', a big 1960 hit in both America and Britain. 'Uh, ah!' he sang (Sam could even *grunt* tunefully!). 'That's the sound of the men, working on the chain gang!' He was inspired to write it by seeing an actual chain gang of prisoners working on a road while he was out on tour.*

It feels odd to me that Sam Cooke was never on Tamla Motown. In many ways, he seems the quintessential Motown soul man. Maybe Sam would have ended up on there one day, if his brilliant career, and life, had not been cut so tragically short . . . but I'm getting ahead of myself here. I'll come to that soon.

I was a big Motown fan, through the sixties and beyond. *I mean, who wasn't?* It is such infectious, life-affirming music. I don't want to be rude, but anybody who can't find joy in Smokey Robinson, Stevie Wonder, Marvin Gaye, Diana Ross and The Supremes or The Four Tops may need new ears!

Although I loved soul music, in my early years I didn't dare to sing much of it live with my band. It was the same story as with Chuck Berry, or The Isley Brothers' 'Twist and Shout' – I wasn't sure that my voice was up to it. My young voice was still quite soft, I suppose, and inexperienced, and those songs were *formidable*.

But I guess your confidence grows with age and experience, and as my career developed I found myself more willing to tackle music I loved that was maybe outside of my vocal comfort zone. And it meant that when I was offered what sounded a challenging project, in 2011, I was willing to give it a go.

Gloria Hunniford first made me aware of the idea. Gloria was friends with David Gest, the American TV producer and

---

* 'Chain Gang' is wonderful, and yet musicians always listen to songs and wonder how they might do them slightly differently. If I ever sang it, I would change things here and there, to make it my own . . . but I would never dare to imagine I knew better than Sam Cooke! His will always be the best version.

celebrity who had been married to Liza Minnelli. She told me that David would like to work with me because he thought I could be 'a great blues singer'.

Me? A blues singer? Well, that kind of surprised me, but I was intrigued as to what he meant. 'What kind of thing is he thinking of?' I asked Gloria.

'David thinks that he could get you into a studio with a whole bunch of Black soul singers,' Glo said, 'and your voice would blend in really well with them.'

Maybe, a few years earlier, I would have been wary of this idea, but now I liked it as soon as I heard it. By then I'd already duetted with a few unlikely people, from Van Morrison to Sarah Brightman. I didn't kid myself that I could sing *the same as* great Black soul singers but, yeah, I thought, I could probably *blend in* with them.

'OK,' I told Gloria. 'If David can arrange it, I'm willing to give it a go.'

Well, I quickly realised that David certainly *could* arrange it. Nobody could accuse that man of not being well connected! Within just a few weeks, I found myself in a studio in Memphis, recording *Soulicious* with a conveyor belt of legendary soul singers. And my jaw was aching from dropping so often!

In through that studio door walked Percy Sledge, Deniece Williams, Candi Staton, Billy Paul, and Dennis Edwards, the singer from The Temptations. *Oh, my word!* Yet, despite the illustrious nature of my star guests, I chose all of the tracks that we were to record myself. It's simple: if I'm making an album under my name, I can't record a song I don't like.

Perhaps the biggest name of all, though, was the legend that David Gest secured as the album's main producer. Lamont Dozier was one of the greatest songwriters and producers in the history of popular music. And, while we were in the studio, he told me *so* many fantastic stories about working with soul-music royalty.

As part of the celebrated Holland-Dozier-Holland songwriting triumvirate, with the brothers Brian and Eddie Holland, Lamont had penned and produced hits for virtually every Tamla Motown icon. The trio wrote more than 400 songs together. Over forty of them went to Number 1 in America. *Over forty!*

'The three of us had about four or five years when we couldn't seem to do anything wrong,' Lamont reminisced to me. 'The songs flowed out of us, and every one of them seemed to become a hit. It meant that everybody wanted to record our songs. Believe me, it was an incredible time!'

Yet for all his stellar history and achievements, Lamont Dozier was a down-to-earth and humble man. He was a joy to work with as he began coaxing the best out of me and the soul stars who were turning up in the studio. He geed us up *and* he put us at our ease – and that is no mean feat!

Candi Staton was spectacular to duet with on 'Teardrops'. *What a voice!* So was the genius Percy Sledge on 'I'm Your Puppet'. I also loved singing 'How We Get Down' with Russell Thompkins Jr, the former singer of The Stylistics, who came in with his new band, The New Stylistics.

I would arrive at the studio and find myself singing 'Are You Feeling Me' with Deniece Williams, whose voice seemed to be hewn from pure crystal. Yet I didn't try to copy, or match, those soul greats: I did just my natural, normal thing, and, *yes*, David Gest was right. Our voices all matched and blended beautifully.

One day, I went in to sing 'Go On and Tell Him' with another Motown great: Dennis Edwards, accompanied by a Temptations tribute act called The Temptations Review. I recorded my vocal first, in front of them. When I had finished, to my shock, those guys started ladling me with praise.

'How did you *do* that?' Dennis asked me.

'Do what?' I replied, genuinely thrown.

'Use your breath like that, when you sing!'

'Well, my vocal cords are different from yours!' I said, hitting them with my pet theory. 'Yours are made of concrete!'

'Oh, yeah? What are yours made of, then?' he asked.

I smiled, and said, 'Cotton wool!'

And Dennis and his band all fell about: '*Ah-ha-ha-ha-ha!*'

Lamont Dozier demonstrated his genius when I was singing 'Oh How Happy' with Marilyn McCoo and Billy Davis Jr, from that terrific soul group The 5th Dimension. We were halfway through the gospel-like song when Lamont told us to stop.

'This one's not quite there,' he pondered. 'It's going on a bit. We need something in the middle to break it up. Give me a few minutes . . .'

Lamont vanished to the back of the studio and started scribbling as we practised and waited for him. He resurfaced twenty minutes later. '*This* is what we need to do,' he said, presenting us with eight lines of music that he had written there and then. And they were perfect. *Wow! Talk about creative talent!*

After we had recorded the majority of *Soulicious*, I moved

over to a studio in New York in June 2011 to finish the album with the famous husband-and-wife, singer-songwriter and production duo, Nickolas Ashford and Valerie Simpson. Well, if you're going to work with the best soul stars, work with the *very* best!

Nickolas Ashford was great. He was a striking-looking guy, with really unusual light-grey eyes. Sadly, he wasn't well at the time. He wasn't able to sing on the album, and wasn't around the studio to play much part on the production. Valerie told me that her husband was suffering from a really sore throat.*

At least I got to sing with Valerie. We did a disco song called 'Every Piece of My Broken Heart', co-written by Lamont Dozier's son, Beau. I used falsetto, and Valerie sang like somebody whose throat was woven from pure velvet. Yet again, I thanked my lucky stars to be amid such towering talents.

I certainly did that on the day that Roberta Flack arrived in the New York studio to duet on 'When I Was Your Baby' – although Roberta promptly kicked me out of the room! She hadn't rehearsed her part of the song in advance, and didn't want to record in front of me in case she sang any bum notes.

Ha! How likely was that?! But I acceded to the great lady's wishes and left her in the studio with Valerie. I found a Starbucks, sat outside with a latte and watched New Yorkers going about their daily business. *You wouldn't believe it,* I told them, in my mind, *but I am duetting with Roberta Flack RIGHT AT THIS MOMENT!*

When I got back to the studio, of course, the vocal that

---

* Tragically, it was a lot more serious than that. I turned on the TV in Portugal just a few weeks later to learn that Nickolas had died of throat cancer. It was a terrible shock. Lovely guy.

Roberta had put down was consummate. I *love* her voice. It's so smooth and soulful, and full of true feeling, yet she's never strident or in your face. She's just a natural, instinctual soul singer, a queen of her rarefied game.

I had already recorded my vocal – and she was so flattering! She liked the way that I softly exhaled on one line of the song: *'Seeing you this way, just takes my breath away.'*

'Yeah!' she said with a smile, nodding her head as we listened back to it. 'Cliff, honey – that breath is the dollars!'

Roberta Flack is a force of nature, and it was a joy to meet her. It was good to see her again when she came to Barbados, a few years ago. Sadly, she's recently had to retire from performing after being diagnosed with motor neurone disease, but as her manager said, 'It will take a lot more than that to silence this icon!' In fact, she's recently co-written an autobiographical picture book for children. I wish her well.

After you've been fortunate enough to make a record with some of the greatest soul stars in history, what do you want to do next? Why, you want to go out and sing live with them, of course! David Gest began setting up a *Soulicious* UK arena tour for the end of 2011 . . . then, suddenly, everything went pear-shaped.

I'm not sure exactly why, but David pulled out of promoting the tour just a few weeks before it was due to happen, saying he no longer wanted to be involved. *Uh-oh! Now what do we do?* We had venues booked, artists lined up, tickets on sale . . . were we going to have to pull the whole thing?

Never! Over my dead body! I've always believed in the old showbiz adage: the show must go on. I told my management that

I still wanted to do the tour. They said it could be possible if all the soul singers remained willing. They did, so we got hold of their tour contracts. And we were . . . quite surprised by them.

It seemed the soul stars had all agreed to do the tour for far less money than they were worth. Was it the Chuck Berry story all over again: *Black artists being seriously undervalued by the music industry?* It sure looked like it. We immediately doubled, or even trebled, their tour fees. It was the right thing – the *only* thing – to do.

They were delighted, naturally, and it made for a positive atmosphere on the *Soulicious* tour. The camaraderie was fantastic. In any case, it was worth any amount of money to be able to sing live with Freda Payne – *Freda Payne!* She was truly astonishing. I think I applauded her as hard as the audience did!

I also felt blessed to stand on a stage, night after night, and sing 'I'm Your Puppet' with a living legend: Percy Sledge. Percy was not in the best of health. He'd be on oxygen in his dressing room just before we went on. But when he got out in front of the crowd, he still sounded wonderful.

Percy gave this great, beaming smile every time I spoke to him, or the audience applauded him. One night, my youngest sister, Joan, came to a concert, and he had her in raptures. 'Oh, Cliff, Percy was fantastic on "I'm Your Puppet"!' she told me after the show. 'I loved his smile, and his singing was beautiful!'

'Yes, it was, Joan,' I agreed, adding, 'And what about me?'

'Oh, you were OK, Cliff. But Percy was *wonderful!*'

Well, fair enough! As I said, I never kidded myself that I can sing the same as soul legends – and, coming back to the subject of this chapter, certainly not the same as Sam Cooke, the man who started my love of great soul music off when I heard 'You Send Me' way back in 1957.

So many great artists in this book met with tragic ends. Sadly, Sam Cooke is yet another. Sam's demise was, in some ways, even more dramatic and terrible than those poor souls who met their makers in plane crashes or car accidents. Because Sam was killed. Maybe even – *who knows?* – murdered.

It happened in December 1964, when Sam was arguably at the peak of his powers – why, it was only four years after I'd witnessed that unforgettable theatre show! He turned up one night at a motel in Los Angeles with a woman called Elisa Boyer, who was not his wife. The pair booked a room and vanished into it.

A short while later, Sam apparently appeared in reception, this time alone, yelling, 'Where's the girl?' The motel's manageress, who was on the reception desk, was later to claim she found his behaviour 'threatening'. She had a gun and shot him 'in self-defence'. Sam Cooke fell to the floor, and died. He was just thirty-three.

The manageress was not charged with his killing. *Why?* Speculation was rife. Etta James, Sam's friend, saw his body and claimed that he'd been beaten. The world champion boxer, Muhammad Ali, implied a racist cover-up: 'If Cooke had been Frank Sinatra, The Beatles or Ricky Nelson, the FBI would be investigating!'

We'll never know now what really happened on that tragic night in LA. What does seem clear is that Sam Cooke was a troubled individual with a lively private life. He was reportedly a drinker and, outside of his two marriages, was known to have fathered at least three children in affairs with other women.

Well, you know what? That kind of behaviour is obviously disappointing, but *let him who is without sin cast the first stone*. Let's face it, nobody is perfect in their private life, so who are we to be judgemental? We are all flawed creatures, so how can we condemn, or *cancel*, artists for their flaws?

Unless they have done something so unspeakable that I can't bear to listen to them, I can always separate the art from the artist. If they've done something wrong in their personal life, they'll usually have paid the price – in Sam Cooke's case, the *ultimate* price. So why should we be no longer allowed to listen to them?

Well, the answer is that we *can*. We *can* still listen to their great music – and, if we choose, we can still sing it. I returned to Sam Cooke in 2014, when I recorded my *Just . . . Fabulous Rock 'n' Roll* album. I dearly wanted to sing his debut song, the one that had swept me away when I heard it back in '57: 'You Send Me'.

It could have been intimidating . . . but it wasn't. Why? Well, I always feel that I don't *cover* a song; I *reignite* it. My new version of 'You Send Me' was a homage to Sam Cooke, sure, but I wasn't trying to impersonate him. I sang it my own way, just as Sam had sung it his. And I was so pleased with how it came out.

For me, Sam Cooke will always be that suave, handsome, peerless performer who swept on stage in that packed American theatre back in 1960, and held all of us in the palms of his hands. He will always be the soul singer with the flawless voice who opened his mouth and crooned those timeless words:

'Oh, you-oo-oo-oo, send me . . .'

Sam Cooke did. *He sent me* then, and he always will.

NINETEEN

'MY FUNNY VALENTINE'
– DAKOTA STATON

When I found there really was *more to life, and music, than rock and roll*

When you're a teenager, you're evangelical about the music that you love. No, it's more than that: you're totally blinkered! You know what you like, you can't begin to understand anybody who doesn't like it, and you think that every other form of music is a total waste of time.

Well, if I'm honest, that was me at fifteen and sixteen, after I first heard Elvis, Little Richard and Buddy Holly. I just wanted *more* Elvis, *more* Little Richard, *more* Buddy Holly; *more rock and roll*, full stop! I thought that any other kind of music was old hat, and boring. I wasn't interested.

I certainly had no time for jazz. To me, it was terminally dull, tepid, yawns-ville; music for old people, or for anyone too square for rock and roll. *Ha! Time to get hip, daddy-o*, as they used to say! I thought jazz was one great big snooze-fest (I believe this is called 'being young and precocious'!).

Well, luckily, you change. You can't only listen to one kind of music all of your life, any more than you could only eat one kind of food. As I left my teens and became more established in my own music career, I began to find myself paying attention to music that I would previously have airily dismissed.

In fact, as I grew more settled in my career, and more comfortable with myself, I heard other musical artists who were a long way from rock and roll, and I realised that I liked what I heard. I began to appreciate their skill. Their artistry.

I thought crooners such as Frank Sinatra were alien to me, then I listened closer to his singing, to his voice, and it clicked: *Wow! He really knows what he's doing!* I came across one of his classic albums, and I found myself enjoying it. Suddenly, I came around to 'Frankie baby'. It didn't *matter* that he wasn't like Elvis.

I developed a more open mind, I'm glad to say, and I learned to appreciate other, more established styles of music surprisingly quickly. Through listening to the BBC Light Programme, and my parents' records, I grew to like music that wasn't rock and roll – and, yes, that even included jazz. Well, some of it, anyway.

In fact, I have an example of just how quickly I changed. In October 1960, just two years into my singing career, and when I was still only twenty, I went to BBC Broadcasting House to choose my eight favourite records for Roy Plomley for the first of my two appearances on Radio 4's *Desert Island Discs*.

I chose Elvis, Dion & The Belmonts, Ray Charles and Bill Haley discs, of course. But I also selected three jazzy, Black, female American singers. I chose 'How You Say It' by actress, singer and civil rights activist, Lena Horne; 'Beat Out Dat Rhythm on a Drum' by a Broadway actress and singer, Pearl Bailey; and *this* song.

'My Funny Valentine' by Dakota Staton.

I first heard Dakota Staton on her classic 1957 debut album, *The Late, Late Show*. I am sure it was Mum or Dad who bought it from Marsden's, not me, but it got a lot of plays in our house and, despite my Elvis fixation at the time, I liked it. To be honest, it would be pretty impossible *not* to like it.

It's so often about *voices* with me, and Dakota Staton had a fantastic voice. It had an ease and a grace that were staggering. I liked its pitch, and depth, and what we musicians call the 'legato': the way her strong tones and timbre connected so perfectly with the rhythms. Her voice *glided* over the surfaces of the music.

The Late, Late Show was a wonderful album, and it was also a huge hit. It got into the Top 5 in America, which was extremely rare then – and still is now! – for a jazz album. And my favourite track? 'My Funny Valentine'.

It was written by the legendary songwriting duo of Richard Rodgers and Lorenz Hart and it originally came from a 1937 musical, *Babes in Arms*, which I had never heard of (again, not my thing, as a teenager!). Apparently, Hart wrote the lyrics to reflect his own insecurity that he was too short and unattractive to be loved!

So, with forensic vocal precision, Dakota crooned to her amour: 'Your looks are laughable! Unphotographable!' Over a velvet swell of music, she inquired: 'Is your figure less than Greek? Is your mouth a little weak?' Yet, she declared, she loved her man just the way he was: 'Don't change a hair for me. Not if you care for me.'

There was a sass, and a stylishness, and a sexiness to Dakota's knowing vocal that was utterly beguiling. The plucked strings, swoops and swoons of woodwind, and gently tinkled piano drew me in, too. I loved rock and roll for so many reasons, but it often wasn't *subtle*. Here was music of subtlety, and nuance and depth.

Even as my own career went crazy, I never forgot 'My Funny Valentine' or Dakota Staton. She released a handful more excellent albums in the late fifties and early sixties, including *In the Night* and a great live record, *Dakota at Storyville*. Then, in the mid-sixties, she moved to England, and I got to see her play live myself.

I saw Dakota Staton sing at Ronnie Scott's, the legendary jazz club in the heart of Soho. It's such a gorgeous venue, with its stained wood, plush red seats, low lights and velvet curtains. You could sit back, eat a meal* and enjoy a glass of wine as you watched the acts. And Ronnie Scott's was *made* for Dakota Staton.

Dakota was extraordinary that night. She was a larger-than-life, charismatic lady, with a lovely line in between-song patter and a voice that could have shattered glass. She was utterly charming, and her vocal skill and dexterity were perfect. Everybody in that luxuriant room knew that we were in the presence of genius.

Dakota Staton must have sung 'My Funny Valentine' a thousand times by then but she eased and coaxed her way through the song as if still enchanted by it, and still discovering new things in

---

* What did I eat at Ronnie Scott's? I don't remember exactly, but I'm afraid this was the era in Britain when chicken-in-a-basket was the height of nightclub culinary sophistication . . .

it. *What a privilege to be there*. It was another of those nights, like Sammy Davis Jr, where I thought, *Well, I might as well give up now!*

Dakota Staton wasn't the only female singer that I discovered as I broadened my musical palate. I really liked Morgana King, who was also a jazz singer, like Dakota, but whose voice was smoother and a tad gentler. Nina Simone was also clearly a formidable talent. I wish I could have seen her live.

Etta James was another brilliant rhythm and blues and jazz singer. The first time I heard her sing her signature tune, 'At Last', I couldn't get it out of my mind for days. In fact, my first listen to it made such a lasting impression on me that I can remember exactly where I was, and what happened.

The Shadows' old drummer, Tony Meehan, invited me back to his house after rehearsal one day. His wife, Bridget, cooked dinner for us, and Tony put a record on. As soon as it began oozing out of their Dansette, my head did a 360-degree turn: 'Wow! What is *that*?'

The strings, the rhythms, the instrumentation, the *voice* . . . everything about 'At Last' was perfect. Apparently, the song had started its life as a trad jazz number, which Glenn Miller used to play back in 1942, but Etta, her band and her producer had given it depth and divinity. Every note, every breath, was exquisite.

'At Last' had so much *soul*. I didn't know much about Etta James, so when there was a TV documentary about her, years later, I eagerly watched it. I was dismayed to learn that she had a really hard life of physical abuse, drug addiction and even imprisonment. Poor woman. At least she left behind a truly magnificent legacy.

I liked some of the female pop singers in my early years. The American Brenda Lee was tiny – only 4'9" in her socks – but they called her 'Little Miss Dynamite' and she was personality-plus! I loved how she belted out 'Sweet Nothin's' in 1959. I could hardly believe it when I learned that she was only fifteen years old!

Brenda wasn't the only school-age female pop star. My record label boss and producer, Norrie Paramor, had his own child star in Helen Shapiro. She was only *fourteen* when she had two 1961 Number 1s: 'You Don't Know' and 'Walkin' Back to Happiness', yet she had quite a deep, masculine-sounding singing voice.

I met a rather more established, and formidable, female singer and showbiz star in the early sixties. I was recording a television variety show at the BBC studios in London. The headline act was Eartha Kitt and, during rehearsals, I was surprised to get a message that she wanted to see me. In her dressing room. *Now.*

Huh? What could Eartha Kitt want with me? I toddled along, nervously, tapped on her door, and heard a bark of 'Come!' I walked in to find Eartha, a vision in a lurid tiger-skin robe, reclining on a chaise longue. She cut straight to the chase.

'Young men like *you*,' she informed me, magisterially, 'are making things very difficult for people like *me*!'

Uh-oh! What do I say to THAT? Fortunately, I managed to think on my feet.

'Miss Kitt,' I replied, 'young men like me can do *nothing* that would make things difficult for people like you!'

Luckily, Eartha liked my reply. She gave one of her trademark throaty growls, and we had a brief chat before she regally waved me away. Yet, thinking back, what a telling encounter!

She was an international icon, but I guess even stars as mighty as Eartha Kitt must have felt threatened by the advent of rock and roll.

So, there are a few jazzy songs I could have chosen for *A Head Full of Music*, but 'My Funny Valentine' is my favourite. Rod Stewart did a great version on one of his *Great American Songbook* albums. He'd just had an operation on his vocal cords and I thought it made his voice even better. I can just picture him leaning against a piano and crooning it.

I haven't yet sung 'My Funny Valentine', but I ventured into interpreting classic show songs and jazzy tunes in 2010, when I made my *Bold as Brass* album. I went to Nashville and sang compositions by the likes of Cole Porter, Hoagy Carmichael, Rodgers and Hart, and George and Ira Gershwin, with a ten-piece jazz band.

Yet, much like when I did *Soulicious* later, I didn't want to begin *impersonating* jazz singers and their mannerisms. I didn't don a beret and start scatting! Nor was I trying to croon 'I've Got You Under My Skin' like Sinatra. Instead, I simply chose tunes, in that genre, that I liked, and I sang them like me. In my style.

Recording a more elaborate record like that is totally different from recording early rock and roll. Back then, we'd go in the studio, pick up our guitars and let rip, letting the music take us where it wanted to. We didn't always know what we were doing and, you know what? That was half the fun of it!

Making an album today is a far more sophisticated affair. I might record a track six or seven times. The producer will take two lines from one version, three lines from another, four from another, and make a composite from the takes. Basically, he will cherry-pick the best bits . . . and there is the finished version!

When I released that *Bold as Brass* album in 2010, I did six nights at my favourite concert venue in the world, the Royal Albert Hall. Normally, in those days, I would open my set with 'Move It' or 'Travellin' Light'. But *Bold as Brass* was a special album for me, so I decided to do something different.

Like what? Like this . . .

I came on in a dressing gown as if I was ill and couldn't perform. My sister, Joan, appeared behind me, holding a giant syringe, and pretended to inject me up the you-know-what. I came to life, threw off my dressing gown to reveal a tuxedo, and fired into 'Fly Me to the Moon'! It was *so* much fun, and the crowd loved it.

I'm so glad that I diversified away from only listening to rock and roll, and discovered terrific singers such as Dakota Staton. Even now, at my ripe old age, I still try to be broad-minded and to keep my ears open for great new music, whatever style or genre it may be.

But I must confess . . . I don't always succeed.

I've had a great relationship with Katherine Jenkins ever since she supported me on my Summer Nights tour of stately homes in 2004. We've always kept in touch, and I was a special guest at one of her Royal Albert Hall shows. I love her light, pop-opera voice – but traditional, hardcore opera is a different story.

When I was doing my stage show of *Heathcliff* in the nineties, my production designer, Joe Vanek, had also done the staging for a major operatic production. It was showing at the Coliseum in

London and Joe asked me if I wanted to go along to see it with him. I'll try anything once, so I said, 'Sure!'

Well, Joe and I went along, and had terrific seats near the stage, but I couldn't make head nor tail of what was going on. The plot seemed like nonsense, the singing was so loud that it was giving me a headache, and I couldn't decipher a single lyric. After half an hour of this (*it felt longer!*), I leaned over to Joe.

'What language are they singing in?' I whispered.

Joe gave me a puzzled, slightly pitying look.

'English, Cliff!' he whispered back.

Oops! Well, it might as well have been Greek to me! I mean, Katherine Jenkins's sweet strains are lovely, but those formidable opera divas who open their mouths and hit a perfect top D, or E, that I could never reach, at ten times the volume and power that I could ever muster . . . do I *really* want to listen to that all night?

No. I really don't. Sorry, opera buffs!

TWENTY

'APACHE' – THE SHADOWS

My band. My gang. My family.

I will freely confess that I've always loved being Number 1 in the pop chart. It means, for one week at least, you're at the top of the tree, and your tune is the favourite song in the whole country – what's not to like about that? So, how does it feel to be knocked off Number 1 . . . by your own band?

Well, let me tell you, it feels absolutely fantastic.

Musicians often say that being in a band is like being in a gang, or even a family. I think there is a lot of truth in that. The Shadows and I have been tight friends for more than sixty years now. Our own little gang has gone on for a very long time – although sometimes, like any gang, the members have changed.

After we did our tour with The Kalin Twins in 1958 – when, in fact, we were still The Drifters – Ian Samwell left the group. It wasn't his choice. We had Hank, Bruce and Jet now, and his guitar playing just wasn't quite on the same level. As ever, the music had to come first, no matter how close our friendship was.

Ian did great things for The Drifters, and for me: he wrote

our huge breakthrough single, 'Move It', and even helped to rename me when I stopped being Harry Webb! I'm sure he was a little hurt at being asked to leave the group but, happily, we stayed close, and Ian carried on writing songs for me.

With the new band line-up in place at the start of 1959, it was also evident that Terry Smart was a little out of his depth as our drummer. He had been fantastic on the primal adrenalin rush of 'Move It', but when we tried to write and record more complex material, Terry's playing wasn't quite up to it.

It was hard for me to tell him he had to go. Terry and I had been in bands together since The Dick Teague Skiffle Group. He was even with me that fateful Saturday in Waltham Cross, when I first heard Elvis! But I couldn't disagree with the others when they said his drumming limited us musically. Because they were right.*

In fairness, Terry acknowledged he was struggling to keep up. 'Yeah, I know!' he agreed, when I had the painful conversation with him. 'I was wondering when this would happen!' He wasn't too devastated, because he'd always wanted to join the Merchant Navy when he turned eighteen. So, he went and did just that.

Luckily, we had a replacement drummer lined up. Hank and Bruce knew Tony Meehan from the 2i's coffee bar, and he had already played with Jet Harris in The Vipers skiffle group – even though he was still only sixteen! Tony slotted straight into The Shadows, and his drumming took us to a whole new level.

With this improved new line-up in place, I was desperate for

---

* This was one of the reasons I hated it when the press started calling me a wimpy Goody Two-Shoes. If only they knew! I was never afraid to make painful decisions for the good of my music and my career.

Norrie Paramor to let The Shadows play on all of my records, rather than hiring session men. Norrie was not convinced at first. He feared my new band members were just young guys off the street, rather than experienced, professional musicians.

'Studios are not cheap, Cliff!' he told me. 'I need you to be recording three songs an hour!' But when I finally persuaded him to give Hank, Bruce, Jet and Tony a chance, and give them a listen in the studio, he was quickly persuaded. 'They're great!' he said, surprised. 'Yes, you can definitely use these guys – no problem!'

In fact, The Shadows were to surpass all of Norrie's expectations. We never wrote or rehearsed material in the studio, as The Beatles were to do: that meant their albums cost a fortune to make. Instead, we'd get the songs down pat first, then just go in and record them: sometimes five songs in a three-hour session. Norrie loved that!

Once the line-up was in place, The Shadows and I went out and gigged and gigged and gigged. We worked so hard. We were spending weeks and weeks at a time in Transit vans and B&Bs. It certainly helped to establish our career, but it also took me away from my friends and family for a lot longer than I'd have liked.

We slogged so hard because we knew what we had could so easily be taken away from us at any moment. We'd seen so many of our musical competitors fall away. The press would sometimes write that we'd be 'here today, gone tomorrow', and I guess we half-believed them. We had no idea how long it would last.

Out on the road non-stop, of course, we were living in one another's pockets. We got to know each other's foibles and idiosyncrasies off by heart. It can be tough to live on top of each other like that. Mostly, we got along, though – and it helped to have not one, but two wisecracking jokers in our midst.

As I said, Hank and Bruce had known each other since they were schoolboys in Newcastle. It meant they had an almost telepathic relationship, both musically and comedically. They were both masters of the one-liner, and would frequently have the rest of us cracking up. Believe me, that helps on the road!

I remember at one gig, not that long after they had joined the band, Bruce sidling up to me on the stage at the end of a song. 'Could you scratch my nose please, Cliff?' he asked me.

'Eh? Why me?'

'Because you're nearer to it than I am!' Well, Bruce did have a bigger nose than the rest of us – but it wasn't *that* big!

There is no doubt that The Shadows, in this new incarnation, were an incredibly talented band. They deserved to be more than, as Jet had archly commented, 'in my shadow', and Norrie Paramor recognised that. Halfway through 1959, he offered the group their own separate recording contract.

This made a lot of sense. Norrie had already started thinking about me recording some tracks on my albums with The Shadows and some with his orchestra, which might free up some time for them. Plus, they were such great musicians that they deserved to be a band in their own right. We all thought it was a terrific idea.

Norrie released a few Drifters/Shadows singles in 1959. 'Feelin' Fine' was written by Ian Samwell and had vocals,* and 'Jet

---

* The Shadows released very occasional tracks with vocals: Hank, Bruce and Jet all had a go at singing. But everybody always thinks of them as an instrumental band – as they nearly always were.

Black' was an instrumental written by Jet Harris. They weren't hits. 'Lonesome Fella', written by radio DJ Charlie Chester's son Pete, and sung by Jet, snuck into the charts at Number 31. Then, their next release struck gold.

A singer turned songwriter named Jerry Lordan came to one of our shows with an instrumental tune he had written. He had originally presented it to Burt Weedon, who had recorded it but, for some reason, not released it. Undeterred, Jerry now thought that it might be good for The Shadows.

The name of the instrumental was . . . 'Apache'.

Jerry initially played it backstage at a show to Jet Harris, on a ukulele. When Jet liked it, Jerry played it to the rest of the band. Everybody could tell it was a great tune. When Hank and Bruce picked up their guitars to run through it, the twang and the rhythms sounded fantastic. It was clearly something special.*

I could see The Shadows were excited by 'Apache', which definitely summoned up mental images of Western films. They practised it a few times in rehearsals before – the big test – playing it to Norrie Paramor. Well, Norrie knew a hit when he heard one. 'That's excellent!' he said. 'We can release that as a single.'

So, that was the plan. But Norrie's promotions guy, whose job it would be to plug the single and get PR for it, foresaw a possible hurdle. 'It's very hard to promote instrumental singles,' he reflected, at one record label meeting. 'Cliff, could you play something on it, so I can tell the press that you are on the record?'

---

* Jerry was to have a golden songwriting spell at the start of the sixties. He wrote a great song for Cliff Richard & The Shadows, 'A Girl Like You', a Number 3 in 1961.

The Shadows liked this idea, and I wanted to help them out – but what could I do? We soon found a solution. I would tap out a few bars of rhythm on a drum at the start of the track, before the song proper came in. It meant the PR guy could put out a press release: 'CLIFF RICHARD PLAYS ON SHADOWS' NEW SINGLE!'

Well, I did – just about! Tony Meehan taught me the opening drum pattern and I played it on what was (appropriately) called an 'Indian drum'. I carefully followed his instructions, and they faded my diligent but amateur percussion out before Hank came in with his characteristic twang.

If I'm honest, I'm not sure 'Apache' needed my low-level contribution. It was a terrific tune in its own right, and the single sounded brilliant. Joe Brown happened to be knocking around the studio and gave Hank a tape echo unit that he didn't like. Hank made use of it then and on many records to come.

Bruce played the acoustic Gibson that I talked about earlier, which I'd bought for us all to use. It was the same guitar that we'd used on hits such as 'Living Doll' and 'Travellin' Light'. Bruce was an absolute wizard on rhythm guitar by then and he made the Gibson sound fantastic on 'Apache'.*

'Apache' sounded terrific, but then there was a twist before it got released. Norrie Paramor preferred the single's B-side, 'Quatermasster's Stores', and wanted to make it the A-side. It was 'Move

---

* I'll tell you how much I love that guitar – the second time I went on *Desert Island Discs*, in 2020, I took it to my island as my luxury item. 'It's got a very gentle and warm sound,' I told Lauren Laverne.

It' and 'Schoolboy Crush' all over again! Luckily, The Shadows gently persuaded Norrie that 'Apache' was the way to go.

The Shadows and I were already having big chart success in 1960. In July, 'Please Don't Tease' became our third Number 1 single, after 'Living Doll' and 'Travellin' Light'. Meanwhile, 'Apache', released two weeks later, was bounding up the hit parade towards it.

On 25 August 1960, 'Apache' hit Number 1, knocking 'Please Don't Tease' off the top. How did I feel? Absolutely delighted! I had been Number 1 for three weeks by then, so I knew something was going to dislodge me soon. What could be better than it being my own band? It was . . . *family!*

The Shadows were absolutely blown away. They couldn't believe it. They'd never have dared say, '"Apache" could be a Number 1' – because there is no way of knowing. You can never say, 'It sounds like a Number 1.' All you can say is, 'It sounds like a hit.' And, right from the off, 'Apache' had sounded like a hit.

The Shadows arrived with 'Apache' and, after that, they enjoyed a string of chart hits. They went to Number 1, again, in 1961, with 'Kon-Tiki'. Then Jerry Lordan wrote them another great instrumental called 'Wonderful Land'. It was to top the chart for eight weeks in 1962, which was an unbelievable achievement.

They were really flying high. When Cliff Richard & The Shadows weren't on tour, The Shadows would head out on their own. They pulled big crowds, but they were notably different! Where our gigs were full of screaming girls, The Shadows had much more of a male crowd, keen to watch Hank and Bruce on guitar.

The Shadows were out on tour with me, though, when they had their next line-up change. As I said, people leave and join gangs, or bands, and the next departure from the ranks was to be Tony Meehan. And it was all down to his time-keeping. Or, rather, complete lack of it.

Tony was a brilliant, classic drummer* but, offstage, 'time' was an abstract concept to him. He did things when he wanted to and when he felt like it. Bands on the road run on tight schedules and timetables, but Tony would pay absolutely no attention to ours whatsoever.

On tour, we would be packed and ready to leave a B&B at 10am to head to the next town, and Tony would wander down from his room at five past and begin to order breakfast. It used to do our heads in – especially Bruce, who was a stickler for punctuality. Once, we left Tony behind to make his own way to the next gig.

Tony always seemed oblivious to the fact we were all fed up with him. 'What's the rush?' he'd ask us. 'Just relax, eh?' His band nickname was Baron Meehan and, yes, he had a certain sense of entitlement. I liked him a lot but, really, keeping us all waiting for him, day after day after day, was just not acceptable.

It came to a head, I gather – thankfully, I wasn't there! – with a stand-up row between Tony and Bruce, after which Tony quit the band. Happily, we managed to recruit a replacement straight away: Brian Bennett, who had drummed with Marty Wilde's Wildcats. Brian was to stay with The Shadows right until the end.

---

* Although Tony was a terrific drummer, he hated doing drum solos! 'Do I have to?' he'd ask us. 'They tire me out.'

As they say, it never rains but it pours. No sooner had Tony Meehan exited stage left than The Shadows lost another member: their bassist, Jet Harris. However, this was a very different turn of events.

Jet had always been an enthusiastic party animal and was a lot of fun backstage and, especially, after the shows in clubs and hotel bars. He had always enjoyed a drink, but as we got into 1962, it was getting out of control. He would turn up for rehearsals drunk, or even get into fights on nights out.

The Shadows would go out on tour with Jet and return with horror stories about him drinking too much before shows. Apparently, when they played the Cavern in Liverpool, which launched The Beatles, Jet fell off the stage and the crowd had to help him back on! It couldn't go on, and The Shadows fired him.

From what I can gather, Jet took the news fairly well. I think he had probably seen it coming, because he had a couple of solo hits in 1962 and then, in 1963, teamed up with Tony Meehan. They had an instrumental Number 1 with 'Diamonds' and a Number 2 with 'Scarlett O'Hara' – both, again, written by Jerry Lordan.

How did we feel about that? We were pleased for them. We bore Jet and Tony no malice, and it was good that they had managed to make something happen for themselves. Shadows fans didn't mind them leaving: they mostly came to watch Hank and Bruce, I guess, anyway. Brian 'Licorice' Locking joined to replace Jet.

As well as backing me, The Shadows continued to have their own hits throughout the sixties. 'Dance On!' was a Number 1 for them at the end of 1962, as was 'Foot Tapper' the following year.

That track was taken from my *Summer Holiday* movie: it was one of the songs that the kids danced to in the scene in the club.

It was a great time, really. We had our joint career, while The Shadows were also scoring plenty of chart action on their own. We'd loosely try not to release singles at exactly the same time, so we weren't up against ourselves, as it were. But I never saw them as competition. *Why would I?* They were my band.

I also really enjoyed what they were doing. I'm a singer, but I've always liked a good instrumental. Indeed, in 1960, I'd been blown away by a song that, if I am honest, could probably have a chapter all of its own in *A Head Full of Music*: 'Honky Tonk', by Bill Black's Combo.

I knew all about Bill Black's Combo for a very good reason: their leader had been in Elvis's backing band! Bill Black played double bass, Scotty Moore played guitar and D.J. Fontana was on drums for Elvis hits such as 'Heartbreak Hotel', 'Hound Dog' and 'Jailhouse Rock'. They were usually billed as The Blue Moon Boys.

Black left Elvis's band in 1958 and started up Bill Black's Combo in 1959. I listened out for them and bought their debut album, *Solid and Raunchy*, in 1960 (they were hard-working guys – they released *three* albums that year!). It was a cool album, with versions of 'Blueberry Hill', 'Bo Diddley' and Elvis's 'Don't Be Cruel'.

My favourite track, though, was 'Honky Tonk', a cover of an instrumental written and first released in 1956 by an American rhythm-and-blues pianist and rock and roller named Bill Doggett. Bill Black's version had such an amazing guitar rhythm, great energy and a cool saxophone break. It was good to jump around to.

The Shadows were up against competition, of course. In 1962, The Tornados got to Number 1 in both Britain and America with 'Telstar', written and produced by Joe Meek. But they were pretty much one-hit wonders. The Shadows had smash after smash. In terms of instrumental groups, they outshone everyone.

They were terrific on their own and they were terrific playing with me. Whenever The Shadows and I hooked up to make a record, or go on tour, we had a great time. We really were a gang, or a family – although obviously, like any family, we had our tensions every now and then.

Ours usually revolved around Bruce. He was a fantastic guitarist and, as I was to learn fully in later years, a brilliant studio producer, but he was also an obsessive perfectionist. Everything had to be just right for Bruce and, if it wasn't, he would certainly let you know about it.

I told the story in *The Dreamer* of how Bruce was once having trouble tuning his guitar before a gig in Blackpool. He couldn't get it right, and got so frustrated that he stormed off, got in his car and drove off back to London, leaving us to play the show without him.

Bruce turned up at the house of our then manager, Peter Gormley, grumbling about his guitar. I don't know if he expected sympathy, but he got short shrift, not to mention a flea in his ear, from that bluff Australian. 'Get back in that car and back on bloody tour!' Peter ordered him. And Bruce did.

At other times, Bruce would arrive at a gig before the rest of us and start cleaning the amps, would you believe! When he was like that, Hank was the only one who could get through to him.

'Bruce, leave that!' he'd say. 'They have people here who can do that for us. Just leave it.'

Bruce was normally a fun guy and, like Hank, very witty, but at times, a darkness would descend on him. You could almost see it. He had such extreme mood swings. Thankfully, he mellowed over the years, as we all do, and nowadays Bruce is always a great laugh to be around.

We got on so well – certainly better than a lot of bands. In 1968, Cliff Richard & The Shadows' tenth anniversary rolled around and we marked it with an album called *Established 1958*. Ten years! Well, there was one in the eye for those early critics who had said we would be 'here today, gone tomorrow'!

It was the first time in my life that I distinctly remember thinking that my career, *our* careers, might have some longevity. So, it was quite a shock, not to mention extremely ironic, when Hank phoned me that August to tell me that The Shadows were to break up at Christmas.

I have to admit that I was very taken aback by the news. *Really?!* At that point in my life, my focus was not quite so exclusively on The Shadows. I had a lot going on: I was making albums with Norrie's orchestra, I had converted to Christianity and I was making TV shows. Even so, they were still my *band!* My *gang!*

It was a totally amicable break-up. We did a farewell tour of Britain and Japan in 1969. Hank wrote a very cool song, 'London's Not Too Far', for my *Sincerely* album that same year, and also became a weekly fixture on my *It's Cliff Richard* Saturday night

BBC TV show in the early seventies. His sense of humour made him a natural for comedy skits.

We all kept in touch and we all stayed best friends. In 1984, Cliff Richard & The Shadows got together for a reunion tour, playing four nights at Wembley Arena and five at the NEC in Birmingham. And which song did we kick-start the set with every night? 'Move It', of course!

We also reunited for my enormous The Event extravaganza at Wembley in 1989, marking my thirtieth anniversary in music. Yet this had its tensions. As I've said, The Shadows and I are family – but while you love your family the most, they can also annoy you and wind you up the most!

The Event was a retro-journey through my career. I wanted The Shadows to play with me right at the start of the night, in the *Oh Boy!* section, before doing their own separate set later in the show. But they wouldn't appear at the start of the show because they didn't want to 'upstage their later performance'. *Huh?*

'We don't want to be seen until we are introduced for our own bit,' Bruce said. I tried hard to change their minds, but they wouldn't budge. I ended up doing the *Oh Boy!* segment with The Kalin Twins, plus singers and dancers from the original cast, and Jet Harris and Tony Meehan joined me for my set at the end of the show.

And you know what? They were all great . . . but I still felt disappointed not to have Hank, Bruce and Brian with me. *Ah, well! That's showbiz!*

The Shadows and I got together again in 2009 for an album

of re-recordings of our classic hits, fifty years after we had formed. We called it *Reunited*, but that was misleading: we were all in different parts of the world so we recorded the record remotely, in different studios. It still worked well, though.

At the end of that year and the start of 2010, we played an arena tour of Europe, the UK, Australia, New Zealand and South Africa. It was terrific that so many fans still wanted to come out and see Cliff Richard & The Shadows . . . yet we butted heads this time around, as well.

I was keen to include some of my solo hits in the set: songs that had sold millions for me, such as 'Devil Woman' and 'We Don't Talk Anymore', but The Shadows insisted that they only wanted to play songs that they had played on. I thought, *Well, if that's the case, they shouldn't play anything I haven't sung on!*

I *thought* that . . . but, to keep the peace, I didn't *say* it. I tried to talk them round, but got out-voted. *Ah, well! That's showbiz – again!*

Yet, ultimately, those disagreements don't matter. The Shadows were my band: *my boys*. They were with me right at the start of my career (even if they *were* called The Drifters then!) and they've been with me through thick and thin. We owe everything to each other, and we'll never not be close.

The bonds run very deep. Hank has written some wonderful songs for me, including my Top 10 hit 'The Day I Met Marie' in 1967. My biggest single remains 'We Don't Talk Anymore' – produced for me by Bruce. We're always together. Even when we're not.

That closeness is demonstrated by the fact we've always kept in touch, over the years. Occasionally, I see the original Drifters. Terry Smart and Norman Mitham have come along to my shows. I last saw Norman when I played the Albert Hall in 2021. He and I recreated an old 1956 photo of us for my Facebook page!

Ian Samwell sadly died in 2003, after a very successful career. He wrote songs or produced records for Dusty Springfield, The Small Faces and Elkie Brooks, and discovered the seventies band America, for whom he produced 'A Horse with No Name'. In the later years of his life, Ian lived very happily in California.*

Tony Meehan remarried, to a lovely lady called Sue, and I'd sometimes visit them in Hampstead when I was in London. It was a shock, in 2005, when Sue called me, out of the blue, to say she had got home to discover Tony had fallen down their stairs and was unconscious. He died in hospital. Tony was a lovely man, even if he *was* always late for everything. RIP.

It's harder to see Hank than any of the other surviving Shadows now, because he has lived in Australia since 1986. He moved Down Under because he wanted his kids to have a healthy, outdoor existence, and he's never regretted it. He loves it there.

Hank has a recording studio at home and plays in a group, Hank Marvin Gypsy Jazz, who interpret the music of Django Reinhardt, the great jazz guitarist, and also write their own tunes. It's a real passion for Hank. They make records, and occasionally do short tours of Australia and New Zealand.

Whenever I toured Australia, I always called Hank and asked him to be a special guest. He always said yes. Hank would walk

---

* And let's not forget that, in 1995, Ian *finally* got around to writing that second verse for 'Move It'!

on, the Aussie crowd would go nuts, we'd do 'The Young Ones', 'Living Doll' and 'Summer Holiday', Hank would wave and walk off, and the crowd would go nuts again.

We did it on four or five tours, and I would always look forward to it for weeks beforehand. Every time, it was such fun to be on a stage with Hank again, even if it was only for ten minutes or so. I really hope that we get to do it again.

Hank is still a master of the one-liner! He turned eighty in 2021. He's a Jehovah's Witness, and they don't celebrate birthdays, but I sent him a little message via email: 'How lucky for you that you'll always be a year younger than me!' Hank emailed me back: 'I hope so!'

Bruce lives in Richmond upon Thames as he has for many years. He has done a lot of interesting projects. From 1998 to 2012, he ran Shadowmania, an annual one-day show of Shadows tribute bands. Bruce would always top the bill. In 2011, the show included a tribute to Jet Harris, who had just died of cancer.

I see Bruce when I'm in London, as I do Brian Bennett, who, since The Shadows, has had a successful career writing theme tunes for TV shows. Remember the theme from *The Ruth Rendell Mysteries*? That was Brian! He was married for more than sixty years to the lovely Margaret, who sadly passed away recently.

Whenever I meet up with Bruce and Brian, the years fall away. When we went to the SODS awards last year, we had a great laugh, as we always do. *As we always will*. If I still lived in England, I'd see those two guys much more than I do. We always miss Hank, though, and the Hank-and-Bruce double act!

I feel so fortunate to have met, and worked with, The

Shadows. It's easy to forget what a terrific band they were and, with due modesty, how fantastic they and I were together. But occasionally, out of the blue, you get a reminder.

Twenty years ago, the people at EMI were poking around in a dusty old cupboard when they found a recording of Cliff Richard & The Shadows playing live at the ABC in Kingston in 1962. They got in touch with me, suggesting they release it as a live CD.

Well, I was horrified! '1962?' I replied. 'It's bound to be rubbish! You can't release *that!* I'll have to hear it first.' So, they sent it to me, and when I listened to it . . . I was amazed. Because I couldn't believe how great we sounded.

That recording of us, still wet behind the ears in 1962, knocked me sideways. My vocal sounded strong and confident. The Shadows' wild guitars made you want to leap out of your seat. The songs cooked, the crowd were going wild and the gig sounded like it was the only place to be. *Wow!*

I was expecting an amateur racket, but we sounded like a skilled, sussed rock and roll band, right on top of our game. In fact, Cliff Richard & The Shadows in 1962 sounded like the music I used to thrill to on AFN, a few years earlier. We sounded phenomenal. *We sounded American!*

So, I opened my laptop, emailed the recording on to Hank in Australia . . . and I added a little note.

'Gosh, Hank, listen to this!' I wrote. 'It's amazing! I don't remember Cliff Richard & The Shadows being *this* good back then!' And Hank sent me a two-word reply:

'*I* do.'

TWENTY-ONE

'LOVE ME DO' – THE BEATLES

Despite my prediction, nobody stepped on them

Around the time that The Shadows were releasing 'Apache', I remember we heard a demo by a new band from Liverpool. It was a cover of 'Dizzy, Miss Lizzy', a 1958 rock and roll song by Larry Williams, and it was dreadful. *Horrible*. 'This sounds like a band who will always be playing their local church hall!' I said to the others.

How wrong can one man be?

Well, The Beatles may have made an unpromising early demo, but they were to get a whole lot better very, very quickly. Later in 1960, they left for Hamburg, where they honed their musical chops by playing more than 250 shows in about two years. Why did they go there? Well, they claimed it was partly down to me!

Paul McCartney reputedly said that one reason The Beatles went off to Germany was that 'Cliff and The Shadows had got everything sewn up in Britain'. We *were* riding high then, but I never imagined we were forcing our rivals to emigrate! But if it's true, I guess we played a big part in their career. Because when they came back, they were terrific.

When The Beatles enjoyed a Top 20 hit in Britain in autumn 1962 with their debut single, 'Love Me Do', they sounded a different band completely. The Shadows and I loved the song from the first hearing. In fact, I can remember exactly what I thought when I heard it: *Oh, I wish WE had that song first!*

'Love Me Do' was a fantastic pop-rock tune. It was beautifully direct and simple. It was a slow-paced rock and roll track with blares of mouth organ, and two voices harmonising sweetly. Paul McCartney had this high, clean voice, John Lennon's was lower and more guttural, and they slotted together perfectly.

In fact, I liked 'Love Me Do' so much that I did some unpaid freelance promotional work for it! Cliff Richard & The Shadows were about to do our second tour of South Africa. On our first visit, in 1961, I'd done a few radio interviews where the DJs asked me if they could play a favourite song for me. I couldn't think of anything quickly enough, so I just said, 'Play anything by Elvis!'

So, on our second visit, I took my copy of 'Love Me Do' with me and asked all of the DJs who interviewed me to give it a spin. I told them all the truth: 'We really wish that *we* had this song!' Everybody liked it, and one DJ asked me on air if I thought that The Beatles might go on to be huge.

'Not really,' I laughed. 'Their name sounds like something you might step on!'

I really was NOT doing well with my Beatles predictions!

By the time we got back to Britain, The Beatles had gone to Number 2 with their follow-up single, 'Please Please Me'. It was clear something big was happening. They didn't really sound like anybody else. Their songs were great, but they also had their finger on the pulse of commercial appeal. Radio loved them.

I thought that I'd like to meet The Beatles, and I was to get the opportunity very quickly. Bruce Welch phoned me up in March 1963. He was having a party at his house that Friday night, and The Beatles were going to drop in after they had played a gig at Lewisham Odeon. Would I like to come along?

Yes, please! It sounded too good to miss. The Beatles turned up pretty early that night (they had only played four songs in Lewisham: they were the support act to two American rockers, Chris Montez and Tommy Roe). And, as you do at all good parties, we quickly found ourselves sitting and chatting in the kitchen.

It was all very relaxed. They were fun to talk to. Paul seemed an easy-going guy, and Ringo was a fun, chatty bloke. John had more of an edge to him but he was a really funny character. George Harrison was friendly, but didn't say very much. Well, I guess they *did* always call him 'the quiet one'!

Mostly we talked, and talked, and talked about music. We compared notes on the artists that we liked, and they were pretty much identical. We raved about Chuck Berry, and John Lee Hooker and Buddy Holly.* And The Beatles definitely shared my passionate, formative love of Elvis.

Paul and John had been in a skiffle band – The

---

* The Beatles adored Buddy Holly. I didn't know when I met them that, even before their lousy version of 'Dizzy, Miss Lizzy', their first demo had been 'That'll Be the Day'. And they called themselves The Beatles in order to be named after insects, like Buddy's band, the Crickets!

Quarrymen – like me, and had been moved to start playing rock and roll by Elvis, like me. I always say that if there had been no Elvis, there'd have been no Cliff Richard. You know what? I think I'd add that without Elvis, there would have been no Beatles, either. He was the catalyst for all of us.

One thing I picked up quickly in the kitchen was that John Lennon was slightly . . . *weird*. He was very witty but, also, he was quite an off-the-wall individual. He made a lot of acerbic comments. While we were talking about music, I told him how much I liked Ray Charles. 'Do you?' I asked him.

'Oh, I *used* to like Ray Charles,' John replied. 'But now that everybody else likes him, I can't be bothered.'

Huh? I thought to myself. *Surely you either LIKE Ray Charles, or you DON'T?*

Don't get me wrong, though. John was very nice to me. I think he was aware that The Shadows and I were established stars at that point, while The Beatles were just starting out. He even made a joke about it: 'Can you delay your next single coming out, please, Cliff? To give our new one a chance?'

'What's it going to be?' I asked him.

'We recorded it three weeks ago, but we're still not quite sure about it,' he said.

Bruce Welch always had guitars and instruments lying around his house, and that evening was no exception. There was a guitar leaning against his kitchen wall. He handed it to John. 'Go on!' Bruce said. 'Play it for us now!'

I have told this story so many times in my life, and it never fails to

Clyde McPhatter was such a gentleman that he didn't even mind that my group, The Drifters, had accidentally nicked his band's name!

A promo poster for The Biggest Show of Stars for 1960 ... hang on, who's this 'Cliff Richards' character?!

Sammy Turner took a 1926 Irving Berlin show tune, 'Always', and turned it into a stone-cold soul classic.

Bobby Rydell was so cool that he even had the high school in *Grease* named after him!

He had a wild life, a ferocious talent, and *he sent me* … every time. Soul giant Sam Cooke.

I'll never forget seeing her at Ronnie Scott's, back in the day: the formidable, personality-plus Dakota Staton.

Hank Marvin tackles the crossword: 'Hmm, four down: Cliff's band: 3, 7?' My boys, The Shadows, in 1963: Brian Locking, Bruce Welch, Hank Marvin, Brian Bennett.

I heard their first demo and predicted they'd never get anywhere. So, they went on to be the most successful band in the history of pop! Paul, Ringo, George, John: The Beatles.

'I'm not hurting your leg, am I, chuck?' With my great friend Cilla Black: people remember her as a TV star, but I'll never forget what a wonderful singer she was.

'There's a train a-coming …': Fred Cash, Sam Gooden and Curtis Mayfield from that wonderful soul band The Impressions.

The day my life changed forever: coming out as a Christian at the 1966 Billy Graham rally in Earl's Court where I sang 'It Is No Secret (What God Can Do)'.

I've always loved being Number 1 in the charts – and was very happy when 'We Don't Talk Anymore' got there in 1979.

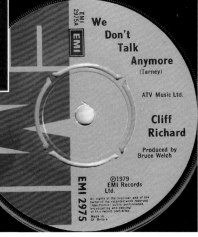

He released my records in America then, decades later, stood by me in my hour of greatest need: the fabulous Elton John.

Ah, those harmonies! My favourite band, now and forever: Maurice, Robin and Barry Gibb, The Bee Gees.

'G'day, Cliff!' With my friend and, yes, soulmate, the irrepressible Olivia Newton-John.

The Queen of Soul, Aretha Franklin, appears on my TV show in 1970. Thankfully, my pith helmet is nowhere to be seen.

Today, I'm happy performing both rock and roll *and* Christian songs – especially when I can sing the latter with somebody as talented as Sheila Walsh. Here we are performing together in 1984.

give me goose bumps. The Beatles looked at one another, shrugged and nodded. John began to strum the guitar, and he, Paul and George started to sing, in beautiful harmony:

'If there's anything that you want . . .'

They fired out the first few notes of 'From Me to You' and it sounded *incredible*. In fact, they played the whole song, as The Shadows and I sat in the kitchen, our mouths hanging open. I don't think I'd ever heard a more sure-fire hit record in my life – yet The Beatles were worried about it!

John finished playing and put the guitar down. 'But we're still not sure about it,' he repeated.

'Oh. My. God! Are you joking?' Bruce asked, incredulously. 'That is amazing! It's a potential Number 1!' Bruce had far more faith in the song than they did. And I've learned, over the years, that nobody – *nobody* – has better ears, or is better at spotting a hit, than Bruce Welch.

Sure enough, 'From Me to You' climbed the chart to Number 1 when it came out the following month. Yet The Beatles still seemed unaffected by that success when we met them again, a few weeks after Bruce's party. This time, it was by the seaside. We were in Blackpool.

The Shadows and I were staying in the town and doing a summer residency, six days per week, Mondays to Saturdays, at the local ABC theatre. The Beatles came up to play two or three Sundays in the same venue. We met up with them.

'How are you going to get away from the ABC after the shows?' I asked them.

'Oh, we'll just walk down the seafront to our hotel,' said Paul. 'It's not far.'

I burst out laughing. 'Are you *kidding*? You have no chance! We get mobbed every night just running from the theatre to our van! Your fans are going potty for you, so it'll be the same for you. Would you like to borrow our van on Sunday nights? Because I think you'll need it!'

'Er, yeah, OK, sure! Thanks!'

So, we left our van outside the ABC every Sunday, and the venue's security men hustled The Beatles to it through the crowds of screaming girls, just as they did for us in the week. I must admit, I thought they were quite naïve to imagine they could take a gentle stroll back along the promenade! But it was sweet, I guess.

After that, The Beatles went into what you might call their imperial period of chart domination. After 'From Me to You', 'She Loves You' had got to Number 1. 'I Want to Hold Your Hand' went to the top of the chart just after we were in Blackpool together. I liked them all. How could you not? They were great singles.

And then The Beatles went to America.

It was February 1964 when they flew into New York. 'I Want to Hold Your Hand' had just gone to Number 1 in the *Billboard* chart. And The Beatles arrived to find an estimated five thousand girls at the airport crying, screaming, waving banners and yelling that they loved them.

It was an incredible sight, and it helped The Beatles to break America virtually overnight – but it had not happened by chance. In advance of The Beatles flying in, their manager, Brian

Epstein, their US record label and a merchandise company had apparently hatched a clever plot to maximise the impact of their arrival.

I have read that their record label PRs were encouraging radio DJs to keep repeating that 'The Beatles are coming!' and to plug the flight arrival time. And that every fan who turned up at the airport was promised a dollar and a free T-shirt. I still wonder if it was true.

If it was, it was a fabulous, slick marketing plan, but I had to chuckle bitterly at the contrast with my own first tour of America in 1960. 'Living Doll' had been a US hit, but nobody from my American label had even bothered to come to see us play! And it's just a fact of life: you can't make it unless your people are behind you.

So, I watched from afar as The Beatles stormed America – then they came home and stormed Britain again. By then, what the papers were calling Beatlemania was in full flow. They couldn't walk down the street without being mobbed. They were basically enjoying the same levels of fame as I'd had for the last six years.

In July 1964, The Beatles launched their first movie, *A Hard Day's Night*, with a big, star-studded premiere in Piccadilly Circus. There were so many thousands of screaming girls outside that it pretty much closed down the whole West End. I saw it on the TV news. 'This has never happened before!' a reporter said.

What? Excuse me! It *had* happened before, twice – for me! We had identical crazy crowd scenes outside the West End premieres of *The Young Ones* and *Summer Holiday*! The hysteria outside

Summer Holiday in Leicester Square, in 1963, had been so wild that the police hadn't let me get out of the car when I arrived. I had missed my own film premiere!

It wasn't The Beatles' fault, at all, but it seemed to me that the media were totally ignoring the fact that I had excited similar scenes in order to big up Beatlemania and sell newspapers. In fact, I was so upset about it that I asked for a meeting with my manager, Peter Gormley.

'Peter, this is ridiculous!' I complained to him. 'What are we going to do about these Beatles? Every time I open a newspaper, they're all I read about! It's like the papers have totally forgotten about me! What's going on?'

Now, as Bruce Welch had learned when he went to Peter complaining about tuning his guitar, our no-nonsense Australian manager was never big on tea and sympathy. Instead, he sighed, rolled his eyes and gave it to me straight.

'Cliff, mate, are you still doing concerts?' he asked me.

'Yes.'

'Do they still sell out?'

'Yes.'

'And are your records still being hits?'

'Yes. All of them.'

'Well, what are you worrying about, then?' Peter concluded. 'Forget about the bloody Beatles! You're got your own career, and it's going very well.'

He was completely correct, of course. And I didn't have any beef with The Beatles, who made terrific records, and had always been friendly to me when I met them. I was disappointed with the press, who always like nothing better than fomenting rivalry between stars, pretending that we're all at each other's throats.

Around this time, the idea sprang up that I was jealous or resentful of The Beatles' success. It simply wasn't true. *Why would I be?* As I said earlier, John Lennon had famously said: 'Before Cliff Richard and "Move It", there was nothing worth listening to in British music.' It meant so much to me then, and it still does. Thank you, John.

But the press wasn't interested in *that*. They were much keener on trying to stoke an imaginary rivalry between us. Because I didn't go around punching people, and was getting into Christianity, they began writing about me as if I wasn't rock and roll at all. It was the dawn of that 'Goody Two-Shoes' tag that I detest.

I remember, in one interview around that time, a journalist asking me, 'How does it feel not to be cool?' *Huh? What the heck?* I replied, 'Oh, you don't think I'm cool? Well, *John Lennon* thinks I'm cool, thank you very much!' But, by then, the media had put me in this category of being strait-laced and po-faced.

There was never any bad feeling between me and The Beatles but the papers kept trying to create it. I recall one interview where they asked what I thought of one of The Beatles' new albums. I answered honestly: that I thought it was cool, but I had noticed one – *one!* – duff note in a guitar solo, which had surprised me.

'They made it at Studio Two at the EMI Recording Studios, which is top-of-the-range,' I said. 'Whenever *we* play a bum note* there, we just correct it, and I'm surprised The Beatles didn't

---

* Certainly, today's technology allows us to correct a 'bum note' very easily. The engineer can simply push the note up or down and put it in tune. I have absolutely zero knowledge of how it works – I just know that it does!

notice it. But it's still a terrific album!' I should have kept my big mouth shut. The interview appeared with this headline:

CLIFF SLAMS BEATLES!

Of course, all The Beatles' fans thought, *Bloody Cliff Richard – who does he think he is?* And I don't blame them for that. But all I'd done was try to make a point about technology. Again, I can only believe it was the press trying to feed a grudge that simply didn't exist.

Well, what can you do? I carried on enjoying The Beatles' music into the mid-sixties – great hits like 'Can't Buy Me Love' and 'A Hard Day's Night', and amazing albums (and movies) such as *Help!* As Peter Gormley said, there was room for all of us, and I certainly couldn't deny their musical brilliance. And they were *so* prolific.

Also, it's true that The Beatles and I *were* taking very different paths at that stage in our careers. I was converting to Christianity, taking a small step back from rock and roll, playing gospel tours and making TV shows. They were becoming icons of the hippy counterculture and going to India to meet the Maharishi.

Or was it so different? It may have looked it from the outside but, for me, The Beatles and I were both *searching*: for something greater, to make sense of our lives. It's not down to me to say what enlightenment they got from the Maharishi. But I knew I felt very comfortable with where I was, once I'd found God.

Unlike The Beatles, I never played psychedelic, hippy music, although I liked some of the songs coming out of that flower-power scene. I was very wary of the drugs that seemed to accompany it, though. Over the years, I saw too many talented artists die young, like Janis Joplin, and Mama Cass from The Mamas & the Papas.

There was no danger of *me* doing that. I was never going to start getting stoned: I hated smoking! When I was a kid, my dad smoked non-stop.* The cigarette smell in our house made me feel sick. Whenever Dad asked me to pass the ashtray, I did it with the very tips of my fingers, or asked my sister, Donna, to hand it to him.

The Beatles got so massive, of course, that in 1966 John Lennon claimed that they were 'more popular than Jesus'. I'm certain he meant it as just a flippant, acerbic comment (like the ones he'd made in Bruce's kitchen!), but it got him in a load of grief. People in America were burning Beatles albums in the street.

I was a Christian by then, and while I could see that John's comment was meant as a joke, I also thought it was a mistake. Pretty stupid, if I'm honest. There are millions of people all over the world who would disagree with him. The Beatles sold more records than Jesus – but, as far as I'm aware, Jesus never made albums! And, if he had, he would have outsold all of us!

I carried on following The Beatles but some of their more far-out, experimental music was not to my taste. I bought *Sgt. Pepper's Lonely Hearts Club Band* in 1967 and thought it was interesting, but I didn't play it all that often. And on the follow-up, the *White Album*, I only liked a couple of tracks: in particular, 'Blackbird'.

---

* More than anything in the world, I wish that my dad hadn't smoked so much. It killed him, eventually, when he was only fifty-six.

Probably my favourite album that The Beatles made was one of their last ones – *Abbey Road*, in 1969. The harmonies on tracks like 'Because' were fantastic and the whole record just sounded to me more professional than many of the others. And, of course, it was to lead to the recording studio changing its name!

Ever since 'Move It', The Shadows and I had made our records in Studio Two at the EMI Recording Studios in Abbey Road, St John's Wood, with Norrie Paramor producing them. As soon as The Beatles began making albums, they were doing them in the same studio, with George Martin.

In fact, I once bumped into Paul McCartney there, and we joked about it. 'Every time we phone up to book EMI Studio Two, we get told we can't have it, because Cliff is using it!' he told me. 'Oh, *come on*, Paul!' I replied. 'Whenever *I* ask to use it, they say, "No – The Beatles are in there!"'

It was their *Abbey Road* album, though, with its famous cover of the band walking across the zebra crossing in the street outside, that led to the studio being given the same name. History will always grant The Beatles that – but it can't take away the fact that I was recording Number 1 hits there years before them!*

Of course, by the end of the sixties, The Beatles were over. I saw a biographer of theirs, on TV, saying that they weren't really talking to one another by the end of 1969 and their last album, *Let*

---

* At the end of 2022, Sara Cox interviewed me in that famous studio, for a BBC TV Christmas special programme. The interview was later broadcast on her Radio 2 show. 'Everyone thinks The Beatles own this place!' I joked to her. 'But I began recording in here five years before them. *I* own it! I just rented it to them . . .'

It Be in 1970, was effectively a posthumous release. They did so much, but they did it all in seven years. Remarkable.

They all went their separate ways and began making their own music. I was having a lot of hits again in the seventies, and would sometimes find myself fighting for chart places with Paul McCartney and Wings (and the fab Abba!). John married Yoko, of course, went off to New York, and they made quite a few records together.

In fact, during the seventies, when Elton John put a couple of my records out in America, I met one of Elton's studio engineers, who told me he had just been working with John Lennon. 'Really?' I replied. 'I met John right back at the start of The Beatles. I thought he was a really strange guy.'

'He was, but he's totally changed now,' the guy said. 'He's completely different these days. He's not nearly as edgy and sarcastic as he was. He's mellowed a lot and is completely charming. He's a baby!' *Oh*, I thought, *that sounds good! I'd really like to catch up with John again!*

And then, of course, in 1980, John Lennon got shot dead. I was so horrified when I heard that. They said the guy that did it was a fan; well, he doesn't sound much like a fan to me! I remember, twenty years later, somebody breaking into George Harrison's house and stabbing him, as well. *What goes through people's heads?*

I've seen Paul McCartney live once or twice, over the years. His shows are always great fun. Paul has so many terrific hits to play, both Beatles classics and from his own later career. But what sometimes frustrates me is that he rarely speaks to the crowd.

When I do my tours, I try to chat to the audience between songs. I'll tell a couple of stories, or maybe even the odd joke (whether they like it or not!). It helps the evening flow better. Paul doesn't tend to do that. He'll just say, 'Good evening!' and 'Are you all doing alright?' and maybe give them the odd double thumbs-up.

It baffles me because, when Paul *does* talk to the crowd, he's really good at it. A natural communicator. When I was recording in Nashville about ten years ago, he came through on tour and I went to the show. He was in a chattier mood that night, and some of the things he said were really moving.

Paul picked up a ukelele and said, 'Y'know, nobody really knows that George was great at playing the ukelele. He wrote "Something" on it.' Then he played the song. And when he said, 'I don't think John knew how much I loved him,' then played a song he'd written in Lennon's honour, I had a tear in my eye.

I love it when artists do that, and I think audiences appreciate it. They might go home thinking they know a little bit more about you than when they arrived. I've always been a chatty soul, and I enjoy going on stage and relating a few real-life stories: 'Hey, you won't *believe* what happened to me yesterday . . .'

I bump into Paul, very occasionally: I suppose it normally tends to be at royal or charity events. We always chat as easily as we did in Bruce Welch's kitchen, sixty years ago, and we always share our joke again about both trying to book Studio Two at Abbey Road:

'Ah, Cliff, you were EMI's favourite! They kept it for you!'

'Are you joking? I could never get in because you Beatles were always in there!'

It never grows old! I like Paul a lot. We've never been close, close friends, but if we had lived near to each other, maybe we'd have gone for dinner every now and then, and got to know each other a lot better. *Who knows?* At least I can imagine it.

I've sung Beatles songs over the years. I covered both 'I Saw Her Standing There' and a Beatles obscurity called 'I'll Be Back' on my *Don't Stop Me Now!* album in 1967. And I was very pleased with the version of 'And I Love Her' that I did on my *Wanted* album in 2001.

And yet, ultimately, I think my favourite Beatles song might still just be that debut single from back in 1962. I would love to sing 'Love Me Do' and find my own way to interpret it. Maybe I'll finally get around to it when I make my next album. Because I *still* wish The Shadows and I had had that song!

I sometimes see statistics about who has sold more records in Britain: me or The Beatles. They say it's The Beatles, and that perplexes me a little. Apparently, if you add up all the weeks that I've spent in the Top 40, it comes to twenty-two years (!), whereas The Beatles were over and done in seven years. Can it be right?

I do wonder if those chart statisticians are adding to The Beatles' total all of the records that John, Paul, George and Ringo sold after they went solo. If they do *that*, there is obviously no way that I can compete. But that would seem unfair to me. The Beatles, as a band, ended in 1970. Solo sales are a different thing.

Ultimately, though, *does it matter?* The Beatles were my

musical competitors for a few years, but I outlasted them. I've been making records for six times as long as they ever did! In fact, I saw quite a funny quote, not so long ago, from Mick Jagger, saying exactly the same thing.

The media (again!) always painted The Rolling Stones as The Beatles' arch-rivals in the sixties, and in a recent interview, Jagger got asked the old question: 'Who was best, The Stones or The Beatles?' 'What, The Beatles?' he laughed. 'That band who were around for ten years, fifty years ago? We've been going for *sixty* years!'

He's right. And I've been going for sixty-five.

I think these supposed musical 'rivalries' are silly. In the end, I believe – and this may sound a bit odd to you, but bear with me – that the rock and roll world is like a great big supermarket, where you do a weekly shop. People can walk through the shelves of all the musical options and pick up whoever they want.

They might say, 'Oh, a Cliff Richard record – shall I take one of those? Nah, I got one last week. What's this? George Michael? Oh, yes, I like him! Let's pop that in my trolley!' We artists are all there, year in, year out, for the shoppers to choose from. And the lucky ones of us get chosen more than the others.

Seeing things that way makes life easier for me. I took Britain by storm when I appeared, but I never took the whole world by storm, including America. Elvis did that, and The Beatles, but I didn't. Well, so what? I've been fortunate that millions and millions of people have put me in their trolleys. And I'm very grateful for that.

I will always go down in music history as the first artist to make a British rock and roll record. I'm proud of that legacy. The Beatles will go down in history for plenty of other reasons. It doesn't make sense to see us as rivals: we artists are all in one big fraternity, a brotherhood, a *family* of rock and roll.

Even if they *did* once make a lousy demo tape . . . (joke!)

TWENTY-TWO

'YOU'RE MY WORLD' – CILLA BLACK

Music's loss was television's gain

The Beatles weren't the only fabulous artists to come out of Liverpool at the start of the sixties, of course. That era also saw the spectacular arrival of an incredibly talented lady who, over the ensuing decades, was to become one of my very close friends.

Cilla Black (or Priscilla White, as she still was then) started out as the cloakroom girl and an occasional amateur singer at The Cavern Club, when The Beatles were still basically the house band there. After The Beatles' manager, Brian Epstein, took her under his wing, she enjoyed a meteoric rise to success.

It came after a false start. Cilla's debut single, 'Love of the Loved', written for her by John Lennon and Paul McCartney, only just crept into the Top 40 when it came out in 1963. Its follow-up, at the beginning of the following year, was a very different matter.

The great Dionne Warwick had had a big US hit at the end of 1963 with 'Anyone Who Had a Heart', written for her by Burt

Bacharach and Hal David. Bacharach and David were a Rolls-Royce of songwriters, of course, and when George Martin heard the song, he thought it could make a great follow-up single for Cilla.

How right he was. Before Dionne's label could put her version of the song out in Britain, Cilla recorded it with George Martin and EMI rushed it out. Cilla was still basically unknown at this point, but when people heard her terrific version, the effect was phenomenal.

She suited the song, and the song suited her. She had such a strong voice – and it was an obviously *English* voice, not mid-Atlantic at all – and the song allowed it to soar. The radio DJs played 'Anyone Who Had a Heart' non-stop, the public fell in love with it, and it raced up the chart to Number 1. What an arrival!

Everybody loved Cilla's take on the song . . . except Dionne Warwick! I have been fortunate enough to get to know Dionne a little, over the years, and she is a truly legendary talent with an extraordinary career that is still going. But, in 1964, she definitely felt Cilla had stolen her thunder – and her song.

In fact, Dionne was pretty miffed! Allegedly, she called Cilla's version of the song 'a copy' and passed some harsh comments in her press interviews. I heard about one where Dionne apparently said, 'If I had coughed when I recorded the song, *that woman* would have coughed as well!'

Now, I understand Dionne's irritation, but I think that comment is a tad unfair. Cilla's version *wasn't* just a copy. She sang the same melody, of course, but she had a different type of vocal to Dionne. Dionne's voice is cool and mellifluous; when Cilla's voice went high, it was tight and strong. Both versions were great.

Thankfully, there was no controversy at all around Cilla's follow-up single: the song I've selected for *A Head Full of Music*. It was absolutely phenomenal, and it equalled the performance of 'Anyone Who Had a Heart' by climbing to Number 1. It was called 'You're My World'.

The song was originally a big Italian ballad, by a guy called Umberto Bindi, called 'Il mio mondo'. The funny thing is that I have heard that version and . . . how can I put this? It is really not my cup of tea! The fact that Cilla and George Martin were able to turn it into something as brilliant as they did is quite miraculous!

Because 'You're My World' is wonderful. It demonstrated just what a marvellous voice Cilla had. She sang the soft, low-end part of the song beautifully, then when she went for the big notes, she hit them gloriously. You felt like applauding! She took that sow's ear of an Italian ballad and turned it into a silk purse.

When those two songs went to Number 1 in quick succession, it felt as if a new musical superstar had arrived. Paul McCartney and John Lennon wrote Cilla's next single, 'It's for You', which went Top 10, then, early in 1965, she sang The Righteous Brothers' 'You've Lost that Lovin' Feelin'' and saw it go to Number 2.

Oddly, Cilla never had another Number 1 single, although she was to have loads of amazing hits through the sixties such as 'Alfie', 'Step Inside Love' and the great 'Surround Yourself with Sorrow'. But then, Cilla Black found another career, and showed that she had so much more going for her than just a voice.

In 1968, she began hosting a BBC TV variety show called *Cilla*. She was a natural. As soon as you saw it, it was patently obvious that she was going to be a massive television star. She had so much character, and she was just so funny! Her larger-than-life personality leapt through the screen.*

That show was where I first met Cilla Black. I went on and duetted with her on 'Walk On By' (another Dionne Warwick song!) and 'Passing Strangers'. I hate to say it, but it was so long ago that the broadcast was in black and white! Cilla was a lot of fun, singing with her felt very easy, and we hit it off straight away.

I had a longer association with the *Cilla* show when the BBC used it to choose the song that I was to sing for Britain in the 1968 Eurovision Song Contest. I did a different song every week for seven weeks, and viewers wrote in to vote for the one they liked the most. The winner was the last one I sang: 'Congratulations'.

I was to make a similar career journey to Cilla in 1970, when I began hosting my own Saturday night BBC show, *It's Cliff Richard*. I enjoyed it but, ultimately, I've always been primarily a singer, and I returned to music. Once Cilla began doing TV, she was so good at it, and loved doing it so much, that it became her world.

Television viewers loved her because she was so quick-witted and warm, and she could talk to anybody and about anything. She had that natural Scouse humour, where she could always think of something to say to make everybody laugh. She became one of the most popular, and highest-paid, telly presenters of all time.

---

* Cilla was so great on telly that BBC chief Bill Cotton wanted her to take over as host of *The Generation Game* when Bruce Forsyth moved on. Cilla was tempted, but declined because she didn't then want to give up her singing career.

I would sometimes watch Cilla hosting *Blind Date* and she made it look so easy, even though I knew enough about TV by then to know that it certainly wasn't! In later years, when we were close, I commented that she always seemed to know which guy, or girl, to guide the contestants towards picking.

'Ah, well, chuck, I'll let you into a secret!' she said. 'I used to have a peek through the curtains during rehearsals, and watch them getting ready and preparing their answers. I could always tell who would be good fun and who wouldn't!'

As I got to know Cilla better, I'd sometimes see her with her husband Bobby, whom she'd met when she was still a barmaid in Liverpool. Bobby was clearly her rock and her anchor. He also took over as her manager after Brian Epstein died. Sadly, Bobby died from cancer in 1999, just after they'd bought a place in Barbados.

I had always got on well with Cilla, but I think to become *really* close friends with someone, you have to live near to them, so you can see them all the time. That's how it was with us. Our friendship really went up a notch, and kicked into gear, when I also got my house in Barbados in the new millennium.

My six-bedroom Barbadian house is by far the most expensive thing that I've bought in my entire life. I helped an architect to draw up the plans and it was to take eighteen months to build. When I finally moved in, in December 2001, there were still windows missing. Lucky it doesn't rain much in Barbados!

I invited Cilla over as soon as I moved in. The builders had done such an amazing job: when you enter, you can see right through the house to a breathtaking view of the Caribbean. Cilla walked in the front door, took it all in, winked at me, threw her arms up in the air and started to sing:

'*There's no business, like show business . . .*'

Once I was settled in Barbados, Cilla and I saw each other all the time. She lived five minutes away. We'd hang out on her beach, and her sense of humour meant that she was really well liked all over the island. She would get invited to a lot of parties, and I soon became her regular plus-one . . . or was it her chauffeur?

Cilla would phone me up: 'Cliff, chuck, would you like to go Lesley's party?'

'Yeah, sure!' I'd reply.

'Great! You couldn't pick me up on the way, could you?'

Cilla couldn't drive so, since Bobby had gone, it was hard for her to get around the island, unless she took taxis everywhere. The first time that I ever picked her up, I was driving a Ford F-150 truck. It's a big, high car, quite a way off the ground, and Cilla stared at it, aghast. 'How am I going to get into *that?*' she asked.

'It's got a running board,' I explained. 'Put your right foot on it, hold on to the door and then lift yourself up and sit down.' She did. When we arrived at the party, she had another question: 'Chuck, how am I going to get *out* of this?'

I walked around, opened Cilla's door, and told her, 'Just turn sideways and slide out.' She slid down, a breeze caught her skirt, and it went *whoosh!* – up into the air! It was so funny! I couldn't help noticing: *Crikey, Cilla's got a fabulous pair of pins!* Her legs were still really long and shapely.

I never minded driving her. We were as thick as thieves by then, and she was always such fun. Yet, for all her natural charm and confidence, Cilla didn't go out much in Barbados for a while after Bobby died. It hit her so hard. She hated arriving anywhere alone.

I remember that she and I went to the theatre in London one night. She was fine when we were in the car, but as we got out and walked to the building, she whispered to me, '*Don't leave me!*'

'Of course I won't!' I assured her. I gave her my arm, and we walked in together.

I never forgot how great Cilla's voice was. I always thought it was such a shame that she largely stopped making records in the eighties and nineties, as her TV career took off. And, early in the new millennium, I had a proposition for her.

In 2004, I was playing my Summer Nights tour of national British landmarks such as Chatsworth House, Edinburgh Castle and Blickling Hall. I knew that Cilla was going to be in England when I played a show at Leeds Castle, in Kent, in July, and I asked her if she would appear as my special guest.

I think, by now, Cilla had actually stopped thinking of herself as a singer, and she stared at me, shocked. 'I can't do that, chuck!' she gasped.

'Oh, come on! You can!'

'But I haven't sung in ages!'

I managed to talk her round, and she came to a couple of rehearsals. We were going to sing 'It Takes Two', the old Marvin Gaye and Kim Weston song. Cilla was very nervous at first, but she didn't sound crackly or croaky: she still *sounded like Cilla Black*. It was such a thrill to hear that fantastic voice again, close-up.

We even learned a few dance steps! On the day, Cilla got an

enormous cheer as I announced her and she came out, and she was sensational, of course. She was always going to be. You don't *lose* talent like Cilla's. She was a born performer. Singing, and entertaining a crowd, came as naturally to her as breathing.

Cilla and I had such a hoot roaming around Barbados together. We simply enjoyed each other's company so much. In fact, I can only remember one occasion when there was ever any tension between us, and that came when I inadvertently re-opened her old grudge match with Dionne Warwick from 1964.

In 2006, I recorded a new album, *Two's Company*. It collected some of the duets I had sung over the years, with artists from Phil Everly to Elton John and Olivia Newton-John. There were also new recordings, with Barry Gibb, Daniel O'Donnell and Lulu, and I was planning to include 'Anyone Who Had a Heart'.

When I heard that Dionne Warwick might be available to sing it with me, I knew immediately that I wanted to do that. I loved Cilla's version of the song but, if I am totally honest, I probably liked Dionne's softer original slightly more, and . . . *she was, after all, Dionne Warwick!* I had grown up loving her voice and music.

Dionne came down to the recording studio late at night, after she had played a concert in London. I'd already put my vocals on and she knew which part she was to sing, so she just pulled up a stool, put the mic a few inches in front of her face, and sang over the track. She sounded unbelievable. *Another pinch-me moment!*

I loved how the finished track sounded, but when I – nervously – told Cilla what I had done, she looked so disappointed. She just stared at me as if she couldn't believe what I was telling her. 'But Cliff, chuck, why didn't you sing it with *me*?' she asked. *Gulp!* I opted to tell a little white lie.

'It was the record company's decision,' I fibbed. 'They told me that Dionne was in town and they wanted her on the album.' I probably should have added that they thought it would help the record in America, but, of course, I never thought of that. *Did Cilla believe me?* I'm not entirely sure.

Cilla was definitely hurt, because we were such big mates that she had assumed I would sing it with her. But we soon put it behind us. We were such good buddies that any tensions weren't going to linger for too long, and we were having such a laugh in Barbados together.

Humour seemed to follow Cilla around. She never liked to go grocery shopping. I once asked her why, and she said, 'I hate pushing a trolley around, chuck!' So I was quite surprised, shortly after that, to be in our local supermarket, Massy's, and bump into Cilla at the end of an aisle.

'I thought you didn't like supermarkets?' I laughed. Cilla just smiled back and gestured behind her . . . where one of her male staff was diligently pushing her trolley for her.

Cilla Black was such a fun person, and she could find comedy in anything, but one thing that she really didn't like was the ageing process. She hated getting old. I can remember going to her apartment for a drink in 2013, just a fortnight before her seventieth birthday, and she was feeling really down.

'I don't *want* to be seventy, Cliff,' she told me, simply. 'I've already got a problem with my eyes.'

'Wear glasses!' I replied.*

'And I can't hear very well.'

'Wear earpieces!' I urged her. 'I do!'

I did my best to cheer her up. 'Look, Cilla, you're going to wake up, in a couple of weeks, on your seventieth birthday, and nothing will have changed,' I said. 'You'll still feel exactly the same.' But she didn't look very convinced. She was feeling so rotten about growing old.

Sadly, Cilla wasn't to last too much longer. She died in 2015, aged seventy-two, at her place in Spain. She fell over and hit her head on a wall, and the autopsy revealed that it might have triggered a stroke. It was a sad way to go: she was on her own at the time, and it was around four hours before anybody found her.

Over the years, I have had a lot of very close friends, and in losing Cilla, I lost one of those special ones. I went to her funeral in Liverpool three weeks later. Jimmy Tarbuck and Christopher Biggins gave tributes and Paul O'Grady (who, sadly, also died in 2023) read a eulogy.

I sang at the funeral. It was a song called 'Faithful One' from an album I made in 2004, *Something's Goin' On*. I practised it a few times, but I hadn't sung it for quite a few years so I put the lyrics on my iPad to ensure that I got them all right.

We got into the church, the service began, and . . . *disaster!* I realised that I had left my iPad in my car! *Uh-oh!* When I went to

---

* I've worn glasses since I was a kid, because I'm short-sighted, but my long sight improved so much a few years ago that I didn't need glasses at all for a while. I loved that, because I could *finally* buy cool-looking sunglasses! Nowadays, I wear glasses to see distances, but I have to take them off to read.

the front to sing, I noticed Tom Jones staring at me, which for some reason made me even more nervous. I just screwed my face up, concentrated hard, and got through the song OK.

After the service, as we were filing out, somebody came up and congratulated me on my rendition. 'You looked so intense as you sang it!' she said. 'You were clearly really into the song!'

'Yes . . . and I was also trying hard to remember the words,' I confessed.

I also paid tribute to Cilla at the funeral. It was hard to find the words because she had meant so much to me. I think she left a big hole in everyone's heart. A nice thing was that, the following week, *The Very Best of Cilla Black* went to the top of the albums chart. It was the only Number 1 album she ever had.

Three years after Cilla died, I sang a duet with her remastered vocals on a tribute album, *Cilla with the Royal Liverpool Philharmonic Orchestra*. Rebecca Ferguson and Sheridan Smith also appeared. It was so moving to sing with my dear friend one last time, and I chose my very favourite of her songs: 'You're My World'.

I know, to many people, Cilla Black will always be a television personality and light entertainer. To me, though, she will forever be that fabulous singer who set the music world alight with those two Number 1 singles in 1964. Just listen to that voice again. Mark my words, *she was a singer* – and a magnificent one at that.

Miss you, chuck.

TWENTY-THREE

'PEOPLE GET READY'
– THE IMPRESSIONS

A gentle genius sings a song that has everything

In my life, and in this book, there have been songs where the sheer beauty and majesty of the music have captivated me. There have been tunes where a great vocal, and wonderful harmonies, drew me in. On some tracks, a brilliant lyric has been an attraction. And there are the rare, special songs that have *everything*.

This is one of them.

The Impressions were a Black Chicago band who started out in the fifties playing gospel, doo-wop, R&B and soul. They were first known as Jerry Butler & The Impressions, after their main songwriter, band leader and singer. In fact, Jerry co-wrote and sang their first big US hit, 'For Your Precious Love', in 1958.

They never had any hits in Britain, which seems crazy to me, so the only way for me to hear them was on AFN. They sounded fantastic. There was a warmth and depth to their sound, and nothing pretentious about their music. You could tell they meant it. They weren't trying to be anything that they weren't.

Another member of The Impressions was Curtis Mayfield, who had first met Jerry Butler in his early teens in a church choir. Those two guys weren't unique in starting out like that, of course. So many great Black artists of that era emerged as singers after being members of gospel choirs.

One great example is Dionne Warwick. I've seen photos, and heard a recording, of a very young Dionne singing in a fifties New Jersey and New York family gospel group, The Drinkard Singers, which also spawned the brilliant singer Cissy Houston, Whitney Houston's mother. They looked, and sounded, absolutely glorious.

Jerry Butler left The Impressions at the start of the sixties, and Curtis Mayfield took over the leadership of the group. Curtis was still in his teens when he wrote and sang a superb 1961 US hit called 'Gypsy Woman'. It had a moment where Curtis changed from falsetto to chest voice, to lift the song into the chorus, that took my breath away when I first heard it. It still does.

Curtis wrote other great hits for The Impressions in the early sixties, such as 'It's All Right' and 'Keep on Pushing'. I'd sometimes pick up their albums when I was on tour in the States. And suddenly I was in love with the music of The Impressions – and particularly the voice of Curtis Mayfield.

Curtis just had this terrific vocal range. He sang so easily and freely. He could do a fantastic low-down husky growl then switch right up to a keening falsetto, if the song required it. It was the first time I had ever heard a male artist sing so high, so purely, and it really grabbed my attention: *just listen to that!*

They called Curtis 'the gentle giant' because of the delicacy of his singing. It suited him. There was nothing raucous whatsoever about his vocal. I think, after Elvis, I would rather have had the chance to sing a duet with Curtis Mayfield than anybody else in the history of music.*

I said as much in an interview, in 1964. I told a music journalist, 'Nothing would make me happier than to record a Curtis Mayfield song, with The Impressions backing me.' And it was true: their music really appealed to The Shadows and me. It is hard to play rhythm and blues as naturally, and as beautifully, as they did.

And then, in 1965, Curtis Mayfield wrote his masterpiece for The Impressions. It was called 'People Get Ready' and I think it is one of the most phenomenal pieces of music ever created.

The greatest compliment you can pay a song is that, as soon as you hear it, you want to sing it. 'People Get Ready' had – *has* – that effect on me. The music is instinctual and Curtis sings as if he is floating on air. He's in that place you always want to get to, as a singer.†

'People Get Ready' is a very spiritual song with its roots firmly in gospel. From the start, its message is transparent and *transcendent*. 'People get ready, there's a train a-coming,' Curtis cooed. 'You don't need no baggage; you just get on board.' It's a rallying call, a message of faith, and the end of the first verse makes it even clearer: 'Don't need no ticket, you just thank the Lord.'

The sincerity in Curtis's voice as he sang those words was so

---

* I'm very happy with my singing voice, but there were a couple of notes in Curtis Mayfield's repertoire that I'd certainly love to be able to hit!
† I try so hard to get to that place when I play live, but normally I'm just trying to keep up with the band!

palpable you could almost touch it. And it is universal. As I say, it is a song clearly rooted in a Black-music tradition, in gospel, yet it also speaks to a white man like me. It speaks to everyone. It's a song about the triumph of getting to heaven.

Curtis said as much. Explaining 'People Get Ready', he said, 'The train takes you back to the old gospel way of thinking, and the teachings of different religions. Black religions, as well as white ones. And the train is a symbol of God, Himself, coming to bring all the other people to venture to the other side.'

I have no doubt that 'People Get Ready' resonated so strongly with me because I had just begun my own spiritual journey and converted to Christianity. I had come to realise: *There must be more to life! We're not all here just because of some cosmic accident, and a scientific Big Bang! There's something ... beyond us.*

In fact, becoming a Christian had led me to see my life, and everything in it, in a very different way. It's not always an easy process, but hearing 'People Get Ready' comforted me, and lifted me. Here was a song that wasn't just suggesting we would get to heaven, but stating it: *We'll be on that train!*

Turning to God made me think very hard about what I did. Initially, I thought I should give up being a singer and spread the word instead, maybe as a religious studies teacher. I called a press conference to announce that I was retiring from music, and sat and passed a religion O-level to get ready for my new calling.

I'm not sure I ever *really* wanted to totally give up rock and roll, though, and it turned out there was no need. I could carry on being a singer, and it would give me a platform to talk about my faith. And the very first opportunity of that kind came when Norrie Paramor phoned me up in 1967.

'Cliff, I think you should make a gospel album,' he said. Initially, the suggestion threw me slightly. 'Really?' I replied. 'Well, you're a Christian now, so why not?' he asked. It was a simple but persuasive argument. And the more I thought about it, the more I liked it.

So, I made *Good News* in 1967, my first album of hymns and spiritual songs, and I began playing gospel tours. I didn't perform any rock and roll, or secular, songs at those shows, but I was delighted to sing 'People Get Ready'. I had to take it down a key from Curtis's falsetto, but what a joy it was to sing those blessed words: *'People get ready, there's a train a-coming . . .'*

'People Get Ready' had so much going on. It wasn't only a religious song. Curtis Mayfield apparently wrote the words the day before Martin Luther King came to Chicago to lead a big civil rights march. In fact, Dr King was later to call it the 'unofficial anthem of the civil rights movement'. He often played it at his events.

The song crossed over between the spiritual and political worlds. In addition to its use at civil rights events, some Chicago churches began using it in their services, and even adding it to their hymn sheets. And, you know what? It's so glorious, and uplifting, that it fits right in there!

The Impressions, and Curtis Mayfield in particular, became even more closely linked with the civil rights cause with songs like 'We're A Winner', a Number 1 on the US R&B chart in 1967.

Well, strong passions can breed great art, because a lot of unbelievable music came out of that point in American history.

Another artist deeply involved in the civil rights struggle was James Brown, with anthems like 'Say It Loud – I'm Black and I'm Proud'. I liked the power of James's music but I didn't play it too often because, ultimately, I always gravitate to more melodic tunes. *But what a performer!* He was fantastic to watch on TV.

I've never really ventured into political music. I have nothing against it at all, it has just never been my thing. The nearest I have got was probably a single that I put out jointly with Hank Marvin in 1970. Hank had co-written it, and it was called 'The Joy of Living'.

'The Joy of Living' was about a 'lovely multi-coloured crocodile . . . growing by the mile' and was about the millions of cars in the world, and the damage that they were doing polluting the planet. It was quite a sarcastic song, I suppose, praising people for taking 'all the air you need' just to 'feed your car'.

A year later, I had a single called 'Silvery Rain', originally recorded by Hank, Bruce and John Farrar as Marvin, Welch & Farrar. This was about the damage done to insects by the use of pesticides in agriculture. It wasn't exactly my usual subject matter, to say the least, but it squeezed into the Top 30.*

Curtis Mayfield left The Impressions in 1970 to go solo. He had the famous funk-soul smash 'Move On Up' the following year, then went on to do songs like 'Super Fly' for the soundtracks of what they used to call 'blaxploitation' movies. I liked some of

---

* OK, these songs weren't social commentary, or political protest, in the style of 'Strange Fruit' or 'What's Going On'. But they still made a point.

them but, if I'm honest, they never moved me as much as 'People Get Ready'.

Good Lord, how many amazing artists in this book have met horrible ends! Curtis Mayfield was such a towering talent that he should have been making wonderful soul and R&B music for decades. He could still be going today. Instead, this great singer was stricken by a tragedy from which he never really recovered.

Curtis was about to play an outdoor show at a park in Brooklyn, New York, in 1990, when the lighting rig for the concert collapsed on top of him. He was paralysed from the neck down. He could no longer perform but, amazingly, was still able to compose and sing in this terribly debilitated condition.

Lying flat on his back, and able only to sing a few lines at a time, he even managed to write and record an album so good that it was nominated for a Grammy, *New World Order*, in 1996. Sadly, he was not to survive too much longer, and died, from complications from diabetes, in 1999. He was just fifty-seven.

It all goes to show: you can be unbelievably talented, and famous, and a sudden accident can take it all away in a split-second. At least Curtis Mayfield will forever be remembered as a musical giant, who left behind the legacy of one of the greatest songs ever written. He is in a better place now. *He's on that train.*

TWENTY-FOUR

'IT IS NO SECRET (WHAT GOD CAN DO)' – ELVIS PRESLEY

The song that I sang on the day my life changed forever

You have some songs in your life that are very occasion-specific. Whenever you hear them, you are immediately catapulted back through the years to the moment when you first heard them, or when they were the soundtrack to a major event in your life – or, if you're an artist, the first time you *sang* them.

'Heartbreak Hotel' is a great example for me . . . and so is this song.

When I became a Christian, in 1965, I kept it very quiet at first. I had been casting around for a greater meaning, a *purpose*, to my life ever since my dad had died in 1961. Welcoming Jesus into my life gave me a great deal of comfort and support, as I struggled to come to terms with that devastating loss.

Yet I didn't want to make a big noise about it. I was still working out what being a Christian *meant* in terms of how I went about my everyday life. I was very wary of going public. My music career was still going great guns – how would people react if I announced I had found God? Would they mock? Would I lose all my fans?

So, I kept my head down and went about my life largely as usual – until the day I was jolted out of my hiding place. The Reverend Billy Graham, the legendary US preacher who held huge 'Crusades' rallies all around the world to spread the word of Jesus, wrote to me. He had somehow heard that I'd become a Christian, and wanted me to speak at one of his meetings.

Uh-oh! I was flattered, and excited, by his invitation, but also terrified. I knew that accepting it would change my life forever. There was a big upside to coming out as a Christian, but also a worrying possible career downside. Did I want to do it, or not? I had sleepless nights, and went back and forth in my mind for days:

Yes, I will!

No, I won't!

I went to my manager, Peter Gormley, for advice. He confirmed that I might lose some fans, but he didn't think it likely, and he didn't tell me not to do it. Peter stressed that it was an entirely personal decision, for me and me alone to take. Well, in my heart, I knew that was true – but that didn't make it any easier.

I only made my mind up when I went along, incognito, in a cap and with my collar turned up, to one of Billy Graham's youth rallies at Earls Court. It set my mind at rest. Reverend Graham invited the young people to take Jesus as their saviour but he didn't *pressurise* them. The tone of the event was positive, and supportive.

On the way home, I made my decision: *OK! I'm in!* My office let Reverend Graham know that I would speak and sing at another meeting, at the same venue, a few days later, on 16 June 1966. It didn't mean that all my apprehensions were gone, far from it, but I was resolved.

And at least I knew exactly which song to sing.

'It Is No Secret (What God Can Do)' is what they call a southern gospel song. It was written by Stuart Hamblen,* a singing cowboy from Texas, after he converted to Christianity in 1949 and had a chat about why he had done so with, of all people, John Wayne. Hamblen had a hit on the US country chart with it in 1951.

If I'm honest, I'd never heard the Stuart Hamblen version. I was only ten when it came out. It pre-dated my interest in music. Nor did I know the 1951 cover by Bill Kenny, the singer of the US rhythm and blues/doo-wop band The Ink Spots. My knowledge of the song began, as so much in my life did, with Elvis.

At the end of 1957, the King released *Elvis' Christmas Album*. I was at the height of my Elvis fixation, so I quickly cycled down to Marsden's to buy it. It had so many great festive songs: 'Santa Claus Is Back in Town', 'White Christmas', 'Blue Christmas', 'Santa Bring My Baby Back (To Me)'. I thought it was fantastic.

The first side was all jaunty Christmas tracks, but Elvis also sang a lot of gospel numbers over the years, and side two was carols and Christian songs. There was 'O Little Town of

---

* Stuart Hamblen's other claim to fame is that he wrote 'This Ole House', the pop-country song that was a UK Number 1 for Rosemary Clooney in 1954 . . . and for Shakin' Stevens in 1981!

Bethlehem', 'Silent Night' and 'Take My Hand, Precious Lord'. And the last song on the record? 'It Is No Secret (What God Can Do)'.*

It was the first time I'd heard it and I liked it straight away. 'The chimes of time ring out the news, another day is through,' crooned Elvis, over angelic backing vocals. 'Someone slipped and fell – was that someone you?' This was mild, gentle Elvis, rather than his rock and roll side, but it still appealed to me.

It was well before my own interest in religion, so I liked the track for the sheer joy of hearing Elvis's velvet tones, rather than for its message. But, nine years later, when I needed a song to sing at Reverend Graham's rally, it came straight into my mind. *Yep*, I thought. *That's the one.*

It ticked a lot of boxes. Its spirituality chimed with the event. I was going to talk about my new life, and turning to Jesus, so it had to be a song which I related to, and which spoke for me. Plus, I'd sung along to Elvis's version so often (and to one by Jim Reeves) that I knew it off by heart. No words to learn, or to forget!

So, I was confident about the song, but that didn't mean that I wasn't terrified on that Thursday evening in June in 1966. Not only was Earls Court full to its 25,000 capacity, but thousands more people were shut out and listening, via speakers, in the car park outside.

I sat on the stage behind the Reverend Graham with some

---

* I've sung so many of those songs over the years, including putting out a version of 'O Little Town of Bethlehem' as a Christmas single in 1982, and including 'Blue Christmas' on my *Christmas with Cliff* album . . . forty years later!

others, including the England cricketer Colin Cowdrey. When it came my turn to speak, I walked to the lectern. The sea of faces before me seemed to stretch forever. I was used to being on stage, in front of thousands of people. But this . . . *this* was very different.

This time, nobody was shouting, or screaming, 'We love you, Cliff!' They all looked serious. They were all waiting for me to speak.

I knew I was about to bare my soul to that hall. To turn myself inside out and say, *THIS is what I am. I've changed. I believe in Jesus.* I hadn't written a speech, but I knew what I wanted to say. So, I took a deep breath, and I began to say it.

I thanked my churchgoing parents for bringing faith into my life as a boy. And I talked about how I felt now that I had accepted Jesus.

'I can only say to the people who are not Christians but are still searching that, until you invite Jesus into your life, you're missing out on so much,' I said. It was comforting to see that people were nodding as I spoke. They seemed to agree with what I was saying.

I don't know how long I spoke for. It may only have been two minutes. Somehow, it seemed both shorter *and* longer than that. But, when I finished, I nodded at the organist, he played those portentous opening chords, and I began to sing:

'*The chimes of time ring out the news, another day is through . . .*'

I sang 'It Is No Secret (What God Can Do)' to the end – then, as I turned to go back to my seat, I had a shock. In my terror, I'd gripped the sides of the lectern so hard as I spoke, and sang, that my arms had gone numb. I couldn't feel them! I had to rub them, surreptitiously, for minutes until the circulation came back.

What an evening. And what a turning point in my life. I'll never forget it. The next day, the newspapers were all reporting my appearance and conversion: some sympathetically, some mockingly. *Well, it's been that way ever since!* What was important was . . . I felt different. I felt *proud* to be out, as a Christian.

I went to more Billy Graham rallies. In 1967, I went to one as a double agent! Unknown to the crowd, Billy was filming a scene for a movie, *Two a Penny*, in which I played a non-believer. I had to sit behind him among his followers, as he preached, pulling faces and rolling my eyes as if thinking, *What a load of crap!**

After my conversion, as I said earlier, I began making spiritual albums and playing gospel tours. Putting a band together was a challenge. The Shadows were not religious, except for Hank, and he was a Jehovah's Witness, with very different beliefs. So, I had to look elsewhere.

I hooked up with a Christian singer named Cindy Kent and her band, The Settlers, and we started doing shows in theatres and churches together. The shows were very different from my usual gigs. They were a lot smaller, to start with. Plus, I would spend a quarter of my time on stage talking about my faith.

My friend Bill Latham, who had helped me start out on my Christian journey, and who was to go on to work with me for many years, helped with those shows. Bill would come on stage with a clipboard of questions, pull up a couple of chairs and interview me. Sometimes, we'd do a Q&A with the audience.

---

* My acting must have been OK! After the rally, a few outraged members of the congregation wrote me letters to say, 'How could you have been so *rude* when the Reverend Graham was talking? You have no manners, young man!'

I remember walking down the aisle of one church with Bill before we gave a talk. Bill was (how can I put this?) bald, but as we passed one of the pews, we heard a small boy whisper to his mum, 'Which one's Cliff?' Oh, Bill *loved* that! We later used it for the title of a religious booklet we wrote: *Which One's Cliff?*

Bill Latham went on to work for Tearfund, the evangelical alliance relief fund for whom I raised funds and visited countries like Bangladesh, Kenya and Haiti. We also house-shared, initially with his mum Mamie, for thirty years. He was a huge figure in my life, and I was saddened when he died at the end of 2022. RIP Bill.

Those gospel shows with Cindy and The Settlers were vastly fulfilling for me. We never misled the fans over what to expect. I always made it clear that we would be playing only spiritual songs, and not 'Move It' or 'Congratulations'. Despite that, a lot of my mainstream pop fans came along anyway.

They saw it as a chance to see me close-up, in a more intimate venue than usual. They were as good as gold, and didn't shout for 'Devil Woman' or 'We Don't Talk Anymore' (in actual fact, I began playing both of those songs at my gospel shows, after some fans explained they held spiritual significance for them).

I loved that, over the years, a few fans wrote to me to say they came along to a gospel show and it started them on a journey to becoming Christians. *That* was wonderful to hear. I don't take any credit for *converting* them, though, because no human can convert another to believe in God.

No. Only God can do that.

I don't play gospel concerts today. I am eighty-two years old, and it's time for someone younger, and fresher, to do it. But I'm proud that, back then, I showed that you can be a Christian *and* a rock and roll singer . . . and you can take that belief, and that music, to church. Because it felt important to me to share what had changed my life for the better.

At virtually every gospel show, I sang 'It Is No Secret (What God Can Do)'. It's a special song. It's where being a Christian pop star began for me, and it will always – *always* – transport me back to that petrifying Thursday evening, in June 1966, when I gripped a lectern so hard that my arms stopped working.

Because that's not the sort of memory that you ever forget.

TWENTY-FIVE

'WE DON'T TALK ANYMORE' – CLIFF RICHARD

The Number 1 that sealed what they called my 'comeback'

As the sixties turned into the seventies, I had become distracted from my music career. It no longer had the same all-consuming prominence in my life. Becoming a Christian had led me to re-evaluate what I was all about, and what my main priorities were, and the answer was my faith.

Accepting Jesus into my life had opened up new lines of activity for me. I was playing gospel tours, speaking at rallies and making religious TV shows. I had also begun hosting my Saturday evening *It's Cliff Richard* show on BBC1. I had probably taken my eye off my recording career. I was basically treading water.

When I made albums, I had got into the bad habit of hardly being in the studio. I'd get together with Norrie Paramor to select the songs from the pile of demos we got sent, then Norrie would get a band together and record the tracks without me. I'd wander in when they were finished and add my vocals to them.

So, I had definitely slipped a little with my music, and in the public's eye, but I'm glad to say that I didn't completely *disappear* as a singer. As I became more settled with my faith, and with who I was, my focus returned to my records. And that coincided with a major change at the head of my musical team.

Norrie Paramor had signed me up in 1958 and put out 'Move It'. It had made me a star. Norrie had also overseen and produced every record I'd made since. However, by 1972 he was nearly sixty, had become resident conductor of the BBC Midland Radio Orchestra, and was winding down his music-executive career.

Norrie told me that he felt he couldn't do any more for me. He thought it was time I recorded with somebody younger than him. I was sorry to see him go, but I guess he and I had maybe slipped into a bit of a rut. But I'll always be grateful for the faith Norrie had in that 17-year-old Cliff Richard.

Luckily, my manager, Peter Gormley, was always a can-do character. He quickly found me a new producer to work with: a fellow Australian called David Mackay.

David was a good guy, and introduced me to two English-born musicians who had grown up in Australia: guitarist Terry Britten and bassist Alan Tarney. They were both to play major parts in my future career. David also diagnosed that I had become detached from the process of making records. He got me back in the studio with the band every day.

That was how I had always worked with The Shadows, and I liked going back to being more involved in the creative process. I even wrote part of my next album, *The 31st of February Street*, myself. I was proud of it, but the public didn't really take to it, and it wasn't a commercial success.

Despite that, I had enjoyed recording it, and it felt like a bit of a comeback. *So, who should produce me next?* The answer was to be found very close to home.

Since The Shadows split, Bruce Welch had kept busy. He had played, with Hank and John Farrar, in a group called Marvin, Welch & Farrar, and co-produced a hit single, 'If Not for You', and album, *Olivia*, by his girlfriend, Olivia Newton-John. Peter Gormley asked what I thought about Bruce producing my next album.

Well, what *did* I think? I thought I'd like to give it a go. I saw our close friendship as an advantage: we should be at ease working together. I knew, from my past experience, that Bruce could be a hard taskmaster in the studio but, well, maybe that was what I needed right now. There would certainly be no slacking!

That preconception was confirmed when Bruce and I had our initial meeting to discuss the project. Bruce explained that he was already chasing up his many songwriter contacts for new songs – then he gave me a steely-eyed stipulation.

'If we're going to do this album, Cliff, we're going to do it *properly*,' he insisted. 'And that means we don't do any songs that sound anything at all like "Living Doll", "Summer Holiday", or "Congratulations".'

Now, Bruce wasn't dissing those hits. He liked them – how could he *not* like 'Summer Holiday'? He had co-written it, with Brian Bennett! He meant that he wanted us to make a record that was current, and contemporary, and didn't slip into a predictable groove. I was pleased. Because I wanted that as well.

The seeds of the album that was to become *I'm Nearly Famous* were planted very quickly. I told the story in *The Dreamer* of how Bruce turned up at my house in Weybridge one afternoon, waving a cassette tape. He sprinted up the stairs to my music room two at a time in his eagerness to play it to me.

As soon as he pressed 'Play' on my tape deck, I understood Bruce's enthusiasm – and I shared it. Over gentle opening music, a male voice sighed, 'I've had many times, I can tell you . . .' and rose to a poignant chorus: 'But these miss you nights, are the longest . . .'

Wow! I held out my forearms to Bruce: 'Look! I've got goose bumps!' I gasped.

'So have I!' He grinned back.

'Miss You Nights' was a lush, gorgeous ballad. When Bruce and I got started on the album in the studio, with the band, I loved recording it. On a lot of my softer, less rock and roll material like that, I take vocal inspiration from the way Peggy Lee sang her hits like 'Fever'. I always loved her gentleness of tone.

One of my band members, Terry Britten, had already played me a song that he had co-written: 'Devil Woman'. I liked it from the off – it had a story, a fab tune and a great chorus – while also having quite severe misgivings about its lyrics.*

'Devil Woman' was the story of a fortune teller ('Crystal ball on the table') who had bad intentions ('evil on her mind'). I

---

* Terry Britten was to tell me the opening riff of 'Devil Woman' was the beginning of 'I Heard It Through the Grapevine' by Marvin Gaye 'turned upside-down'. I had no idea what he was talking about. Then I listened to it again, and I got it.

wasn't sure how my fans, used to gentle songs such as 'Summer Holiday', would react to such edgy material. Also: should a practising Christian *really* be singing songs about dabbling with the occult?

I thought it through, decided recording it would do no harm, and sang it well (or so I thought) on the first studio take. At the end, I looked to Bruce, awaiting his approval. It didn't come. 'Cliff,' he sighed, from behind the production desk, 'can you do it again, please, and *this* time in the same key as the song?'

Bruce's legendary – or is it notorious? – perfectionism in the studio was in full force. One day, I walked in . . . and into a very tense atmosphere. The musicians and engineers all had their heads down while Bruce had his ear glued to one of the giant speakers, listening to a track.

'Play it again, with the lead guitar taken out!' he instructed an engineer. The guy did so. It sounded fine to me.

'Right, now take the bass out!' Bruce ordered. Yep, still sounded OK.

'OK, now take Cliff's vocal out!' *Huh? Just what is going on here?* Bruce listened intently to the drum track.

'A-ha! That's it!' he declared, triumphantly. 'That cymbal is off the beat!'

'Bruce, nobody in the world will hear that!' I told him. 'I don't care! *I* heard it!' he barked. I made a joke, managed to snap Bruce out of his bad mood, and we got cracking. Afterwards, an engineer took me to one side. 'Cliff, I'm glad you turned up!' he whispered. 'Because that session was going *badly* downhill . . .'

Yet occasional aberrations like that were worth it for what

Bruce brought to the sessions, and to the album. His obsessiveness and attention to detail meant that he was right on top of all the latest recording techniques. As he'd promised, he made *I'm Nearly Famous* a current, contemporary album.

You have to bear in mind how much studio technology had changed since 1958, when 'Move It' was released in mono, with a sleeve promising 'also available in stereo'! They had invented four-track machines, then eight-track, and then digital technology came in, and I could suddenly sound like a hundred-voice choir.*

Bruce also shares my love of great harmonies, and enlisted the help of a backing vocal group led by a guy called Tony Rivers. Now, Tony, as I mentioned earlier, is the *king* of harmonies. Bruce would ask, 'Do you have a harmony for here, Tony?' and he'd have the exact right answer. Every time. Tony thought – he *dreamt* – in harmonies.

It all meant that the songs sounded thoroughly modern. That was as important to me as it was to Bruce. We didn't want anyone to listen to *I'm Nearly Famous* and say, 'Oh, it's the same old Cliff Richard.' Because it really *wasn't*. Musically, it was bang up-to-date.

In the seventies, artists such as Mud, Showaddywaddy and Alvin Stardust† were reviving fifties rock and roll. I had nothing against those guys, who were very good at what they did. But I

---

* I remember asking how digital recording technology works, and being told, 'It remembers music in numbers.' I was baffled: *Huh? How do you remember music in numbers?* If I'm honest, I'm still none the wiser.

† Alvin Stardust always wore leather gloves when he sang. I knew Alvin (by his real name, Shane) and his wife, the actress Liza Goddard. I always thought of him as an actor, rather than a rock and roller, but he was a good singer.

didn't want to be a retro-rocker (even if I *had* been there the first time around!). I wanted to be current. Relevant.

We succeeded. *I'm Nearly Famous* sounded sharp, and fresh, and it got terrific reviews. Critics *and* real people began calling it my renaissance or 'comeback' album. I wasn't so sure about the 'comeback' bit – after all, I'd never really been away! – but it felt good to be back in the game.

As I said earlier, where I used to be competing with Marty Wilde for chart places, now I was competing with his daughter, Kim – and with Adam Ant, Duran Duran, Spandau Ballet and The Eurythmics. And I loved it. I wasn't afraid of any of them. I felt that I deserved to be in that fight. It's where I belong.

I've never tried to hide that I'm competitive about chart positions. Any musician who tells you they don't check the charts is fibbing. Nobody makes a record and hopes to get to Number 38 – you want to be Number 1! And if you can't, you want to be as close as possible.

I'm Nearly Famous wasn't a Number 1 album, but it got to Number 5, my best performance in ten years, and I was delighted with that. Especially as it came out at a time when the atmosphere wasn't the best for long-standing recording artists such as me.

I'm Nearly Famous was released in 1976, at the height of punk rock, when bands like The Clash and The Sex Pistols were sneering that established stars like Elvis, Elton, Rod Stewart and me were boring old hat. I have to say that the feeling was mutual, because I thought they were . . . *what's the word I'm looking for? Oh, yes* . . . rubbish!

Most of the punk bands were just a racket. For me, they

hardly even qualified as music. They would hit one chord – *CLANG!* – and then shout over the top. It was absolutely awful stuff, and for me, the big question is, *Where are they nowadays?* Hardly any of them lasted. Frankly, I'm not surprised.*

Punk rock was all about attitude, really. You still sometimes get people copying it. I remember Chris Evans, the DJ, claiming he'd burned all of my records! He was trying to be a bad boy and, for his trouble, he found my fans picketing his studio! Today, Chris is charming, and great to be interviewed by.

After *I'm Nearly Famous*, Bruce Welch was to produce my next two albums: *Every Face Tells a Story* and *Green Light*. After that, I felt it was time for a change, so I made my following album, 1979's *Rock 'n' Roll Juvenile*, in Paris, with Terry Britten producing. Bruce had wanted to carry on doing so, and was a bit miffed.

Yet it was still Bruce who came up with the masterstroke that was to give me the song that I have chosen for this book: 'We Don't Talk Anymore'. And it all came about because, as I said, Bruce Welch has the best ears going when it comes to spotting a hit.

Two musicians I had recently worked with, Alan Tarney and Trevor Spencer, had a side-project, Tarney/Spencer Band. Alan had written 'We Don't Talk Anymore' for them to perform, but when he happened to play it to Bruce, Bruce had other plans. 'I know who needs to record this!' he said. 'Cliff!'

Terry and I had pretty much wrapped up *Rock 'n' Roll Juvenile*

---

* I did like one singer from the punk era, Elvis Costello, and his song, 'Watching the Detectives'. But he is talented, so he was hardly a punk at all. I've met his wife as well, the jazz singer Diana Krall, who is absolutely delightful.

by now, and were putting the finishing touches to the album in a studio in Wimbledon when Bruce and Alan turned up one day. They played me 'We Don't Talk Anymore'. I loved it from the off, and asked them to keep it for me.

'*Keep it for you?*' asked Bruce, incredulously. 'You need to release it *now*!'

Peter Gormley and EMI had also heard the song and loved it, so we recorded it – with Bruce producing – and put it out as a single. It entered the chart at Number 35 on 15 July 1979. And then it began climbing.

The following week, it was Number 23. Then Number 14. The next week, it shot up twelve places to Number 2! *Crikey!* It was there for two weeks, behind 'I Don't Like Mondays' by Bob Geldof's band, The Boomtown Rats. Had it peaked? *No.* On 19 August 1979, 'We Don't Talk Anymore' went up one place to Number 1.

Wow! It was my first Number 1 in over ten years, since 'Congratulations' in 1968. It made me feel my 'comeback', if that was what it was, was complete. 'We Don't Talk Anymore' topped the chart for four weeks, was Number 1 in seven countries, and even got to Number 7 in America, thanks to Elton John (more on that in the next chapter!)*

'We Don't Talk Anymore' went on to sell more than four million copies. It remains my best-selling song ever. Tragically, while

---

* The funny thing was, I still didn't want to include 'We Don't Talk Anymore' on *Rock 'n' Roll Juvenile*. I felt it didn't fit. EMI overruled me, and it was probably for the best, as the album was to go to Number 3 – also my best performance in years.

it was Number 1, Norrie Paramor passed away, aged sixty-five. I was broken-hearted ... yet also glad that dear Norrie, who took me to the very top of the pop world, had lived to see me back there again.

Because I think he will have enjoyed that.

TWENTY-SIX

'YOUR SONG' – ELTON JOHN

I don't know him incredibly well but he is a real friend

I could easily have met a very young Elton John.

Sadly, I didn't.

Elton tells me that in 1960, when he was thirteen, he badgered his mum to take him to see Cliff Richard & The Shadows play live. His constant pleas worked, and they came to the London Palladium, where we were doing a residency in a variety show called *Stars in Your Eyes*. He reckons it was my twentieth birthday.

He wasn't Elton John then, of course. He was still Reg Dwight, probably in the big specs that he didn't need, but that he wore in order to try to look like Buddy Holly. He remembers that he and his mum had a great time, and hung around the stage door after the show because he wanted to meet me.

'But you never came out!' he complains, laughing.

'Oh, that's a shame!' I reply. 'I could have given you an autograph!'

Elton is seven years younger than me, and yet he got into rock and roll at exactly the same time, and in the same way, that I did. He was only *nine* when his mum brought home Elvis's 'Heartbreak Hotel'. The effect was precisely the same on him as it was on me.

'I'd never experienced anything like this in my life,' Elton was to recall in his autobiography, *Me*. 'As "Heartbreak Hotel" played, it felt like something had changed, that nothing could really be the same again. As it turned out, something had, and nothing was.'

Yep! Tell me about it!

The young Elton collected all the same records as me – Buddy Holly, Jerry Lee Lewis, Little Richard – and left school as soon as he could to try to start a music career. He played piano in a pub, got a job as an errand boy at a music publishing company in Denmark Street (London's 'Tin Pan Alley') and played in bands. He also met a gifted young lyricist called Bernie Taupin and began writing with him.

Elton was trying hard to get started but his early years were tough. He used to be a session singer on those old 99p Pickwick *Top of the Pops* covers albums. I never bought them – I didn't want to hear other people singing my songs, badly! – but, apparently, Elton did backing vocals on 'Goodbye Sam, Hello Samantha'.*

I was blissfully unaware of all of this, of course. Nor did I hear any of the seven or eight singles that Elton released at the end of the sixties and start of the seventies that never got

---

* That wasn't all. Elton also sang Bee Gees covers on those *TOTP* albums. He used to wobble his throat with his hand to replicate the Gibbs' vibrato!

anywhere. No, the first time I was aware of the existence of Elton John was in 1970, when I heard 'Your Song'. And I absolutely loved it.

'Your Song' is a fantastic tune. It had me hooked from the opening gentle tinkles of piano. Elton's voice sounded terrific: soft, strong and distinctive. It was nothing at all like mine, but I loved his phrasing: he was clearly a proper singer. It was evident right from the start that here was a major new talent.

Most of all, 'Your Song' had that magic ingredient, the X factor: *it sounded like a hit.* It sounded fantastic wafting out of the radio, and entirely in place as it raced up the charts to the Top 10. I wasn't surprised to see it do so well. If somebody had offered me that song, I'd have snatched their hand off!

I kept an eye on Elton John after that, as he had a string of terrific Top 10 hits. 'Rocket Man' was great, and 'Crocodile Rock', and particularly 'Daniel', with its lovely melody. 'Saturday Night's Alright for Fighting' . . . I could go on. It's that age-old showbiz story: Elton worked hard for years to become an overnight success.*

Elton was able to come up with this conveyor belt of hits because his songwriting relationship with that lyricist, Bernie Taupin, had struck gold. They were a perfect creative match. They had written a stockpile of songs in Denmark Street together, and they always seemed able to come up with new material.

As a partnership, they were unbelievable. Bernie would

---

* Because I really liked Elton's music when he appeared, I bought a couple of his early albums. They credited his orchestral arranger: Paul Buckmaster. For some odd reason, I really liked that name!

knock out a sheet of lyrics – brilliant, original ideas, never clichés – and hand it to Elton. Elton would sit at the piano, scan the words, and write melodies on the spot. I don't know how he did it. Elton says he doesn't, either: the tunes just came to him. *What a talent!*

Elton and Bernie wrote hit after hit. I'm surprised it took them so long to have a Number 1. It didn't come until 1976, when Elton and Kiki Dee topped the chart with 'Don't Go Breaking My Heart'. In a fair world, though, 'Your Song' would have been Number 1 for weeks. I think it certainly deserved to be.

That fateful year, 1976, was also when Elton John entered my life in a big way. I could not have been more dumbfounded when it happened. Because, out of the blue, he phoned up and asked if he could release my new album in America.

I knew that *I'm Nearly Famous* was my strongest album in years. Its lead single, 'Miss You Nights', went Top 20 in Britain, and everybody was raving about its follow-up, 'Devil Woman'. But EMI America had no interest in me. They'd never supported me, and decided they wouldn't bother putting the album out in the US.

Elton heard 'I Can't Ask for Anymore Than You' on the radio and couldn't believe it was me, singing falsetto. Then he heard 'Devil Woman' and loved it. He had his own record label, Rocket Records, and when he heard EMI America were passing on *I'm Nearly Famous*, he called up Peter Gormley and asked to meet us.

Peter and I saw Elton and his manager, John Reid, at their office in London. It was the first time I'd met Elton, and he could not have been friendlier. He got straight to the point: 'I think your album is fantastic, and "Devil Woman" is amazing,' he said. 'I want to release them in America.'

Let me tell you, Elton was a breath of fresh air! He was positive, enthusiastic and passionate about my music, and the album – everything EMI America were not! He was funny, great to talk to and super-excited about how my records might do in the US. It was a complete no-brainer to agree to his plan.

Elton and John Reid asked if I'd be willing to go out to America and do weeks of promo interviews. *That* was music to my ears. You only have a hit if your record label supports you, and I was impressed that they were so committed to getting behind me. 'Of course!' I assured them. 'When do I start?'

So, John Reid fixed me up weeks of interviews in the major US cities, from New York right across to Los Angeles. It was fascinating. Some journalists knew all about my long back story and realised that I had released the first British rock and roll record. Other interviewers hadn't got a clue *who* I was.

John Reid and Elton went all out on the promotional front. They got thousands of button badges made, with my album title on them: I'M NEARLY FAMOUS. And, because Elton knows every celebrity in the world, those badges began appearing in the *most* unlikely places.

Elton always had one pinned to his lapel. Jimmy Page from Led Zeppelin got photographed wearing one. And then, somehow, a picture appeared of *Elizabeth Taylor*, of all people, with an I'M NEARLY FAMOUS badge fastened to her famous chest. I did a double-take when I saw that!

And the campaign worked. *I'm Nearly Famous* got to Number

76 in the US: my first hit album over there. And 'Devil Woman', the single EMI America didn't think even worth releasing, climbed up, and up, and up the *Cashbox* singles chart, week after week, until it peaked at Number 5.* *Amazing!*

While I was doing my interviews in America, Elton was playing a concert tour of stadiums and arenas across the country. We happened to be in Atlanta, Georgia, at the same time. 'Do you want to come and see me play tonight?' he asked me.

'Yes, of course!'

'Good! Come on down, and come backstage to see me afterwards.'

The show was in a huge sports stadium and it was absolutely terrific. Elton was an incredible performer by then. He was so flamboyant, and larger than life, and the crowd loved him. He would play the piano like a demon, then leap on top of it and jump up and down. I was getting flashbacks to Jerry Lee Lewis!

Elton took things even further than Jerry Lee, though, because as well as the rock and roll, and theatrics, he also had gobsmacking clothes! *Such* wild costumes! He had eight-inch silver platform boots, glittery suits, dresses, over-sized spectacles with their own windscreen wipers . . . you name it! It was incredible.

At the end of the show, I went to the stage door to see him, as he had suggested. As I waited, a limousine suddenly swept past outside . . . with Elton in it! He didn't see me, and had forgotten that we'd arranged to meet. I wasn't offended. After a show like that, he needed a good lie-down!

---

* It got to Number 6 on the *Billboard* chart, *Cashbox*'s slightly more important rival – but, obviously, I always tell people the higher placing!

When I returned to England, *I'm Nearly Famous* continued to sell well, both in the UK and America. I would call John Reid's office to check on its sales figures. And it led to Elton inventing a new comedy nickname for me.

Elton has always given his close male friends female nicknames. He says they are their 'drag names', i.e. what they would be called if they were drag queens! He called himself 'Sharon', John Reid 'Joy' and Rod Stewart* 'Phyllis'. His chauffeur was 'Betty' after Betty Driver, who played Betty Turpin on *Coronation Street*.

So, I wasn't totally surprised when Elton began addressing me as 'Sylvia'. But I did ask him how he had chosen it. 'Well, John Reid says that you're always calling the office, asking if your record has gone silver,' he explained. 'So, I thought "Sylvia Disc" might suit you . . .'

America has never really worked out for me, but after 'Devil Woman' did so well there, I wondered if it might be worth giving it another crack. I went to see Peter Gormley, to ask him what he thought.

'Cliff, you've got two choices, son,' he told me. 'If you want to give up Europe, and Southeast Asia, and Australia, and go and live in America, you may have a chance.'

'But why would I have to give up the other places?' I wondered.

'Because there is no way to break America without being

---

* I bumped into Rod Stewart at a charity event a while ago. He said he wished he was starting out on his career today, and asked me if I felt the same. 'No way!' I answered. 'Rod, you and I have sold millions of records! We'd never do *that* now it's all about streaming.'

there,' he replied. 'You have to really want it, and you have to work bloody hard.'

He was right: Elton had spent *a lot* of time in Los Angeles. I thought of trying to do something similar, but I quite quickly decided against it. It seemed crazy to give up so many countries in which I was successful, in the hope of breaking one where I wasn't. And, also, I didn't really want to live in America.

Elton put out my next two albums, *Every Face Tells a Story* and *Green Light*, on Rocket in America, but they didn't do as well, and our arrangement came to an end. We were both so busy that we drifted apart a little, but we still bumped into each other occasionally.

Towards the end of the seventies, a friend invited me for dinner in London. When I got to the restaurant, Elton was also there. It was great to see him and catch up and, as ever, he was riotously entertaining company.

He had been losing his hair for years and had decided to take the plunge and have a hair transplant. Elton had just come back from seeing a specialist in Paris and he wasn't at all embarrassed at sharing the gory details of his painful scalp treatment at the dinner table. 'Well, it looks good – but how does it *feel?*' I asked him.

'How does it feel, Cliff? It feels bloody sore!' he replied, wincing and rubbing his head. 'It hurts!' Elton was to have a few more attempts at transplants over the years, before giving up and wearing wigs. And, you know what? He's never tried to hide the fact, and they suit him, so good for him!

Our paths crossed again in 1986. Elton was making an album,

Leather Jackets, and asked me to duet with him on a track called 'Slow Rivers'. I liked the song when I heard it, so it was an easy decision to say yes. It wasn't one of Elton's most successful albums, but we did release it as a single.

I read one or two interviews that Elton gave around *Leather Jackets'* release. He was very kind and complimentary about me. He told one journalist, 'It's really extraordinary. Cliff opens his mouth to sing, and *this soft voice* comes out.' Well, I *hope* it was a compliment, anyway!

I've never met anyone quite as generous as Elton John. On my forty-sixth birthday, he and I were appearing on a TV show to promote 'Slow Rivers'. When I arrived, Elton handed me a gift-wrapped box. I unwrapped it to find . . . an engraved gold Cartier watch. Heaven only knows how much *that* must have cost!

'Elton!' I said, astonished. 'There is no need to give me this!'

'Well, I just wanted to thank you properly for doing the song,' he said with a smile.*

Elton and I didn't socialise too much for years after that. There was no reason for this, except that we are both super-busy, we live thousands of miles apart from each other, and, well, *life took over*. But they say that a friend in need is a friend indeed – and, by that measure, Elton John is a true friend.

As everybody now knows, in 2014 I was falsely accused of historic sex crimes, a hideous ordeal which the BBC amplified by live-broadcasting a police raid on my apartment in England. I'll

---

* I still wear that Cartier watch. I have two reasons. The first one is that it's an excellent timepiece. The second is that I always hope people will compliment me on it, so I can say, 'Oh, *this*? Yes, it was a gift from Elton John!'

never forget the horrors of that day, and it began a period of my life for which the word 'hellish' is woefully inadequate.

When those awful events began, I went to ground at my home in Portugal. I didn't know, or understand, what was going on, or even what I was accused of having done. I felt like a leper, a pariah: incredibly alone. And the first person – the *very* first – who phoned me on that terrible day of the police raid was Elton John.

Elton had his own grim experience of sex allegations. In the late eighties, the *Sun*, who in my experience do not seem bothered if their stories are true or not, or who they harm, had accused him of sleeping with young rent boys. It was utter lies, and Elton had fought them in court until he got £1million in damages and a front-page apology as part of a settlement.

Elton was in bullish mood when he called. He said that he knew the allegations against me were rubbish, and urged me to fight back against my accusers and the media. I'm not a big fan of the F-word, but Elton has never minded swearing. His memorable advice for me was this: 'Cliff – go for their f***ing throats!'

And I guess that's what I did. My lawyers and I rebutted all of the accusations, the CPS realised that the whole ridiculous case was the work of a fantasist, and I sued the South Yorkshire Police *and* the BBC and got damages from both of them.* But I'll never forget that the first person in my corner was Elton John.

I went to see Elton live in 2018, when he was doing months of shows in Las Vegas. The contrast with the gig I'd seen forty years earlier in Atlanta was amazing. He doesn't charge around

---

* I also got a full apology from the South Yorkshire Police, but I never felt that the BBC really apologised.

stage in silver platform boots or stomp up and down on his piano anymore. He just sits down at the piano and he plays the songs.

Well, that's fair enough. It's called getting old. When I see footage of *my* early years, or even of The Event in 1989, I was running around stage like a maniac! I can't do that anymore, and nor can Elton, but it doesn't matter. Because his songs are so fantastic that his Las Vegas show was still utterly mesmerising.

Just after that, I had a very glamorous trip to see Elton! He was playing a charity dinner in St Petersburg organised by a friend of mine, Richard Caring, who owns The Ivy chain of restaurants. Richard invited me to go and see him, chartered a jet and flew a whole plane-load of people to Russia.

It was a very glitzy evening and a lot of fun. Everybody stood up, and I couldn't see, so when Elton came on, I put two chairs together and stood on them to gawp over all the heads. Elton was great, then after he'd finished, Tina Turner came on, all in black leather, and was fantastic. Now *that* was a good night!

In 2019, I went to the cinema to see the official biopic of Elton's life, *Rocketman*. I thought it was great, and the young guy who played Elton, Taron Egerton, was terrific. I only had one issue with it, and it was the same one as with the Freddie Mercury film and the Elvis movie: *Why don't they use the original music?*

In all of those movies, the actor who played the lead role was fine, but when they came to sing the songs, they didn't sound like Elton, or Freddie, or Elvis. I mean, *how could they?* They are three of the most legendary singers in rock and roll history. You can't expect an actor to just open their mouth and reproduce what they did.

I can understand actors in a stage musical singing their lines, but *films are forever*. If it's a movie, they should mime to the original vocals. If they ever film the Cliff Richard movie – and it would be quite a story, what with one thing and another – I will insist that they do that. I don't want anybody else singing 'Move It' for me!*

As I write, Elton John is on his farewell tour of the world's stadiums. I'd like to go see him one last time, because he is always fantastic – Captain Fantastic, in fact! And yet, I must admit, I wonder how long he will stay retired for.

Elton is seventy-six now, it's been more than half a century since he recorded 'Your Song', and he has definitely earned a good rest, if he wants one! But I wonder if he'll get bored after a while, if he'll miss what they call the smell of the greasepaint and the roar of the crowd, and he'll want to come back. Because it's a lot to give up.

'Retirement' is such a big word. I've thought of stopping playing live, but when my manager, Malcolm Smith, asks, 'Are you going to retire?' I say, 'No, I'm *not* retiring. I'm *stopping*.' Because then, if I get the urge, a year later, to play a week or two somewhere, I could phone him and say, 'Can you try to get me the Albert Hall?'

I wonder if Elton might get that urge, too? I'm guessing that he might.

Ultimately, I still don't know Elton John super-well. People assume we're showbiz pals, and always going out to dinner, but

---

* And I think the public would prefer it, too!

our relationship isn't like that. Because of geography, and our schedules, we don't see each other from one year to the next. I mostly tend to bump into him at charity events, or Royal Command shows.

But I know that, when I *do* see Elton, we'll always give each other a big hug, have a great catch-up, and he'll make me laugh my head off. And I will know that this is the man who helped me to have my greatest success in America, and who stood by me in my hour of need, when it felt like the world was against me.

And that is what I call a *real* friend.

TWENTY-SEVEN

'STAYIN' ALIVE' – THE BEE GEES

My favourite group in the world ... bar none

Some people might find it tough to name their all-time favourite singer. They may change their minds, and go back and forth. I have never done that. Ever since I first heard him, on that fateful May Saturday afternoon in 1956, it's been Elvis. And I am equally definite about the identity of my favourite group of all time.

Because that is The Bee Gees.

I've loved The Bee Gees right since I first became aware of them, back in 1967. They had this cool single with the unusual title of 'New York Mining Disaster 1941'. Then, later that year, they had a terrific Number 1 smash with a song called 'Massachusetts'. And they were both astonishing.

The Bee Gees arrived fully formed. Before they broke through, the Gibb brothers had been singing together for years, and it showed. Their records were so precise and honed that it was miraculous. They didn't have the slightest flaw. It was pop perfection, and it got me right from the off.

Robin was the lead singer in those early days, with his fabulous, tremulous voice, rich with vibrato. Barry and Maurice also both had pitch-perfect falsettos, and the sound they conjured up was out of this world. The production on their records was so immaculate that it appeared to have a glistening sheen.

From the get-go, my love for The Bee Gees had the same root as my love for The Everly Brothers: my passion for harmonies. They took the two-part-harmony thing that Don and Phil had perfected, and broadened it into *three*-part harmonies. It meant more things to go wrong: but they never did. They were *never* out of tune.

I bought The Bee Gees' first two albums, *Bee Gees 1st* and *Horizontal*,* and learned a little more about them. They certainly had an unusual background. Barry, Robin and Maurice were born on the Isle of Man in the 1940s. Their family then moved to Manchester, and the boys formed a skiffle band, The Rattlesnakes.

In 1958, the Gibb family emigrated to Australia under the 'Ten Pound Poms' scheme the Aussie government introduced to increase the country's working population. The brothers began singing between races at a Brisbane speedway track, from the back of a truck being driven around the course!

In their teens, they played holiday resorts, got a record deal and slowly built a reputation in Australia. If you search YouTube, you can find ancient footage of the three of them sweetly

---

* Those were The Bee Gees' first two *international* albums. They had, apparently, made two previous records that were only available in Australia.

harmonising on a 1960 Aussie TV show. They're so young, yet you still hear the beautiful balance of their voices.

They returned to England in 1967, and had their big break-through the same year with 'Massachusetts'. They had another great Number 1 in 1968 with 'I've Gotta Get a Message to You' – *what a song!* – then ticked over until they had their purple patch as part of the mid-seventies disco explosion.

I enjoyed a lot of the disco acts that were around in those days. It came down to the individual song. If the song was good, I liked it, and dance artists such as Kool & The Gang, Chic and Sister Sledge had loads of good songs. Another band that I liked were Earth, Wind & Fire.

I liked to sing along with Earth, Wind & Fire when they came on the radio, but some of the high notes were beyond me! Their singer, Philip Bailey, had an amazing full-chest falsetto at the top end of his voice. It belonged in the female range! They played Barbados a while back. I went to see them, and Philip *still* sounded fantastic.

Those guys were cool but, for me, The Bee Gees stood head and shoulders above all of the other dance and disco groups. *Those harmonies*, again, set them apart. When I heard 'Jive Talkin'' and 'How Deep Is Your Love', they sent shivers down my spine. *Wow!* 'Angelic' doesn't begin to describe their harmonious voices.

It's hard to choose a favourite song from that golden Bee Gees era, but I think I'd go with 'Stayin' Alive'. It was just the song where it all seemed to come together. The beat sounded elastic, *irresistible*, the chorus zinged, and the voices . . . well, words fail me! Angelic? Yeah, and then some. It was *celestial*!

The message of the song also chimes with me. There are times in your life when it feels like the best you can hope to do is to survive: to stay alive. I felt absolutely lost when I had to endure those awful false sex allegations in 2014, but I told myself: 'I *will* survive this!' And, thanks to my faith (and the occasional Bee Gees record), I did.

The Bee Gees' profile went sky-high in 1977 when songs like 'Stayin' Alive', 'Night Fever' and 'More Than a Woman' featured on the soundtrack of *Saturday Night Fever*. That iconic image of John Travolta in his white suit, his finger pointing in the air, was everywhere, and The Bee Gees were just as inescapable. I loved it!

It's hard to believe now, but some rock fans took against disco. They thought it was effeminate. In 1979, at a 'Disco Demolition Night' in Chicago, thousands of people chanted 'Disco sucks!' as a local radio DJ blew up a crate of records by The Bee Gees and others in the interval of a baseball game. The night ended in a riot.

Crikey! How do you *begin* to explain stupidity like that? Especially as there was a far easier solution: *if you don't like disco, don't listen to it! Turn the dial, and tune in to a different radio station!* Or was that too simple for those guys?!

The hysteria surrounding *Saturday Night Fever* passed, as these things do, and The Bee Gees settled down to being quietly excellent in the eighties. They wrote great songs like 'Islands in the Stream', for Kenny Rogers and Dolly Parton, and released the odd cool single like their 1987 Number 1, 'You Win Again'.

I'd occasionally see The Bee Gees perform on TV. Their harmonies were always as impeccable as on the records. To my regret,

I never saw them live. However, I reached out to Barry in 2004. I was recording my *Something's Goin' On* album in America, and I asked if he would be willing to do something on it. I couldn't have been more pleased when he invited me over to a studio in Miami.

Barry wrote a track for me, 'I Cannot Give You My Love'. He also produced it and sang backing vocals on it. *Singing with a Gibb brother? Yes, please!* Well, the only thing better than singing with a Gibb brother is singing with *two* Gibb brothers, so I asked Barry if Robin might be willing to join us.

He smiled. 'Robin doesn't sing on my songs, and I don't sing on his,' he explained, politely. 'That's how we keep them different.' *Oh, well!* It was still an incredible thrill to hear Barry's fabulous falsetto vibrating in my headphones. I released 'I Cannot Give You My Love' as a single, and it went Top 20.

During that session, Barry also wrote and duetted with me on a B-side, 'How Many Sleeps'. We were to work together again. When I made my *Two's Company* duets album in 2006, he and I hooked up to sing together on a haunting version of Sting's 'Fields of Gold'.

In 2009, Cliff Richard & The Shadows were to record our fiftieth anniversary album, *Reunited*, but we were scattered all over the globe: me in Barbados, Brian and Bruce in England, and Hank in Australia. I knew that, by then, Barry had a home studio in Florida, so I phoned him up: 'Can I hire your studio, please?'

The Shadows and I made the album remotely. Barry left me alone to work in the studio during the day, then, in the evenings, I'd go to his house for a coffee or a glass of wine with him, his wife

Linda and their grown-up kids. I got to know Barry a lot better. For all of his success, he's such a normal, laid-back, Mancunian-via-Australia bloke.

I may never have seen The Bee Gees live but, in 2012, I saw Barry do a solo show at the Hard Rock Hotel and Casino in Hollywood, Florida. I went with a female lawyer friend, Pat, who is also a Bee Gees nut. And Barry's voice had not deteriorated in the slightest. The whole show was unbelievable.

Pat and I had aftershow backstage passes, and when I saw Barry, despite having worked with him and knowing him quite well by now, I became a total over-awed fanboy.

'*HiBarrynowIknowwhyIthinktheBeeGeesarethebestbandinthe-world!*'* I gabbled at him. 'Yes, me too!' squeaked an equally excited Pat.

I'll always love The Bee Gees. They made the best dance music ever – and, despite my great age, I still love dancing! On one of my tours, a few years ago, I was told by my tour manager to take it easy and rest my voice between the shows. So each night, after the gig, I'd retire to my hotel room early.

The final night of the tour was different. *Time to let rip!* I headed down to a club with eight of my dancers, all at least half a century younger than me. Well, come 3am, I was still out on the dance floor . . . and where were they? Sitting in a corner, drinking! They couldn't keep up with me!

Sadly, not all The Bee Gees survive. Maurice had a heart attack and died in 2003. Robin passed away in 2012. On my short,

---

* Whenever anyone ever says anything like that to me, and about me, I'm always tempted to joke, 'Thank you, you have terrific taste!'

open-air tour of British landmarks such as Lincoln Castle and Greenwich Old Royal Naval College in 2017, I sang one of Robin's songs, 'Don't Cry Alone'. I found it very emotionally affecting.

Seeing so many great music artists of my generation – and younger – pass away is poignant for me. Well, that's just the age I am at now. Even *I* will go at some point, although who knows when that will be? All you can do is, as they say, keep calm and carry on. And, if you're like me, make a joke about it.

I sometimes tell people about the new eating regime that I began twenty years or so ago, where I only eat food that's right for my blood type. 'Oh, really? What's it done for you?' they ask. And I reply, 'Ask me on my 150th birthday!'

Well, whatever age I go at, The Bee Gees will be my favourite band until the end. Because of that, I'm delighted to learn a biopic movie is currently being made about their life and career. It should be tremendous: Sir Kenneth Branagh has been involved in the filming, and Barry Gibb is executive producer.

I can't wait to see it! But, I've gotta get a message to Barry, or to anybody else involved in the movie: *Please. Use. The. Bee Gees.' Original. Music!* As I said, *film is forever*. Don't ask three actors, however good, to reproduce the best harmonies in the history of pop! Because, no matter how hard they try, they won't be able to match the vocal sound of The Bee Gees.

But I'll still go along to see it, either way!

TWENTY-EIGHT
'I HONESTLY LOVE YOU'
– OLIVIA NEWTON-JOHN

My Livvy, from the day we met until the end

Some words get badly misused, and 'soulmate' is a great example. I know there are people who appear willing to describe somebody as their 'soulmate' if they merely get on quite well. Well, if I've ever had a *true* soulmate, in the course of my long life in music and in show business, it was Olivia Newton-John.

I first met Livvy in around 1969. She had been born in England, but grew up in Australia (another of those Ten Pound Poms!). She'd returned to England in the mid-sixties to try to launch a music career. At the end of that decade, she formed a female singing duo called Pat and Olivia with an Australian friend, Pat Carroll.

I remember seeing them singing on a TV show. Pat was also a dancer, so she had choreographed their dance routine. They were two gorgeous young women, with fabulous hair and, to cap it all, they could actually sing in tune! So, naturally, I was interested when Peter Gormley told me he had taken them under his wing, and was to manage them.

'Oh, what are they going to do first?' I asked him.

'I don't know,' Peter said. 'Do you want to use them as your backing singers?'

Yes, please! I was about to do a short tour of the Far East and thought they would be perfect for it. So, Peter introduced me to Pat and Olivia, we had a lovely chat, and we headed off to Japan together. We were also lined up to play some dates in Germany.

Pat, Olivia and I got on famously from day one. They were both such fun, sunny, easy-going people to be around. Livvy had this great Aussie accent – 'G'day, Cliff!' – and a smile that would light up the room. She also had this exuberant, loud, happy laugh, the sort that made you join in as soon as you heard it.

Olivia and Pat told me that they liked my 'good manners'. I wasn't quite sure what they meant at first, and asked Olivia to explain. 'Well, if you're driving me in your car, Cliff, when you park, you always jump out of the car and run round to my side to open my door for me,' she said. 'You're the only guy I know who does that!'

Really? That was second nature to me! My dad had taught me to do it. Likewise, if I walked down the pavement with a woman, I always took care to walk on the outside, in case a car drove through a puddle and splashed their clothes. I still do. Dad had drummed that into me, as well.

'There's more,' laughed Livvy. She and Pat also liked that, when we went for dinner, I stood up if one of them went to the bathroom, and did the same when they returned. We had one meal with the band where I was the only guy doing it at the start. By the end, every bloke at the table was jumping to their feet! Ha!

I still do that today, as well. Again, it's just the way I was brought up: *if a lady leaves the table, stand up as she goes!* Maybe some women today may not like it, or think it implies they're the weaker sex, but I would certainly never mean it that way, or want to offend anyone. For me, it's just being respectful and polite.

Olivia, Pat and I had a great time on those tours. Our voices worked like a dream together – and we had such a laugh! During a show in Germany, I noticed that a lot of male members of the audience were constantly gazing past my left shoulder. And, when I looked behind me, I saw why.

Pat and Livvy had moved their mics closer to the front of the stage, and they were doing some great dance moves. So, the next night, unknown to them, I had their mics moved to behind the grand piano. When I was introduced, I came on, all smiles, and opened the lid of the piano. They disappeared from view!

Well, I let my glamorous backing singers stew for thirty seconds or so, and then put the lid back down. Let me tell you, we have laughed at that episode so many times over the years!

Pat had to go back to Australia for a while because she had some visa issue. While she was there, she married John Farrar, the guitarist and singer who was to play with Hank and Bruce as Marvin, Welch & Farrar. And, when everyone was back in England, Olivia was to have her own romance with one of that band.

Livvy began dating Bruce Welch. They were two of my favourite people, so if they made each other happy, I was pleased for them. And those two were already an item in 1970, when

Olivia began appearing as a regular special guest on my *It's Cliff Richard* TV show, along with Hank Marvin and Una Stubbs.

This came about because Livvy had a new single and Peter Gormley suggested she might perform it on one of my shows. Of course! Well, I've often joked since that Olivia came on for one show, and stayed for eight. 'I just couldn't get rid of the woman!' I laugh. But, believe me, I didn't try.

Because Olivia was a natural for telly. She exuded that same natural, ingenuous positivity as she did in normal life. Her upbeat nature lit up the screen, and everybody on the programme loved her – as did the viewers! It was no surprise that her musical interludes became one of the weekly highlights.

It was Peter Gormley's idea that Olivia should sing Bob Dylan's 'If Not for You' on the show, and it was a very good one! I've never been a huge Dylan fan, but it was one of the rare things he'd written that was actually a *pop song*, with a tune, and Livvy brought it to life. She turned it into a blinding ray of sunshine.

It was such a winning number, and her record label naturally wanted to put it out as a single. Bruce and John Farrar produced it together, and it began flying out of the shops. It zoomed up the chart to Number 7 in Britain and was a big hit in America: a Number 1 on the *Billboard* 'easy-listening' chart!*

This was the start of an exciting time for Olivia, when she really broke through. In Britain, she had big follow-up hits with 'Banks of the Ohio' and a C&W song by John Denver, 'Take Me Home, Country Roads'. Then, in 1973, she had a Top 10 hit in the

---

* I've no idea *what* Bob Dylan made of one of his songs topping an 'easy-listening' chart, but I'm sure he enjoyed the royalties!

US with 'Let Me Be There', a song that also won her a Grammy (and was written by a former Shadow, John Rostill, who had replaced 'Licorice' Locking on bass in my band in 1963).

Livvy was suddenly a big star, but sadly her relationship with Bruce was not to last. They broke up after two or three years. It must have been difficult, for both of them, when the relationship ended, and it was certainly sad for all of us when they split up.

Because Olivia and I had such a natural chemistry on my TV show, the newspapers would sometimes speculate that *we* had something going on. We didn't. We were just really, really close friends. We loved each other, but we weren't in love, in a romantic sense – and that was *why* we could be really, really close friends.

In any case, *everyone* was in love with Olivia! That was just the effect that she had on people. Men would go weak at the knees and tongue-tied, and women loved her fun nature and wanted to be her friend. The attraction was her naturalness, I think. People just fell over themselves to be near her.

It was the same on stage. Olivia was a very attractive, and sensual, performer, but a lot of her appeal was that she wasn't trying to be aggressively sexy. She'd wear a demure, buttoned-up dress, and look sexier than Madonna,* say, in her giant pointed brassieres! I guess Livvy just knew that less is more.

Livvy and I stayed thick as thieves as she carried on having hits, both in Britain and the US, in the early seventies. And, in September 1974, she came on the *It's Cliff Richard* show again, and

---

* I have nothing against Madonna, who I think is a very good singer and pop star. She just has a . . . different approach.

she sang a song that was to change her life and catapult her into superstardom. Because it went to Number 1 in America.

'I Honestly Love You' is my favourite out of all of Olivia Newton-John's songs. John Farrar produced it again, and it is a masterpiece. It has an incredible smooth flow throughout, the lyrics are so poignant, and Olivia's voice is crystal-clear, as it rises from a whisper to ring out like a bell. It's unbelievable, as I'm sure you agree.

People underestimate what a good singer Olivia Newton-John was. Critics would sometimes carp and say she had 'a small voice'. *What does that even mean?* Who, out of all of us, had a *big* voice? None of us were Pavarotti! Olivia's singing was always impeccably in tune, and after vocal coaching it was even stronger.

Ironically, it was the quality that made Livvy so attractive that led some people to underrate her. Because she had the image of a smiley, happy-go-lucky girl next door, critics got her wrong and thought she wasn't a serious artist. Well, I reckon a Number 1 in America was a good way to put *that* misconception right!

Olivia knew how to use her voice to convey emotion and passion. She might have sung softly, but it had a powerful impact. 'I Honestly Love You' was a song about love not working out that *ached* with meaning. I think the nearest I have to a song like that is 'Miss You Nights'. They have the same feel, and yearning.

After that huge hit, Olivia moved to live in California. I missed her, and yet the distance didn't damage our friendship. We talked on the phone all the time, and every time I was over there, I'd visit her. When I did my 1976 interview tour, for *I'm Nearly Famous* and 'Devil Woman', she threw a party for me.

The wonderful thing about Livvy was that, despite her huge success in America, and the fact she was world-famous, *she never changed*. She was always exactly the same each time I met her – that big smile, and 'G'day, Cliff!' – and totally unaffected. And that was just as true after she had her huge movie break.

When Olivia told me that she was going to star in *Grease*, with John Travolta, I was delighted for her. It sounded a fantastic project for her (plus, a musical that was set at the birth of rock and roll? Talk about right up my street!). And when the finished movie came out in 1978, the world went crazy for it.

Grease could hardly have had a bigger impact. When it was released, it was the highest-grossing film musical of all time. It received five Golden Globe nominations – including one for Olivia, as best actress. Her duet with John Travolta, 'You're the One that I Want', was Number 1 for *nine weeks* in Britain. *Extraordinary!**

I told the story in *The Dreamer* of how, to my huge shame, I never got around to seeing *Grease* when it came out. I can't even imagine now why that would be. In fact, I didn't see it until Livvy asked me to accompany her to the London premiere of a twentieth-anniversary reissue of the movie in 1998.

I didn't want to tell Olivia that I'd never seen it, but I was so impressed by the film that I accidentally blew my own cover! As she and I left the screening, I excitedly told her, 'Wow! That was so much better than my expectations . . .'

---

* Both 'You're the One that I Want' and Olivia's follow-up solo single from *Grease*, 'Hopelessly Devoted to You', were written by our mate, John Farrar. Largely due to them, John is one of the twenty best-selling songwriters of all time!

Oops!

Olivia looked at me as if she should be cross with me, but she really wanted to laugh. '*Expectations?* You *had* seen it before, hadn't you, Cliff?'

'No!' I admitted. And we both fell about.

I was so blown away by *Grease* largely because Olivia was so amazing in it. She had really been an unknown quantity as an actress when they had hired her for that huge role opposite John Travolta. Sure, a lot of singers can also act – but can they act well enough to carry off a leading role in an A-list movie?

Well, Livvy could, and then some! She was totally convincing as Sandy, the sweet and wholesome Australian teenager who moves to America, enrols at Rydell High School and falls in love with John Travolta's bad-boy rock and roller, Danny Zucco. The two of them had an amazing onscreen chemistry.

It was inspired casting, and I think one reason it worked was Olivia's own public image. Because she *was* seen as a naïve girl-next-door, it made her believable as the innocent, unworldly Sandy – and her transformation, at the end of the film, into a black-leather-wearing, gum-chewing vamp all the more spectacular!

After that huge box-office success, Hollywood naturally very quickly asked Livvy to make more movies. She signed up to star in a musical film fantasy, *Xanadu*, in 1980 (its theme tune was to be a UK Number 1 for her). She was shooting the film when she put in a transatlantic phone call to me.

'G'day, Cliff!' it began, as usual. 'Look, I'm making this movie, and they want to release a single from it. But there's a problem . . .'

'Oh, really?' I replied casually, thinking, *I know what might be coming here – and I hope I'm right!*

'My co-star can't sing.'

'Oh no, poor guy!' I said, trying (and probably failing) to hide my delight. In truth, I was almost punching the air!

'So, I want to ask you a favour,' Olivia continued. 'Would *you* sing it with me?'

Livvy said that the song was called 'Suddenly' and was written by John Farrar. *And that was enough for me!* I normally have a hard-and-fast rule when it comes to singing duets, whether they're with Elton John or Van Morrison. I have to hear the song, and I have to like it. Well, this time, I broke my own rule.

'I'd love to do it!' I told Olivia. 'Just tell me when, and where!'

Well, 'when' was a few days later, and 'where' was . . . in someone's garage, in Los Angeles! John Farrar rigged up a small studio in his engineer's garage, and we did the song right there. It was a lot of fun. We had to abort a couple of takes, due to the noise of huge trucks thundering by, but the session went really well.

And the song was great. It reminded me, yet again, just how well Olivia's and my voices melded together. On 'Suddenly', they just seemed to flow into each other utterly effortlessly. Please forgive me but, at the risk of being immodest, I genuinely believe it is one of the best male-female duets ever.*

'Suddenly' went Top 20 on both sides of the Atlantic – and even jeopardised my anonymity in America! Because I never broke in the US, I can walk around unrecognised. But after

---

* I struggle to think of another duet that I like as much – except for maybe 'The Prayer' by Andrea Bocelli and Celine Dion. That always has me in tears.

'Suddenly' hit big, I bought a shirt in a New York clothes store with my credit card and found the sales assistant staring hard at me.

'Excuse me, but are you *the* Cliff Richard?' he asked.

'Yes,' I confessed. 'But how do you know me?'

'Oh, I'm a big fan of Olivia Newton-John!'

Olivia married in 1984 and became a mother, to Chloe, in 1986. She and I carried on talking regularly, and meeting up whenever we could. In 1992, the two of us were in Monaco, to appear at an awards show. We sang 'Suddenly' together, and then had dinner on a boat. It was a terrific evening.

But the following morning, Olivia called me up, sounding notably more subdued than usual. She got straight to the point. 'Cliff, I've seen a doctor, he's got my test results, and he's just called and given me the diagnosis,' she said. 'I have breast cancer.'

It was devastating news, and yet the way that Livvy tackled her disease was so typical of her. She threw herself into her debilitating treatment and, while she naturally had to pull back from her normal show-business activities, she made an album about what she was going through.

Olivia recorded *Gaia: One Woman's Journey*, chronicling her disease and her fight to overcome it. She wrote all the songs herself, with titles like 'Why Me' and 'Not Gonna Give in to It', and co-produced the album. It was intended to help women going through the same thing. And I'm sure it did. I was *so* proud of her.

At the end of her treatment, Olivia was declared in remission and clear of cancer. But she was still keeping a low profile in 1995, when I was getting ready to star in my theatre show of *Heathcliff*.

So, I decided to call in the favour that she still owed me from 'Suddenly' and coax Livvy a little more back into the limelight.

I needed someone to sing with me on a single, a duet between Heathcliff and Cathy, to promote the musical. It was called 'Had to Be' and Olivia was the *only* person I had in mind for it. She agreed straight away, we recorded it in John Farrar's home studio, and Olivia nailed it first time. As always.

Olivia had carried on making records but she hadn't toured for fifteen years or so. At the start of 1998, I was celebrating forty years in show business with a few dates in Australia, so I decided to see if I could do something about that. I asked her to be my special guest, sing a few songs of her own, and duet with me.

Livvy seemed a little startled at first: 'I can't do it! I haven't sung live in years!' But once I'd talked her round, she absolutely loved it. Our dates went great, and when they'd finished, she went off on tour with one of Australia's biggest stars, John Farnham.* Then she did a big tour on her own. You couldn't stop her!

By now, Olivia was in the position where she could pick and choose what she did, and she did some interesting projects in the 2010s. She made movies, appeared in US TV shows, including *Glee*, and performed at Sydney Opera House with the Sydney Symphony Orchestra. She really seemed to be living her best life.

In 2013, her cancer came back. Olivia kept it low-profile this time, but she kept us in touch with how she was doing, and she beat it again. But things looked more ominous in 2017, when it

---

* I think John Farnham is *such* an underrated singer outside of Australia. If I could clone certain bits of his singing voice and add them to mine, I'd do it tomorrow!

returned for a third time. By now, her medics told her that it had spread to her lower back, and progressed to stage four.

Yet she would *not* let it beat her. On the phone, she was the same upbeat, cheery Livvy as ever: 'G'day, Cliff!' She didn't complain about the pain she was in when we hung out. And in 2019 she signed up to a fun live project: reuniting with John Travolta for three *Grease*-themed shows at open-air theatres in Florida.

These were to be events where the T-Birds boys' gang from the original cast led the audience in singalongs of the songs from the movie. *Fantastic!* I happened to be in Florida just before the shows, and Olivia invited me to go to lunch with her and catch up.

Well, I always loved one-on-one time with Olivia, and we had a terrific time, as usual. At the end, we were just saying goodbye when Livvy asked me: 'Oh, one more thing, Cliff. Will you join me, John Travolta and some of his team for dinner tomorrow?' And I jumped at the chance!

I had no idea what to expect when I met John Travolta. I'd always figured, *Well, if Olivia likes him, he must be OK*, because, for all her niceness, Livvy didn't suffer fools. Well, John was phenomenal to get to know, the absolute epitome of charm. I've rarely met anybody that famous who has stayed so resolutely ordinary.

We met at a restaurant, and John was completely bald. He didn't have a hair on his head, and yet he was stunning. He looked so masculine: I remember thinking, *If I ever lose my hair, I hope I look like that!* And he had absolutely no side to him at all. He was bowing to Olivia at the table, and making her laugh.

We all enjoyed that dinner so much that the time just flew

by. We had such a good laugh. I could certainly see why Olivia held John in such high regard – and now I agreed with her! Even so, when one of his management team gave a speech at the table about the two of them, I made a cheeky interjection.

'Well, John is Olivia's best friend . . .' the guy said.

'Ahem! Her second-best friend!' I corrected him. Everybody laughed.

The day after that dinner was the first sing-along *Grease* show. I had a prior commitment so I couldn't go, which was a pity. But I saw footage on the local news of them arriving at the theatre. Olivia looked radiant, as always, and John had, overnight, sprouted a full head of hair! A Danny Zucco quiff, no less!

Wow! Now, that was what you CALL a good wig! It looked totally natural.*

Yet in recent years, it was evident that Olivia was struggling with her cancer. But, again, she didn't complain. Olivia never liked talking about 'fighting her cancer'. The nearest she would say was, 'I'm trying to rid myself of something I don't want in my body.' And I guess that, towards the end, she just knew it was an uneven struggle that she couldn't win.

On my eighty-first birthday, in October 2021, Olivia wrote me a lovely email. It could not have been more affecting. She said the sweetest things to me, the kind of things she and I had always

---

* I've thought of getting a wig made for my bad-hair days. At the end of a show, when I'm asking the audience to applaud my band, it bugs the hell out of me if I glance down at my silhouette, in the spotlight, and see a tuft of hair sticking up. A wig would make that one less thing to worry about!

known about each other, but had left unsaid. And it really took me aback. Livvy wrote:

> *You are such a special person and have meant so much to me in my life, both professionally and privately . . . I wanted to take a moment in your special day to tell you how grateful I am for your friendship and mentorship. To have known you for most of my life, and to call you my friend.*
> *Love you very much. Olivia*

What an email to receive. I felt my tears welling up as I read it. I went to find my good friend John McElynn in the next room. 'I've just had the loveliest email from Olivia,' I said. 'Let me tell you what she said.' And John listened closely as I read it to him.

'She's saying goodbye, Cliff,' he said.

'What?!'

'She knows that she's going. And she's saying goodbye.'

Of course, as soon as John said that, I knew that he was right. And the realisation was just heartbreaking. I freely confess that I was in tears.

I called Olivia just three weeks before she died. When she picked up, I said hello. To hear the gale of laughter – 'G'day, Cliff!' – and the cheerful voice that followed, you'd have thought she was still in rude health. She was still the bubbly, joyous force of nature that she always was. That she had always been.

She passed on 8 August 2022. I didn't get a phone call. I heard it on the TV news: *'The singer and actress, Olivia Newton-John, has died at the age of seventy-three . . .'* I'd known it was coming but it was still a devastating shock. I felt the kind of emptiness you only get when someone very special passes. *When you lose a soulmate.*

Tania, my personal assistant in London, phoned me up. 'Cliff, the press and the media are all over us,' she said. 'They want a statement on Olivia's death.' I knew that I just couldn't do it. 'I can't look into a camera and talk about Olivia right now,' I said. 'There is no way I'd get through it.'

Instead, I wrote something for my Facebook page. We found a photo of Olivia and me hugging each other, when she came on stage with me at the Albert Hall, on my seventy-fifth birthday, to duet on 'Suddenly'. It's a nice picture: we look so happy in it. And I wrote this:

> *I find myself at a loss as to what to say. Death . . . well, he is a vicious enemy, and all of us will be taken by him. But all of us are not taken by him at the same time and so while Olivia remains in our minds and memories, she remains very much alive!*

I remembered how Livvy had made music to help other cancer sufferers, and I paid tribute to how she had remained so upbeat as she endured the disease. I talked of our last phone conversation, just three weeks earlier, and how she had still been her 'bright, positive self'.

> *From now on, I will only believe that our gorgeous Olivia simply stopped living. I will miss her. The world will miss her, so let's all keep her alive in our hearts and memories. God bless you Livvy. Rest in Peace . . . Cliff xxx*

John Travolta also paid Olivia a lovely tribute. He said:

My dearest Olivia, you made all of our lives so much better. Your impact was incredible. I love you so much. We will see you down the road again and we will all be together again. Yours from the first moment I saw you, and forever! Your Danny, your John.

I thought that was beautiful when I read it.

Olivia's family held a small, private memorial service for her in California, a few weeks after she died. The actress Susan George and I flew in for it, from England.

We were hoping to speak for a while about what she had meant to us, but the event was on a tight schedule, so we only got thirty seconds each.

As you would expect, it was a very emotional gathering as we all said goodbye to Olivia. John Farrar read a tribute, and he broke down halfway through and had a cry, before collecting himself and carrying on. Well, *good for John.* We all felt for him. It just demonstrated how much Olivia meant to all of us.

I thought the tone of the gathering was a little more sombre than Olivia would have liked, with her sense of fun, so I dug out my old joke: 'I asked her on my TV show, then I couldn't get rid of the woman!' Pat Carroll laughed.

'Thank goodness you made people laugh!' she told me later. 'Livvy would have liked that!'

I had hoped to sing one of the songs in this book at the service: 'Let It Be Me' by The Everly Brothers. Because, as I said, everybody who met her loved Olivia: men *and* women. So, I thought it might be nice to sing it for her, and to dedicate it to all the people in the world who had loved her throughout her career.

Sadly, it was not to be. John Easterling, Olivia's husband, said he would rather I didn't, as it might be 'uncomfortable'. I'm not sure if John had totally understood the reason that I wanted to do so. Well, I have to respect his wishes: he was her husband, and he was grieving. But I thought it was a shame.

I *was* able to say a better farewell to Livvy, though. I performed a tribute to her on my 2022 BBC Christmas TV special. I wanted to duet on 'Suddenly', and contemplated asking Kylie Minogue to sing it with me, or Delta Goodrem, but neither of them were around. And then, I had an even better idea.

If I'm going to sing 'Suddenly', I thought, *it has to be with Olivia.* And so, we took her vocal from that duet we did at the Albert Hall, on my seventy-fifth birthday, and I sang live with it. We showed footage from that 2015 night, and from our 1980 video for the song, plus photographs going back fifty years of the two of us together.

I have to admit, I'm still finding it difficult to get over losing Livvy. It remains an awful shock. I still tear up when I think I'll never hear that cheery voice say, 'G'day, Cliff!' again. But one of the great things about being a Christian is that your faith sustains you. You know, in your heart, that *death is not the end*.

We will meet again. I'm sure of it.

TWENTY-NINE
'ROLLING IN THE DEEP'
– ARETHA FRANKLIN

The Queen of Soul (and a courtier in a pith helmet)

When I first started going to America, at the start of the sixties, I wouldn't always be able to sleep when I got there. The jet-lag would kick in, and I'd have a sense of excitement – *Wow! I'm in America! Me! Right now!* So, I would sometimes get up, go out and walk around the streets in the early hours, soaking it all in.

I was doing that in New York City one time when I stumbled across a record store in Manhattan that seemed to stay open all night. I walked in and got talking to the young guy behind the counter. He was very friendly, and once he found out I was a singer, from England, he started talking to me about new US music.

The guy recommended one or two upcoming artists and I bought their albums off him on spec, without hearing them, and played them when I got home to the UK. They were terrific. I went back the next time I was in New York, and the same guy had another suggestion for me: 'Have you heard of Aretha Franklin?'*

I hadn't, but I bought the album he recommended, *Aretha*, and carefully carried it home across the Atlantic. And, when I played it, it absolutely blew me away.

I didn't know anything about Aretha Franklin, but the power of her vocal stopped me in my tracks. Its strength was amazing. The Shadows and I had cut our teeth on big, bluesy songs, and Aretha clearly came out of that area. She could throw her voice anywhere she wanted, and hit the note spot-on every time.

It was impossible to listen and not think, *Wow! What a voice!* And, after that, I listened out for Aretha Franklin. She released a load of jazz standards throughout the sixties, such as 'Runnin' out of Fools', but they only just crept into the bottom half of the *Billboard* 100. That all changed in 1967.

Aretha changed record labels, and released a full-on R&B and soul album named *I Never Loved a Man the Way I Love You*. It was a phenomenal record. Her vocal soared to new heights. The album gave her a Top 10 US hit with the title track . . . and then a Number 1 with its follow-up, a ferocious song called 'Respect'.

Her jazzy records had earned her a cult following but now, suddenly, *everybody* knew about Aretha Franklin. And quite right, too! She could sing anything she wanted because her voice was so versatile and had so much freedom. She had a four-octave range, which really is absolutely extraordinary.

---

* I made late-night trips to see this record-store guy for years, whenever I was in New York. He was an amazing conduit to new talent for me, including, a few years later, introducing me to the music of the great Bonnie Raitt.

'Respect' was her first Top 10 hit in Britain. Other terrific songs followed in its wake, such as '(You Make Me Feel Like) A Natural Woman', 'Chain of Fools' and the amazing 'I Say a Little Prayer'. People began calling her the Queen of Soul and it was a title that she totally deserved. She was the ruler.

So, you can imagine how I felt, in August 1970, when the producers of my *It's Cliff Richard* TV series informed me that they had managed to book Aretha Franklin to appear on the show.

This was a *serious* coup for us. It is possible that Aretha had heard of me, but it is probably unlikely, as I'd never broken America. More likely, her management just thought it was a good idea for her to promote her new record on a Saturday-night prime-time BBC1 show. *Well, who cares? We'd got her!*

We had other big stars on *It's Cliff Richard* over the years – Elton John, Labi Siffre, Petula Clark – but I must admit that Aretha Franklin is the one that lives on in my memory. Yet, despite my admiration for her, I didn't feel nervous meeting her. I rarely get nervous when I meet new people. Luckily, that's just the way I am.

Aretha sang 'I Say a Little Prayer' on *It's Cliff Richard*, as well as her new single at the time, which was an old Ben E. King song called 'Don't Play That Song (You Lied)'. You can still see that performance on YouTube today. Unfortunately, this means that you can also still see me introducing it!

Aretha followed one of the comedy skits on the show, so I was still in costume for it as I introduced her. It meant that I was wearing a pith helmet, had a curly fake moustache scrawled under my nose, and was clutching a balloon, as I declared, in a put-on Cockney accent: 'Aretha! Franklin!'

Ah, well! I could have been wearing a clown costume and deely boppers, and it wouldn't have detracted from the magnificence of what followed! In a chiffon top and hoop earrings, and with a fantastic Afro, Aretha sat at a piano and unleashed a vocal that lifted all of us in the studio into the stratosphere.

The funny thing is that if you play it back now, on YouTube, it sounds tinny. Well, that was the *last* thing it was close-up! Backed by three grooving backing singers, Aretha's range was unbelievable. She didn't even need to take a breath to hit the top notes. The song, the *music*, appeared to flow through her.

I watched transfixed. I had absolutely no doubt that I was in the presence of greatness. At the end of the song, I went on, held Aretha's hand and raised her arm to take the studio audience's applause. I still have a photograph of that moment, and I treasure it. Thank goodness I'd taken my pith helmet off.

Unfortunately, I didn't get to spend any time with Aretha on the show. Like a lot of American acts, she came in, did her songs, and got out. It was a shame, really. I'd love to have been able to chat with her, and maybe even gone to dinner. Just *imagine* being able to say, '*Oh, I know Aretha Franklin! We hung out once!*'

Well, no matter. At least I got to hear that unbelievable voice close-up. And I must be honest – I may not have been nervous *meeting* Aretha Franklin, but I *certainly* would have been nervous if I'd attempted to sing with her! Because I'm not sure that I would have been able to cope with that.

I'm a pretty game character, and I'm sure I would have

conquered my nerves and given a duet a go, but would I have measured up? In one corner, Aretha Franklin, with her four-octave range! In the other, Cliff Richard, who might have three octaves on a good day, but can barely reach the top or bottom ones!*

It's bizarre, really, that the woman known as the Queen of Soul never signed to Tamla Motown. It just never worked out that way, although I believe that Berry Gordy described Aretha as 'part of the Motown family'. She would certainly have fitted perfectly into that stable of soul giants.

Over the years, I've bought *so* many records by female Motown artists such as Martha & The Vandellas, Gladys Knight & The Pips, and Diana Ross & The Supremes. In fact, I met Diana Ross once. It was in an airport lounge, years after she'd gone solo. She was friendly, and *didn't* insist that I called her Miss Ross.

Aretha's career went a different route. In the eighties, her biggest hits in Britain were duets: 'Sisters Are Doin' It for Themselves' with the Eurythmics, and a huge 1987 Number 1, 'I Knew You Were Waiting (For Me)', with George Michael. Yet the song I have chosen for this book comes from much later. It's an Adele cover.

I first heard Adele, like everybody else, when her debut album, *19*, was hitting Number 1 and breaking sales records in 2008. I quite liked it without thinking it was extraordinary. It's one of those instances where I can see that somebody is very good, and talented, but at the same time, I'm not a fan.

I'll never deny that Adele has a good voice. I've never heard her sing a bum note. But I grew up listening to Ella Fitzgerald,

---

* I would feel the same about attempting a duet with Mariah Carey. She also has a voice so fabulous that it is intimidating.

Etta James and Aretha, and Adele just doesn't do it for me in the way that they did. But she has sold millions of records, and *any* artist with huge record sales is great for our industry.*

While we're talking about Adele, I was perplexed, at the start of 2022, when she postponed a Las Vegas residency the day before it was due to begin. She said that she wasn't happy with the staging of the show, and she didn't feel able to go ahead with it until it was completely right.

Well, I don't get that. *How could she only realise the day before the show?!* When I go on tour, I rehearse for weeks beforehand. I talk with the sound guys, the lighting guys, the staging guys – everybody. My next tour is eight months away, as I write, and I'm planning it *now*! I get everything nailed down in advance.

I thought Adele pulling the dates so late must have been a big disappointment for her fans, who'd not only paid for tickets, but probably also shelled out for flights and booked time off work. But she offered refunds for tickets and for accommodation at the venue, Caesars Palace, and the show got great reviews when it went ahead. I guess that's what matters.

Adele has got *one* song that I like a lot. It's called 'Rolling in the Deep' and was on her second album, *21*. When I first heard it on the radio, I didn't realise that it was by Adele, so I began trying to track it down. I kept typing 'We could have had it all' into Google, and getting nowhere. It was frustrating!

---

* I felt similarly about Amy Winehouse. She could certainly sing, and I've met so many people who loved her that I feel left out! But . . . you can't like everyone. Does it *matter* that I'm not a fan? No! Also, I didn't like the lyrics of her song about not going to rehab: 'No, no, no!' A lot of people *need* rehab to survive.

When I *did* track it down, I got hold of the song and listened to it now and again. Then, three years later, at a tour rehearsal, I was talking to one of my backing singers, Suzie Furlonger, who sang with me for five years before leaving to start a family. I mentioned to Suzie how much I liked 'Rolling in the Deep'.

'Have you heard Aretha Franklin's version?' she asked.

'*Really? Aretha* has sung it?'

'Yep!' Suzie played Aretha's version, loudly, through our speakers. And it was fabulous. It was quite early to cover a song which had been such a huge hit so recently, but Aretha had made it her own. She unleashed that incredible octave range on 'Rolling in the Deep' and completely reimagined it.

Aretha's singing style is totally different from Adele's. I guess I shouldn't say that her version is *better* than the original, but what I *can* safely say is that I enjoy it more, due to a couple of beautiful high notes Aretha threw in. Let's face it, her voice has forever struck a chord deep inside of me. It always will.

I'd like to sing 'Rolling in the Deep' one day. I think it's a great rock and roll song. I'd love to record it in Nashville, with the band I use there. We'd keep the melody, of course, but work out a new arrangement that would suit my voice. If we do it, maybe not everyone will like it . . . but I will!

Sadly, the great Aretha Franklin died in 2018, at the age of seventy-six. It's a measure of what a colossal figure she was in American music and culture that Stevie Wonder and Jesse Jackson visited her on her deathbed. Former president Barack Obama paid tribute, saying that she had 'helped to define the American experience'.

You know what? I think it's true. Aretha Franklin had one of the greatest voices in music history. She truly was the Queen of Soul, and I shall forever be proud and honoured that, one evening in 1970, I was able to witness her unique talent close-up, and introduce her, on British TV, to millions of enthralled viewers.

Even if I *was* holding a balloon and wearing a fake moustache and a pith helmet.

THIRTY
'IT IS WELL' — SHEILA WALSH
(FEATURING CLIFF RICHARD)

To help me feel well in my soul ... even
on a desert island

As I explained earlier in this book, there was a time in my career when I didn't feel able to be both a pop star and a Christian. I didn't think that show business was an appropriate calling for someone who had welcomed Jesus into his life, and I wasn't sure whether my fans would accept me singing religious songs.

Thankfully, those doubts have long since passed. I am just as comfortable singing spiritual numbers and gospel as I am doing secular songs and rock and roll. Some of my favourite tunes, in my head full of music, are Christian songs ... including this one, with a lovely lady whom I first met more than forty years ago.

When I first started doing gospel tours in the late sixties, I cast around for artists to play with me. Initially, a guy called Dave Pope – naturally, we all called him The Pope! – would play support when I did my spiritual shows with Cindy Kent and The Settlers, and my on-stage interviews with Bill Latham.

I was always on the lookout for talented new Christian musicians, though. And I was visiting a minister in Cobham, in around 1978, when he introduced me to a friend who was staying with him, Norman Miller. We talked about my gospel shows and Norman said, 'I think you should meet my wife, Sheila.'

How right he was! Sheila was a young Scottish woman who was just finishing studying music and theology, and also sang in a Christian group called The Oasis.* She was also involved with a spiritual group called Youth for Christ, who were similar to a movement called The Crusaders, whose meetings I often spoke at.

Sheila and I met up. We hit it off straight away. She was a fabulous, gorgeous woman and so much fun. She was also a terrific singer, and soon began playing support at my gospel shows. We struck up a close friendship, a little like my relationship with Olivia, and we'd go out to dinner with her hubby, Norman.

Sheila was very talented, and had her own Christian-music career outside of doing shows with me. She made gospel records and, in 1983, we duetted on the title track of one of her albums, *Drifting*. The album was called *War of Love* in America, where it got Sheila nominated for a Grammy for best gospel performance.

Her career was going well in the US and, towards the end of the eighties, Sheila and Norman, who by now was also her manager, moved to America. Sheila was asked by the evangelist preacher Pat Robertson to co-host a religious television programme with him, which she did for five years.

I wasn't in regular contact with Sheila at this point, but I

---

* They were nothing like the Britpop band Oasis, I'm happy to say!

gather she had a bit of a rough patch in the early nineties. She fell out with Pat Robertson and left his TV show. She and Norman also split up and divorced, and Sheila sought therapy for depression before enrolling at a seminary to take a doctorate in theology.

I wasn't surprised when Sheila fell out with Pat Robertson. I think he was quite a fire-and-brimstone, fundamentalist preacher, and that has never been my kind of faith. I found my way to Jesus through moderate, rational discussions, not being bludgeoned over the head. I don't like that extremist wing of Christianity.

Yet Sheila rallied. She has a kind soul but she is also a tough cookie when it comes to knowing what she wants to do, and going for it. She has since released sixteen gospel albums, and written more than thirty books about her faith and theology. One of them, *Honestly*, about overcoming her depression, became a bestseller.

Sheila and I have kept in touch over the years, and in 2020 she reached out to me and asked me to duet with her on a song, 'It Is Well'. I applied my usual rule of asking her to send me the song to see if I liked it. When she did, I was pleased to discover that I liked it very much – especially as it came with quite a story.

'It Is Well' is based on a hymn called 'It Is Well with My Soul', which was written right back in the 1870s. It was penned by a Chicagoan Presbyterian church elder and hymnist named Horatio Spafford, who wrote it to reassert his faith in God in the face of almost unbearable personal tragedy.

In 1873, Spafford, his wife Anna, and their four young daughters were to sail to England for a holiday. Spafford was also a lawyer, and right before the trip, some work came up that he could not postpone. Anna and the girls set sail on a steamship, the *Ville du Havre*. Spafford was to follow on a few days later.

During its voyage, the *Ville du Havre* was hit by a huge iron ship. No fewer than 226 people were killed, including all four of the Spaffords' beloved daughters. Their mother, Anna, survived the collision and, once on shore in Britain, sent her husband a telegram with a terrible, two-word message: 'Saved alone.'

The grieving Spafford left America to join his devastated wife. Alone on his ship, as it passed near where the *Ville du Havre* disaster had occurred, he wrote 'It Is Well with My Soul' to pledge his devotion to God, even despite his terrible loss. It is hard to imagine the strength of faith he must have needed to do so.

'When peace, like a river, attendeth my way/When sorrows like sea billows roll,' Spafford wrote, 'Whatever my lot, Thou hast taught me to say/It is well, it is well with my soul.' And the chorus repeated the devout, defiant message: 'It is well, it is well with my soul.'

It is such a moving story, and hymn, and I liked Sheila's idea of setting the words to contemporary music. I also relished the challenge of singing them: how do you convey the emotion of a man of God who has endured such cataclysmic loss and despair, yet come out the other side with his faith intact?

By that point in 2020, the COVID-19 pandemic had struck across the world, and nobody could go anywhere, so Sheila and I recorded the song remotely. It had a gorgeous electronic musical backdrop and our vocals came out beautifully. In fact, Sheila was so pleased that she had another question: 'Can we make a video?'

Huh? I was in lockdown in Barbados, and Sheila was stuck in the States! But it's amazing what you can do when you put your mind to it. We came up with a plan whereby we would be filmed, separately, singing our parts of the song, then someone would splice the footage together into a video.

I have to say, that was easier said than done! My good friend John McElynn has many talents, but he has never been a video director! Despite this, John managed to film some nice footage on his phone of me crooning away in a corner of the house. Sheila liked it and, in the circumstances, the video came out well – and the production costs were certainly low!

There again, I think sometimes those kinds of rudimentary, home-cooked videos can work just as well as glossy, big-budget productions. I did a very similar thing, during the long corona-virus hiatus, when Gary Barlow got in touch asking me to be involved in a fun project he had going.

To lift people's spirits during Covid, Gary launched The Crooner Sessions, which saw him duetting online every week with a wide range of music stars. He put the results on Instagram, YouTube, Facebook and Twitter. 'We can't go on stages or into theatres,' Gary said. 'Maybe this is our new stage.'

Now, there were a *lot* of people with time on their hands during Covid, so Gary got some big names! He sang 'Your Song' with Elton, and Robbie Williams, Brian May, Katherine Jenkins, Elaine Paige, Chris Martin, Lulu and Jane McDonald all appeared. And Gary invited me to sing 'We Don't Talk Anymore' with him.

I was pleased to be asked, and I was up for it – like everyone, I didn't have a lot else to do! So, we hooked up via the modern miracle of Zoom, Gary sat in front of his laptop camera, and I jigged around as we duetted. I was really pleased with how it came out: I had no idea that my bathroom had such terrific acoustics!

* * *

Singing 'It Is Well' with Sheila Walsh confirmed, yet again, what I've known for a long time now: *I don't have to compartmentalise my life*. I can sing rock and roll and gospel music concurrently. I can be a Christian *and* be a pop star. And my stardom can, maybe, help me spread the word of my Christianity.

This is quite funny. A few years ago, there was an online vote that asked people to name the most famous Christian they could think of. I came first in the poll! I was surprised by this, but even more gobsmacked when I read who came second, right behind me: Jesus!

I must admit that made me laugh! Unlike John Lennon, I have *never* claimed to be more popular than Jesus, and nor would I! I suspect that poll question could have been better worded – maybe by asking people to name the most famous *earthly* Christian? Because Jesus wasn't 'a Christian'. He *is* Christianity.

Today, in this late stage of my career, I combine singing Christian songs and rock and roll more than ever, and I'm delighted to have the freedom to do so. I happily mixed and matched songs from both areas of music at the end of 2022 when I put out my Christmas album, *Christmas with Cliff*.

One of my favourite songs on it was 'Mary, Did You Know?' It was first recorded in 1991 by a Christian singer called Michael English, but I came across it, five years later, being sung by two country singers: Kenny Rogers and Wynonna Judd. And I thought it was absolutely fantastic.

The song's lyric puts questions to Mary, mother of Jesus. It opens by asking her: 'Did you know that your baby boy would one day walk on water?' And it goes deeper: 'When you kiss your little baby, you've kissed the face of God.' The lyrics are so clever, and I loved Kenny Rogers's deep, rich voice.

I had a hurdle to get over when I sang it on *Christmas with Cliff*: a high section in the middle of the song. Kenny had Wynonna Judd to sing that for him; I didn't! I wondered about also doing it as a duet but, in the end, I just switched to falsetto for that bit. A bit of a cheat, but, when I heard the studio playback, I liked it.

Yet, along with 'Mary, Did You Know?' and carols such as 'Joy to the World', I also sang fun Christmas songs such as 'Rockin' Around the Christmas Tree' and 'Jingle Bell Rock' . . . plus a bit of Elvis! I revisited 'Blue Christmas' and loved it just as much as when I first heard it, on Elvis's own Christmas album, back in 1957.

When I go out on tour again, at the end of 2023, I want to do a gospel song or two. I'm not sure yet whether or not I'll do 'It Is Well', but I definitely want to sing 'Two Worlds', a Christian number that was the B-side to 'The Millennium Prayer' when it got to Number 1 at Christmas 1999.

'Two Worlds' has a beautiful message: 'Everyone knows there's something beyond us.' It's gospel, but not in-your-face: the words are there to take or leave, as the listener sees fit. I was thinking of trying to play guitar on it, but two of my backing singers, David Luke and Tim Bonser, are guitarists, so I'll leave it to them.

I'll be eighty-three when that tour comes around, and I think about how to change my performance style as I get older. I've been singing for sixty-five years now, and I know my vocal cords aren't in the same shape as when I did 'Devil Woman'! I don't think they've deteriorated *too* much, but there are a few notes I can't hit these days.

An example: I sing a high falsetto '*whaa!*'* in the first guitar solo of 'We Don't Talk Anymore'. I can hit it on the first night, but I certainly struggle on the next! It's one of the reasons that I try to schedule a night off between shows.

Likewise, I can't charge around stage like a teenager nowadays. I still love rock and roll, and I don't want to stop rocking, but I'm also in my eighties. I don't want to look . . . *undignified*. So, I've a developed a new, age-appropriate signature move that is getting plenty of work at my shows.

Which is? Basically, I glide over to one side of the stage, rocking my hips slightly. Then I glide over to the other side, doing the same. After my last tour, in 2022, I had people saying, '*Wow!* I don't know how you can still *move* like that!' Well, it's very kind of them. But, if they look closer, I'm not moving as much as they think!

So, here we are. I still have *A Head Full of Music*, and I'll keep singing these songs until I can't sing them anymore. I still love Elvis, and Buddy Holly, and Jerry Lee Lewis, and Chuck Berry as much as I did when I was starting out, in 1958. And, in my later years, I love gospel songs just as much.

Here's how I've changed. When I went on *Desert Island Discs*

---

* Yeah, you know the one!

in 1960, and Roy Plomley asked me to name one disc to save if the rest were washed away, I chose Bill Haley & His Comets' 'Rock Around the Clock': *'One, two, three o'clock, four o'clock, rock!'* I figured, if I were shipwrecked, at least I could jump about to it!

Well, when I went back in 2020, and Lauren Laverne asked me the same question, I gave a very different answer. I chose this book's final song: 'It Is Well'. I imagined being alone on that island, until I died, and I knew what I'd need. 'I'd need to feel that God was with me,' I told Lauren. 'And I *would* feel safe, and I *would* feel well.'

But, do you know what? If only she had let me save *two* records, I'd have kept 'Heartbreak Hotel' as well!

AFTERWORD BY BOB STANLEY

Cliff's career has outlasted all of the rock and roll pioneers. How did he survive? He kept up. He remained a fan, and he wanted to discover new writers, new sounds. He discovered Neil Diamond before anyone – paycheques from Cliff's recording of 'Just Another Guy', 'I'll Come Runnin'' and 'Solitary Man' kept a roof above Neil's head long before 'Sweet Caroline'. What else? He recorded Burt Bacharach songs that no one else did, like the gorgeous 'Through the Eye of a Needle'. He unearthed unusual and atmospheric obscurities like Brian Hyland's American Civil War-themed 'I'm Afraid to Go Home'. And when tastes changed, Cliff and The Shadows were sharp enough to keep pace, antici-pating The Searchers' jangle on the Cliff- and Bruce-penned 'Don't Talk To Him' in 1963, dipping into bossa nova for 1966's *Kinda Latin* and reaching for blue-eyed soul on 1967's *Don't Stop Me Now!* album. Cliff may not have thought he could match Little Richard or Larry Williams for sheer firepower, but – with help from arranger Mike Leander – here he found a way to give 'Good Golly Miss Molly' and 'Dizzy Miss Lizzy' new relevance and excitement in the late sixties.

He has never lost that wide-eyed joy over pop's life-affirming powers – and so he made room in *A Head Full of Music* for the unavoidable Beatles, the unstoppable Aretha and, of course, his 'soulmate' Olivia. The Shadows had to make an appearance too – as he says, Cliff played the Indian drum at the front of 'Apache' that introduced not just that one song, but the group's instrumental thunder to the world. If this book had been twice as long, I'm pretty certain that Cliff would also like to have included something by Neil Diamond. Or by Clifford T. Ward, the Worcestershire schoolteacher who wrote the fragile 'Up in the World', one of the highlights of 1977's *Every Face Tells A Story* album. Or something new he only heard last week.

Cliff's still a fan, it's obvious in every line of this book, and he can communicate his enthusiasm with almost child-like glee. When he hears these records today, he is once again that teenager who is still getting used to his mum calling him Cliff rather than Harry.

ACKNOWLEDGEMENTS

My thanks to Malcolm Smith, my manager, for emailing and letting me know that I was on the right track, and Tania, who was always available as go-between for Ian and me. Ian, of course, is my co-writer and all I can say is this book wouldn't have happened without him. Thanks, Ian, for having the patience to work with me, doing extensive research for me and helping me relive my extraordinary musical history. It's been a joy.

SONGWRITING ACKNOWLEDGMENTS

1. 'In a Persian Market' – Sammy Davis Jr (Albert Ketèlby/Mack David)
2. 'Heartbreak Hotel' – Elvis Presley (Mae Boren Axton/Tommy Durden/Elvis Presley)
3. 'Blue Suede Shoes' – Carl Perkins (Carl Perkins)
4. 'Lucille' – Little Richard (Albert Collins/Little Richard)
5. 'School Day (Ring! Ring! Goes the Bell)' – Chuck Berry (Chuck Berry)
6. 'Rock Around the Clock' – Bill Haley & His Comets (Max Freedman/James E. Myers)
7. 'Twenty Flight Rock'- Eddie Cochran (Eddie Cochran/ Ned Fairchild)
8. 'Great Balls of Fire' – Jerry Lee Lewis (Otis Blackwell/ Jack Hammer
9. 'Stood Up' – Ricky Nelson (Dub Dickerson/Erma Herrold)
10. 'Move It' – Cliff Richard & The Drifters (Ian Samwell)
11. 'A Teenager in Love' – Marty Wilde (Doc Pomus/Mort Shuman)

12. 'When' – The Kalin Twins (Paul Evans/Jack Reardon)

13. 'Peggy Sue' – Buddy Holly (Jerry Allison/Norman Petty/ Buddy Holly)

14. 'Let It Be Me' – The Everly Brothers (Pierre Delanoë/ Gilbert Bécaud)

15. 'Treasure of Love' – Clyde McPhatter (Joe Shapiro/ Lou Stallman)

16. 'Always' – Sammy Turner (Irving Berlin)

17. 'Sway' – Bobby Rydell (Luis Demetrio/Norman Gimbel)

18. 'You Send Me' – Sam Cooke (Sam Cooke)

19. 'My Funny Valentine' – Dakota Staton (Richard Rodgers/ Lorenz Hart)

20. 'Apache' – The Shadows (Jerry Lordan)

21. 'Love Me Do' – The Beatles (John Lennon/Paul McCartney)

22. 'You're My World' – Cilla Black (Umberto Bindi/Gino Paoli/ Carl Sigman)

23. 'People Get Ready' – The Impressions (Curtis Mayfield)

24. 'It Is No Secret (What God Can Do)' – Elvis Presley (Stuart Hamblen)

25. 'We Don't Talk Anymore' – Cliff Richard (Alan Tarney)

26. 'Your Song' – Elton John (Elton John/Bernie Taupin)

27. 'Stayin' Alive' – The Bee Gees (Barry Gibb/Robin Gibb/ Maurice Gibb)

28. 'I Honestly Love You' – Olivia Newton-John (John Farrar)

29. 'Rolling in the Deep' – Aretha Franklin (Adele Adkins/ Paul Epworth)

30. 'It Is Well' – Sheila Walsh (featuring Cliff Richard) (Horatio Spafford/Philip Paul Bliss)

INDEX

IMAGE CREDITS

Plate Section 1

Everett Collection Inc / Alamy Stock Photo (Image 1, 11)

Michael Ochs Archives / Stringer (Image 3, 4, 5, 6, 7, 14, 15)

Bettman / Contributor (Image 8)

V&A Images / Contributor (Image 9)

Pictorial Press Ltd / Alamy Stock Photo (Image 10, 17)

Beverly Lebarrow / Contributor (Image 12)

GAB Archive / Contributor (Image 13)

Popperfoto / Contributor (Image 16)

Plate Section 2

Michael Ochs Archives / Stringer (Image 1)

Pictorial Press Ltd / Alamy Stock Photo (Image 3, 5)

ITV / Shutterstock (Image 4)

GAB Archive / Contributor (Image 6)

Popperfoto / Contributor (Image 7)

Alpha Historica / Alamy Stock Photo (Image 8)

Mirrorpix / Contributor (Image 9)

Gilles Petard / Contributor (Image 10)

John Downing / Stringer (Image 11)

Jack Robinson / Contributor (Image 14)

Richard McCaffrey / Contributor (Image 15)

Doug McKenzie / Contributor (Image 16)

Radio Times / Contributor (Image 17)

Alan Perry www.concertphotos.uk.com (Image 18)